The Anti-Intellectual Presidency

THE ANTI-INTELLECTUAL PRESIDENCY

*The Decline of
Presidential Rhetoric from
George Washington to
George W. Bush*

ELVIN T. LIM

OXFORD
UNIVERSITY PRESS

OXFORD
UNIVERSITY PRESS

Oxford University Press, Inc., publishes works that further
Oxford University's objective of excellence
in research, scholarship, and education.

Oxford   New York
Auckland   Cape Town   Dar es Salaam   Hong Kong   Karachi
Kuala Lumpur   Madrid   Melbourne   Mexico City   Nairobi
New Delhi   Shanghai   Taipei   Toronto

With offices in
Argentina   Austria   Brazil   Chile   Czech Republic   France   Greece
Guatemala   Hungary   Italy   Japan   Poland   Portugal   Singapore
South Korea   Switzerland   Thailand   Turkey   Ukraine   Vietnam

Published by Oxford University Press, Inc.
198 Madison Avenue, New York, New York 10016
www.oup.com

First issued as an Oxford University Press paperback, 2012

Oxford is a registered trademark of Oxford University Press

Library of Congress Cataloging-in-Publication Data
Lim, Elvin T., 1976–
The anti-intellectual presidency : the decline of presidential rhetoric
from George Washington to George W. Bush / Elvin T. Lim.
        p.   cm.
Includes bibliographical references and index.
ISBN 978-0-19-534264-2 (hardcover); 978-0-19-989809-1 (paperback)
1. Presidents—United States—History.   2. Presidents—United States—Language—
History.   3. Presidents—United States—Intellectual life—History.   4. Rhetoric—Political
aspects—United States—History.   5. Communication in politics—United States—
History.   6. Political oratory—United States—History.   7. United States—Politics
and government.   8. United States—Intellectual life.   I. Title.
E176.1.L457 2008
973.09'9—dc22   2007050230

9 8 7 6 5 4 3 2 1

Printed in the United States of America
on acid-free paper

To my parents

Everything should be made as simple
as possible, but no simpler.

—*Albert Einstein*

PREFACE

The state of presidential rhetoric today has taken a nosedive from our founding era. The influential journalist and satirist H. L. Mencken once wrote of President Warren Harding's inaugural address: "It reminds me of a string of wet sponges; it reminds me of tattered washing on the line; it reminds me of stale bean soup, of college yells, of dogs barking idiotically through endless nights. It is so bad that a sort of grandeur creeps into it."[1] Mencken's assessment would not have been too far off in describing the speeches of Harding's successors in the White House, but his complaint also addresses a deeper problem with an ancient pedigree. Our society's disquiet toward presidential rhetoric is as old as Plato's belief that "oratory is a spurious counterfeit of a branch of the art of government," and it is as entrenched as the conventional diagnosis that presidential leadership has become too "rhetorical."[2] There is widespread sentiment today that the pathologies of modern presidential government derive from the loquaciousness of the office and that if presidents spent less time talking and campaigning, they would spend more time deliberating and governing. But the Greeks were not straightforwardly opposed to rhetoric. After all, their arguments were put forth in Socratic dialogues. It was a particular *type* of rhetoric that Plato decried, the type that was used to pander to and seduce the people. Already at the inception of rhetorical studies, Plato had distinguished "mere rhetoric"—words crafted to equivocate, flatter, or seduce—and meaningful rhetoric, which facilitates rational disputation, a distinction that is at the heart of this book's (reconceived) critique of the contemporary presidency. My thesis is this: the problem of presidential rhetoric in our time resides not in its quantity, but in its quality. The problem is not that "going public" has become a routine presidential practice; it is that while presidents talk a lot, they say very little that contributes constructively to public deliberation.[3] Our problem is the anti-intellectual presidency, not the rhetorical presidency.

Although presidential anti-intellectualism has become a defining characteristic of the contemporary presidency, we have been slow to call it as we see it. Perhaps scholars have assumed a synthetic link between the quantity and quality of presidential rhetoric and have focused on the former, assuming that the pressure to speechify has contributed to or is the same pressure that has given presidents the incentive to go anti-intellectual. But of course they are distinct. On the demand side of citizen-auditors, we do not lower our expectations about the substance and quality of what is communicated to us even as we insist, perhaps unreasonably, that presidents have something to say about almost everything. On the supply side, presidents today have an extensive speechwriting apparatus at their disposal. It is unlikely that problematic catchphrases such as the "axis of evil" or the "war on terror" emerged inadvertently as a result of overwhelming presidential speech loads.

Perhaps we have resisted making the charge of presidential antiintellectualism because it is difficult not to sound elitist when laying the charge and even more difficult to prove it. Or perhaps anti-intellectualism creeps up on one. Simplifying rhetoric to make it more accessible to the average citizen is a laudable enterprise, but at some point simplification becomes oversimplification, and the line between the two is often difficult to define, especially in a polity committed to democracy. But whatever the reason, I suspect that the scholarly animus toward the rhetorical presidency would be significantly tempered if contemporary presidents spoke more like Washington and Jefferson with greater frequency and less like Ford and Carter with equal frequency. If this intuition sounds correct, then what really bothers us about contemporary presidential rhetoric is not how much is said, but what is being said. Rather than harp on the problem of the rhetorical presidency, this book addresses presidential anti-intellectualism head on. This is a critical enterprise because much that is wrong with American politics today begins with the words that emanate from the nation's highest officeholder and principal spokesperson. When presidents lie to us or mislead us, when they pander to us or seduce us with their words, when they equivocate and try to be all things to all people, or when they divide us with wedge issues, they do so with an arsenal of anti-intellectual tricks, with rhetoric that is linguistically simplistic, reliant on platitudes or partisan slogans, short on argument, and long on emotive and human-interest appeals.

Let me state upfront what I am *not* addressing in this book as a means of clarifying what I *am* addressing. First, I am concerned with anti-intellectualism only in the political and not in the philosophical sense. I am not concerned with Kierkegaard's doctrine of anti-rationalism, the view that moral truth cannot be derived from an objective judgment of right and wrong, nor with Hume's theory of knowledge that none of our ideas are analytically prior but all are the result of sensational "impressions," nor with Henri Bergson's theory that it is more the intuition and less the intellect that is the driving force behind human thought, nor with Nietzsche's and Freud's theories of unconscious motivation in human decisions. I am interested in the political uses and consequences of anti-intellectualism as manifested in American presidential rhetoric.

Second, this book is not concerned with unintelligence but with anti-intellectualism. Intelligence, as I argue in chapter 2, pertains to the first-order functions of the mind which grasps, manipulates, adjusts, and so forth; intellect evaluates these activities and involves the activities of the mind's eye on itself, such as in theorizing, criticizing, pondering, and so forth. Apart from the conspicuous exceptions from the patrician era, it appears that most presidents were not, especially when we think of the nineteenth-century "dark-horse" candidates, been exceptionally intelligent men because the electoral process (and in particular the Democratic Party's two-thirds rule for nominating its presidential candidates) selected not for intelligence, but for bland standard-bearers who were politically inoffensive enough to garner votes at the nomination convention. In the twentieth century, a first-past-the-post two-party system militated against the selection of a person of exceptional qualities in favor of a candidate that could appeal to the median voter. Thus, Harding was described as a "second-rate provincial" and Franklin Roosevelt as "a second class intellect."[4] What is noteworthy for my purposes, however, is that despite their alleged mediocrity, most presidents in the past preferred to appear less, not more, intellectually inclined than they actually were. And they pursued this strategy even though they had no lack of access to both intellectuals and very intelligent aides who could have been easily deployed to cultivate an image otherwise.[5] A president who assiduously adopts, with the aid of an extensive and professional staff, an anti-intellectual posture cannot be, at least straightforwardly, unintelligent. Indeed, it is the paradoxical fact that the anti-intellectual presidency qua institution is composed of a collectivity (and indeed, an increasing co-optation) of experts that makes my story particularly poignant.

Because anti-intellectualism denigrates the *intellect* and *intellectuals* rather than *intelligence*, I have used "dumbing down" sparingly in this book even though the phrase may appear to be an obvious signifier of the phenomenon I am tracking. Dumbing down, which I approximately understand to be some excessive degree of linguistic simplification, pejoratively supposes a "dumbness" or unintelligence presumed to be the state of the median auditor-citizen. By appropriating the term dumbing down, we implicitly endorse the idea that citizens are unintelligent and presidents are merely calibrating their messages as such. I reject the premise and therefore the conclusion of this idea. Citizens are not dumb, and they deserve more, not less, information from presidents so that they are equipped to make competent civic decisions. Though he will often be the first to make this charge, it is the anti-intellectualist who underestimates citizens and who assumes that citizens cannot digest anything more than platitudes and simplistic slogans. Further, dumbing down does not fully capture the scope of the wily anti-intellectualist's tactics. Linguistic simplification is typically a major component of going anti-intellectual, but the former is neither necessary nor sufficient for the latter. For instance, a major anti-intellectualist strategy is to fudge and to equivocate by the use of platitudes and abstract concepts. This strategy is not accurately described as dumbing down since platitudes can be both trivially true and profound; but they are anti-intellectual in the rejection of precise argument as a basis for deliberation and rational disputation. For example, some defenders of Ronald Reagan's soaring rhetoric have contended that his speeches, in appealing to the mythic chords of collective national identity, were not dumbed down, but recondite and even sublime.[6] In chapter 4, I will suggest, with the different and more precise locution of anti-intellectualism, exactly what is wrong with and anti-intellectual about an excessive reliance on inspirational platitudes.

Third, my purpose is not to provide an instruction manual for presidential leadership in the way Richard Neustadt's *Presidential Power* was written for John Kennedy.[7] I do not expect presidents to voluntarily eschew the anti-intellectual path of least resistance; only citizens can force them to do so. I also reject institutional partisanship—a partiality toward the prospects and accretion of presidential power—because the view from behind the president's shoulder justifies and anticipates the fulfillment of presidential priorities, often at the expense of other branches and institutions of American government.[8] What works, rhetorically or otherwise, for the president may not be best for the country. So my aim is not to assess the marginal political gain to the president of "going public"—a subject that has already produced an extensive and illustrious literature—but to rearticulate the systemic costs of the rhetorical presidency, which is better read, I will argue, as the "anti-intellectual presidency." As such, this book is as much about the presidency as it is about American democracy, for in diagnosing the quality of presidential discourse, I am also offering a barometer for the state of presidential leadership and the health of American democracy.

There are three other prefatory points I want to make. First, throughout this book, I will use masculine pronouns to refer to presidents because, as of 2007 (when this is being written), there has not been a female president in American history. My second point pertains to sources. So as not to clutter the text with too many cumbersome notes, I have indicated only the titles, dates, and the *Public Papers* in which the speeches I have quoted in the twentieth century and beyond are collected, and not the full publishers' and page citations. This is all the information a reader needs to search the solid and accessible digital record of the *Public Papers* of the presidents on the Internet and to retrieve the relevant full-page documents. In particular, I recommend the Web site of the American Presidency Project run by John Woolley and Gerhard Peters at http://www.presidency.ucsb.edu/ws, the University of Michigan digital library at http://quod.lib.umich.edu/p/ppotpus, and for newly minted presidential documents, the GPO Web site at http://www.gpoaccess.gov/wcomp/index.html provides a weekly compilation of presidential documents (all accessed on 8/28/2007).

Today, more than ever, it is imperative that we attend to the substance of presidential rhetoric as we observe the expansion of the rhetorical presidency into the rhetorical executive. Not only is over one-third of the contemporary White House staff engaged in some aspect of public relations or political communication, it is now routine practice for a president to deploy and coordinate his cabinet and staff to do his rhetorical bidding.[9] The expectations for public officials to "go public" is now so heightened that for the first time in the history of the office, James L. Pavitt, chief of the CIA's clandestine service, was called to testify in a public hearing before the 9/11 Commission. This expansion of the rhetorical executive was such a break from precedent that one of the commissioners, former senator Bob Kerrey (D-NE), observed that his "stomach's been turning as Mr. Pavitt's been answering questions here this afternoon."[10] Yet, more words do not necessarily mean more answers, as the regular deployment of top administration officials to toe the White House "line of the day" evidences. My broadest aim in this book is to invite readers to look more closely at the quality of presidential rhetoric and where it has fallen short of the purpose it should serve in a democracy. We must not rest content with relegating presidential rhetoric to "mere rhetoric," because our inattention to mere rhetoric, or our failure to pierce through it, can and has landed us into trouble.

ACKNOWLEDGMENTS

The research for this book was generously funded by the Potter Foundation, the University of Oxford's Andrew Mellow Fund, the Franklin and Eleanor Roosevelt Institute, the George Bush Presidential Library Foundation, the American Political Science Association's Presidency Research Fellowship, and the Faculty Development Fellowship at the University of Tulsa. I would like to thank the late Phillip J. Stone of Harvard University for allowing me to use the *General Inquirer* to analyze the data presented in chapter 4. I am grateful to the 42 former presidential speechwriters I interviewed for their time, candor, and intellectual engagement. I would like to thank the archivists and staffs at the Franklin D. Roosevelt Library, Jimmy Carter Library, George Bush Presidential Library, Green Library and Hoover Institution Library at Stanford University, Perry-Castañeda Library at the University of Texas at Austin, Nuffield College Library, Social Studies Library, and Rothermere American Institute at the University of Oxford, and Sterling Memorial Library at Yale. I would also like to gratefully acknowledge my former colleagues at the University of Tulsa, who provided a supportive and intellectually stimulating environment for my research, and Dean Tom Benediktson, who graciously granted me a semester off to write. Many thanks are also due to David McBride, Brendan O'Neill, and Christine Dahlin at Oxford University Press for holding my hand through the publishing process. I owe an intellectual debt to Nigel Bowles, Roderick Hart, David Mayhew, Byron

Shafer, and Christopher Wlezien, senior colleagues and mentors who have helped to shape and sharpen my thoughts. I am very grateful to Jeffrey Tulis, whose work inaugurated a whole subfield in presidential studies and inspired this book and who so kindly took time out to read and comment helpfully on the manuscript. I am especially indebted to Stephen Skowronek, who saw promise in this project before I saw it and nurtured it with insights that helped me to clarify what I wanted to say in this book. Many thanks are also due to Edward Biedermann, Jeff Hockett, Michael Mosher, Mana Tahaie, and Nicholas Carnes for taking the time to read and comment on various portions and previous iterations of this book, to Ronnie Farhat for his research assistance, to Sonu Bedi for many productive and clarifying conversations, to Melvyn Lim and Ty Voliter, who helped me to resolve many a software and computing issue and for their friendship, and to Ai-leen, for always being there. All remaining errors are mine. I dedicate this book to my parents, to whom I owe an eternal debt of gratitude and love.

CONTENTS

The Anti-Intellectual Presidency

1

The Problem of Presidential Rhetoric

The title and timing of this book may suggest to some readers that my aim is to add to a hackneyed sequence of rants on the intellectual limitations of the current president or other recent presidents. It is not. The problem of anti-intellectualism in the White House has an institutional pedigree that precedes President George W. Bush, even if the culmination of these long-term trends have made the most recent incarnation of the anti-intellectual presidency exemplary. We underestimate the extent of presidential anti-intellectualism if we allow it to become a partisan critique. Indeed, this book is not about intelligence or anti-intelligence, for these are separate categories. The anti-intellectual president is certainly intelligent or at least crafty enough to recognize the political utility of publicly rejecting the "highfalutin" ruminations of the intellectual and to affirm the soundness of "common sense." As I will argue, Bill Clinton was one such intelligent but anti-intellectual president.

The denigration of the intellect, the intellectual, and intellectual opinions has, to a degree not yet acknowledged, become a routine presidential rhetorical stance. Indeed, intellectuals have become among the most assailable piñatas of American politics. For President Herbert Hoover, intellectuals exhibited an "unbroken record of total abstinence from constructive joy over our whole national history."[1] President Dwight Eisenhower had little sympathy for the "wise-cracking so called intellectuals going around and showing how wrong was everybody who didn't happen to agree with them."[2]

Intellectuals, according to President Lyndon Johnson, are "more concerned with style than they are with mortar, brick, and concrete. They are more concerned with the trivia and the superficial than they are with the things that have really built America."[3]

Since Richard Hofstadter's magisterial *Anti-Intellectualism in American Life* was published in 1963, the subject of anti-intellectualism has been given little scholarly attention, and it survives today mostly only in the literature on education.[4] This is partly because the phenomenon, though endemic, is hard to define and even harder to measure. Few people will disagree that elements of it pervade our culture and politics, but disagreements emerge as soon as claims are specified. In politics, observers have long noticed "the special connection between politics and the debasement of language."[5] Murray Edelman observes that political language is "banal...highly stylized and predictable most of the time."[6] For Kenneth Burke, democratic political language serves to "sharpen up the pointless and blunt the too sharply pointed."[7] More specifically, presidential rhetorical efforts have been described as "a linguistic struggle," "rarely an occasion for original thought," like "dogs barking idiotically through endless nights," bordering on "demagogy," and "pontification cum anecdotalism."[8] Yet while many will endorse these declension narratives, we have yet to provide an evidentiary basis for such claims.

Most important, the declining quality of presidential rhetoric is exactly what unifies several scholarly accounts of the contemporary presidency. What connects the scholarly characterizations of the "permanent campaign," the "sound of leadership," the "presidential spectacle," the "symbolic presidency," the "public presidency," and the "rhetorical presidency" is the consensus that the pressure on presidents to go public has created a pathology of vacuous rhetoric and imagery that has impoverished our public deliberative sphere. Democratic politics in our time, according to Hugh Heclo, passes "from degradation to debauchery...when leaders teach a willing people to love illusions—to like nonsense because it sounds good."[9] "The natural inclination of one who speaks for a living is," according to Roderick Hart, "to become less and less inclined to examine one's own thoughts analytically and more and more attentive to the often uncritical reactions of popular assemblages."[10] Presidential "spectacles," which promote "gesture over accomplishment and appearance over fact," have, according to Bruce Miroff, become the mode of governance.[11] Bereft of argument and substance, the language of government is now, according to Robert Denton, "the dissemination of illusion and ambiguity."[12] "All a president can do," according to George Edwards, "is rely on rhetoric and symbols to obscure perceptions enough to be all things to all people."[13] Similarly, James Ceaser and his colleagues argue that the framers created a tripartite governmental system so that members of each branch "would be forced to deal with knowledgeable and determined men not easily impressed by facile oratory." But in the context of today's rhetorical presidency, "argument gives way to aphorism."[14] The anti-intellectual presidency is an underlying thesis in all of these accounts. Whereas these scholars address these similar rhetorical manifestations as symptoms of larger problems differentially specified, I address presidential anti-intellectualism as the problem itself.

These scholarly observations are, curiously enough, matched by presidential speechwriters, partners in crime with presidents in driving the alleged degeneration of presidential rhetoric. Peggy Noonan observes that "the only organ to which no appeal is made these days—you might call it America's only understimulated organ—is the brain."[15] Another speechwriter observes, "I think there was a time when speechwriters were far more conscious of the literary quotient in their prose than is true now."[16] Landon Parvin, a speechwriter for Ronald Reagan, complains, "The reason why I don't like most political speeches is that they don't deal with logic at all."[17] Another speechwriter observes that rhetoric today is "much more of a matter of attempting to put your position in terms that are most familiar and appealing... than it is a matter of attempting to move people and to cause people to adopt a different point of view by the strength of your argument."[18] According to William Gavin, a staff assistant to Richard Nixon, "the whole question of argument is something that has been totally lost in American rhetoric."[19] Speaking in 1976, a former Nixon speechwriter and future Reagan chief speechwriter correctly foretold the future:

> I'm afraid that the quality of public debate is not improving. People
> are not getting a more enlightened argument being presented to
> them.... Now it really is much more a matter of imagery. I think it's an
> unfortunate thing and it's going to get worse, not better.[20]

Other speechwriters have observed our entry into an "unrhetorical age," that political speech has become "run of the mill," "a dying art form," and "rose garden garbage."[21] That the very authors of presidential rhetoric should lament the collective products of their profession smacks of hypocrisy, but it is also a critical telltale symptom of a tyrannical decisional logic that I will examine in greater detail in chapter 3. The pressure to "go anti-intellectual" in American politics is so powerful that those who drive it also decry it.

For now, it is sufficient to note that however one characterizes the contemporary presidency, scholars and speechwriters alike have noticed the declining quality of presidential discourse. The aim of this book is to provide a measure of this decline beyond the anecdotal accounts already offered by demonstrating the relentless simplification of presidential rhetoric in the last two centuries and the increasing substitution of arguments with applause-rendering platitudes, partisan punch lines, and emotional and human interest appeals. I characterize these rhetorical trends as manifestations of the anti-intellectual presidency.

The Rhetorical Presidency

At least since the 1980s, presidential scholars have inverted the presidential instinct that "rhetoric is the solution to the problem" with the diagnosis that "rhetoric is the problem itself." What exactly is this problem though? The conventional wisdom is that presidents are talking too much, in part because "deeds [are now] done in words."[22] Today, we hear the ceaseless "sound of leadership."[23] As campaigns turn seamlessly into governance, we are told that we have entered the loquacious era of the "permanent campaign."[24] To resolve the fissiparous and fragmented institutional environment of American politics, going public to reach the people directly, rather than interbranch deliberation, has become the efficient strategy of choice.[25] The American executive today is preeminently a "public presidency."[26] Notice that all of these accounts focus on the iterative act of rhetoric, rather than its substance.

The dominant and, I think, most sophisticated account of presidential loquaciousness is Jeffrey Tulis's theory of the "rhetorical presidency."[27] The problem of the rhetorical presidency, for Tulis, is not just in the observation that presidents now talk a lot, as he had already noted in an earlier version of the theory, but in the simultaneous existence of two antithetical constitutions guiding presidential rhetorical choices: first, the original, formal constitution, which respects the equality of the three branches of the federal government and interbranch deliberation and correspondingly envisions a more reticent president; and second, an organic constitution, which has evolved into being by a combination of necessity and practice that encourages and legitimates presidential rhetorical leadership.[28] Tulis's insight is in characterizing the rhetorical presidency as a "hybrid" institution that emerged in the early twentieth century. The rhetorical presidency was a product of the second constitution superimposed on the original, with the attendant "dilemmas of modern governance" emerging because of the incongruous coexistence of two antithetical constitutions: one proscribing presidential rhetoric, another prescribing it.[29] The dilemma emerged because presidential rhetoric directed "over the heads" of congress toward citizens preempted congressional and interbranch deliberation during the course of routine politics, but yet was required in moments of emergency. While this insight has advanced our understanding of the processes of institutional change—which are often incomplete and layered—it has distracted us from a proper diagnosis of the pathologies of presidential rhetoric.

Beyond Rhetorical Dilemmas

Most critiques of the rhetorical presidency thesis have challenged Tulis's bifurcation of presidential history and, in particular, the caricaturing of nineteenth-century rhetorical norms as something genuinely distinct from twentieth-century practice. Scholars tell us that presidents in the nineteenth century have in their own ways but with equal enthusiasm taken their case to the people, denying Tulis's claim that nineteenth-century presidents were all that reticent.[30] They go some way in challenging Tulis's thesis, for if nineteenth-century presidents went public as often as twentieth-century presidents did, there would be just one constitution vacillating at different times in American history, not two, and therefore no modern constitutional dilemma to speak of. Presidents would only face the dilemma of reticence versus loquaciousness if the tug of two opposing constitutional injunctions operated on them *simultaneously* rather than sequentially at different times.[31] But these arguments, while persuasive, do not go far enough because they only challenge the empirical premise of Tulis's argument—that there are two antithetical constitutions operating side by side—rather than challenge the argument on Tulis's own terms, granting the author that there are indeed two constitutions, but rejecting his conclusion that the dilemmas of governance emerge from their interaction.

Tulis's developmental insight about the emergence of a distinct, second constitution prescribing presidential loquaciousness is possibly correct, but his diagnosis of what is problematic about the rhetorical presidency is incomplete and does not go far enough because he is constrained by his "hybrid" argument. Here is how. Dilemmas are characterized by more or less equal motivational tugs from opposite directions, so that whichever way one succumbs, one pays an equal cost for the abandonment of the other. If the costs were not approximately equal, then there would be no dilemma to start with. Now, if the problem of the rhetorical presidency were derived from the tension between two constitutions, the pathologies of presidential leadership could be removed if we could surgically remove one constitution, leaving the other intact, so that we either have the unfettered continuation of the original constitution, or a complete displacement of it with the new. *Either* hypothetical solution would remove the conditions for a dilemma. Crucially, Tulis ought to have been indifferent to either hypothetical alternative since for him, the problem of the rhetorical presidency was its *hybridity*.

Yet Tulis was not indifferent to the alternatives, but partial to the merits of reticence as prescribed by the older constitution. Tellingly, his solution to the rhetorical presidency was the deroutinization of going public, while allowing for rhetorical leadership only in moments of crisis, *and not vice versa.* When Tulis lamented that the rhetorical presidency had brought on "an erosion of the processes of deliberation, and a decay of political discourse," he was clearly laying the blame unequally on the new constitution, rather than the old.[32] Dilemma aside, Tulis was partial to the older constitution's prescription of presidential reticence, betraying his view that there is something inherently troubling about the new constitution. And so we are back with an essentially quantitative critique of the problem of presidential rhetoric. As the title of his book tells us, the problem of the rhetorical presidency is that it is, well, too rhetorical.

If Tulis was correct in intuiting that there is something inherently troubling about the new state of affairs wrought by the rhetorical presidency, his characterization of the constitution in terms of its hybridity obscures rather than clarifies his diagnosis. Indeed, the problematic diagnosis translates into an undeliverable solution—a dilemma within a dilemma—that has made an exit from the rhetorical presidency forbiddingly difficult. It reveals the weakness of a quantitative critique of presidential rhetoric. Recall that the ideal presidential rhetorical situation, according to Tulis, would minimize routine appeals to the public while allowing for rhetorical initiative in moments of crisis. But here is the implemental dilemma Tulis himself recognized:

> How would one return to an earlier polity, and who would bring us there? Wouldn't we need to be led by one regarded as the legitimate spokesman for the nation as a whole—that is, by a president appealing to us directly?...Refounding or restorative leadership, even in the service of the "old way," seems to require practices proscribed in the nineteenth century.[33]

By Tulis's own account, the rhetorical presidency cannot be silenced because, paradoxically, only a rhetorical president can rescue us from the rhetorical presidency. This is a paralyzing conclusion, and needlessly pessimistic. It emerges from a failure to distinguish the quantity of rhetoric from its quality. This book proposes a different diagnosis of the pathologies of the rhetorical presidency by shifting our attention away from the dilemma posed by two constitutions and away from the *quantity* of presidential rhetoric toward its *quality*. The "old way" of silence or reticence that Tulis looked nostalgically toward is not a solution because the problem, I propose, is not the rhetorical presidency but the anti-intellectual presidency.

To effect this analytic shift, we need only drop Tulis's untenable assumption that the "surfeit of speech by politicians constitutes a decay of political discourse."[34] More talk does not have to mean less substance, though the assumed causal relationship between loquaciousness and vacuousness has been exaggerated to such an extent that the two have practically come to mean the same thing. Tulis may have assumed a synthetic link between more talk and less substance, between going public and going anti-intellectual, but to diagnose the problem purely in quantitative terms is to miss the essence of the pathology. What bothers us is not the fact the presidents talk a lot, but that they say very little even when they talk a lot. Conversely, if presidents talked a lot but made a lot of sense, it would be unclear what, if any, objections would remain of the rhetorical presidency. We would then be left with the problem of the unequal rhetorical balance of power between the president and congress, but then this becomes a problem of *congress* failing to talk back, not a clear-cut matter of presidential wrongdoing. Indeed, because Tulis represents the decay of political discourse as merely a function of the surfeit of presidential speech, he inadvertently exonerates presidents by characterizing them as passive actors responding to the speechifying demands exerted on them by the new constitution. I will show, in chapter 3, that the anti-intellectual presidency emerged deliberately and calculatedly, rather than inevitably from the relatively independent fact of a more rhetorical presidency.

If speechwriters and scholars alike lament the degeneration of presidential rhetoric, then it is a problem that we must confront head on. I extract the underlying critique of the anti-intellectual presidency, which is embedded in the rhetorical and public presidency literatures, and place it front and center in this book. The anti-intellectual presidency, understood as a problem of rhetorical quality, not quantity, is what properly articulates our intuitions and unifies scholarly lamentations about the rhetorical presidency.

There is another benefit to my thesis. By assigning no inherent fault in presidential appeals to the public but only, potentially, to their content, we can rehabilitate Theodore Roosevelt and Woodrow Wilson, who are relegated to a needlessly ambiguous station in the rhetorical presidency literature. These presidents may have legitimated the routine recourse to going public, but they did not, on my account and by themselves, inaugurate the anti-intellectual presidency. Tulis's bittersweet characterization of TR's "middle way" of rhetorical moderation, I argue, equivocates revealingly on the founding status of TR.[35] Why the equivocation? Why not just concede that TR *was* a founding rhetorical president, who popularized the frequent use of "swings round the circle" and the "bully pulpit," as the conventional wisdom attests? I propose that because Tulis recognized, correctly, that TR was inaugurating something rather new (the rhetorical presidency), he did not want to go as far as to say that this was a corrupt institutional innovation (as the anti-intellectual presidency would be). The distinction I make here allows us to properly locate the developmental innovations of TR and Wilson, both founders of the rhetorical presidency, but less so of the anti-intellectual presidency.

The experience of these two presidents reveals the distinction between the rhetorical and anti-intellectual presidencies. "Cromwell, like so many a so-called 'practical' man," Theodore Roosevelt once wrote, "would have done better work had he followed a more clearly defined theory, for though the practical man is better than the mere theorist, he cannot do the highest work unless he is a theorist also."[36] Insofar as the leader of the Rough Riders valorized action over reflection, the anti-intellectual impulse was latent in his presidency, but TR also knew well that the "practical man" must also be a "theorist," and this was evident in his rhetoric. TR's first communication and annual message to congress after becoming president, complained Secretary of the Navy John D. Long, "might have been shorter" and exuded "a sort of academic flavor."[37] This passage on the antitrust movement from the message gives us a sense of that flavor:

> The mechanism of modern business is so delicate that extreme care must be taken not to interfere with it in a spirit of rashness or ignorance. Many of those who have made it their vocation to denounce the great industrial combinations which are popularly, although with technical inaccuracy, known as "trusts," appeal especially to hatred and fear. These are precisely the two emotions, particularly when combined with ignorance, which unfit men for the exercise of cool and steady judgment. In facing new industrial conditions, the whole history of the world shows that legislation will generally be both unwise and ineffective unless undertaken after calm inquiry and with sober self-restraint.[38]

In his call for moderation, Roosevelt correlated rashness with "ignorance," "technical inaccuracy," and a lack of wisdom—all enemies of "steady judgment" and "calm inquiry." Here was a president who was telling members of congress that the legislative issues they faced were "delicate," for which there were no straightforward (modern presidents would say "commonsensical") answers. He was specifically rejecting the place of passion or the emotions in guiding policy; and he was explicitly advocating accuracy, judgment, and inquiry.

The *New York Times* praised Roosevelt's message in ways that reveal a very different standard of appraising presidential rhetoric from today's anti-intellectual paradigm. The following account of Roosevelt's literary talent seems almost quaint by today's standards:

> Certainly no President's message has ever contained better writing than some passages in the State paper sent to congress yesterday. He writes with the lucidity and the power of a man who commands his subjects and has mature ideas to express and positive beliefs and opinions to present. Moreover, he does not misuse the English language, a fault from which some very great men among our presidents have not been free. The whole range of affairs to which the President may or should invite the attention of congress appears to have been swept by the conscientious and comprehensive Executive pen.[39]

Though TR's "executive pen" produced rhetoric that was qualitatively very different from the one produced by his successors, there was no doubt that he was a rhetorical president. Indeed, his contemporaries tired of his speeches. On the eve of Roosevelt's speaking tour to sell his railroad bill, an editorialist wrote:

> Mr. Roosevelt has had so many opportunities to catch the public ear within the last four years and he has made such assiduous use of them that he cannot be expected to have much that is unfamiliar to offer.... He repeats himself in a remarkable degree, but always with the same earnestness, with the same certainty that he is right and that it is important for his countrymen to hear again and again until they heed.[40]

The assumed synthetic link between the rhetorical and anti-intellectual presidencies is also tenuous in the case of another founding rhetorical president, Woodrow Wilson. The former professor and president of Princeton University definitely envisioned and practiced a more rhetorical presidency, but it would be difficult to argue that he would have unhesitatingly endorsed an anti-intellectual one. In his senior year at college, the budding scholar-statesman articulated an exacting standard of political rhetoric: "in the unsparing examination and telling criticism of opposite positions, the careful painstaking unraveling of all the issues involved...we see the best, the only effective, means of educating public opinion."[41] Wilson, who was no fan of the "hide and seek vagaries" of accountability in the American constitution's checks and balances, would have been just as unimpressed by the hide-and-seek vagaries of authorial responsibility for today's delegated speechwriting environment, a situation I will describe in chapter 5.[42] All this is to say, then, that there is something odd in an account of presidential history that puts Theodore Roosevelt and Woodrow Wilson in the same group of presidents as Bill Clinton and George W. Bush. Legitimate cases can be made for each of these four presidents as eloquent speakers and rhetorical presidents, but these judgments would conceal the qualitatively different types of rhetoric the two sets of presidents produced. TR and Wilson may have inaugurated something that Clinton and Bush inherited, but the latter two presidents transformed their inheritance into something completely different. While Roosevelt and Wilson were founding rhetorical presidents, Clinton and Bush were distinctly anti-intellectual ones.

By distinguishing the rhetorical and anti-intellectual presidencies, we can avoid the charge of flattening out nineteenth-century presidential history, rehabilitate the Roosevelt and Wilson presidencies by acknowledging that these rhetorical presidents were nowhere near as anti-intellectual as their successors, and come to a clearer diagnosis of what is wrong with contemporary presidential rhetoric. And it is important that we get the diagnosis right. We should not assume that presidential reticence alone would solve the problem of a substantively impoverished public sphere. Rather than seek self-defeating strategies by which we can silence presidents, we should seek to elevate the quality of presidential rhetoric. If we see the problem in qualitative rather than quantitative terms, we bypass Tulis's dilemma (and the implemental dilemma within it) altogether. By zooming in on the problem of anti-intellectualism, we stand a greater chance of finding leaders who satisfy the democratic citizen's demand for public leadership and who also refuse to coddle us with vacuous talk. A rhetorical presidency can rescue us from the anti-intellectual presidency after all.

Analyzing Presidential Rhetoric: Some Observations on Methods

To advance our understanding of the rhetorical presidency, we must look squarely and systematically at presidential rhetoric.[43] Part of the reason that political scientists have tended to focus on the quantitative problem of presidential rhetoric is their understanding of presidential speeches as acts—encapsulated by the widespread scholarly adoption of the term "going public"—rather than as processes infused with meaning. Recent scholarship has treated going public as strategic acts with measurable effects on the president's approval ratings, policy agenda, and legislative success and on the nation's economic performance.[44] Yet the measurable impact of speeches derives not just from when or how frequently they are made, but from what is actually said.[45] To assume that the act of saying something generates a certain reaction without close attention to what is being said is to miss the most crucial stage in the causal process and the scope of its impact. Not surprisingly, rhetorical and communications scholars have taken exception to this omission.[46] Yet their scholarly enterprise is not without limitations either. Focused on textual and contextual particulars, most rhetorical scholars have not ventured beyond piecemeal accounts of individual presidential rhetorical efforts to understand the presidency and its collective rhetorical record qua institution. For many rhetorical scholars, "each speech is a problem that has to be solved by using specific kinds of rhetorical devices."[47] This particularism coheres well with a biographical approach consisting of "a study of individual speakers for their influence upon history."[48] The resilience of the biographical approach coupled with a bias for "great" presidents have produced a body of work heavily weighted in treatments of Lincoln, FDR, and the like, and rather thin on the speeches of Buchanan and Hoover. Paradoxically, if rhetorical scholars tell us that content matters, their selectiveness of what is deemed worthy of examination has the opposite implication that most presidential rhetoric does not in fact matter. Piecemeal approaches to presidential rhetoric that select and differentiate between "great" and "ungreat" rhetoric do little justice to the forensic potential in the entire historical record of presidential rhetoric. In this book, I invert the conventional direction of rhetorical analysis by asking what rhetoric tells us *about* the presidency rather than what rhetoric can do *for* the individual president.

This conceptual shift adds an important normative dimension to my analysis. A scholarship that only focuses on rhetoric as personal resource will tend to be uncritically focused on whatever is persuasive and will neglect the systemic costs of successful, and sometimes anti-intellectual, rhetorical acts. The extant scholarship has come almost exclusively from the former camp. As a leading authority on the subject puts it, "Presidential rhetoric is a study of how presidents gain, maintain, or lose support of the public."[49] The predominant focus of scholarship has been on the "principles of rhetoric, understood as the human capacity to see what is most likely to be persuasive to a given audience on a given occasion."[50] A rhetor- and persuasion-centered approach will tend to be "institutionally partisan" in favor of the president, rather than constitutionally objective about the systemic impact of these rhetorical efforts.[51] It must, ultimately, endorse the winning tactics of presidential ant-intellectualism. The anti-intellectual presidency, I argue, has arisen at least in part because of our presidents', their advisors', and scholars' instrumental preoccupation with persuasion.[52]

Content Analysis

In this book, I apply the rhetorical critic's concern for the substance of presidential rhetoric systematically, using presidential words en masse as archaeological data to tell a developmental story about the American presidency and the changing nature of its political communication. While I will deploy a variety of methods, a general statement about computer-assisted quantitative content analysis, which is a relatively new method used in this book, is warranted here. For interested readers, a more specific note on the *General Inquirer*, which is the software I used for content analysis to measure substantive simplicity, can be found in appendix I. Readers who simply want to get on with the story I have to tell should skip ahead to the chapter synopses below.

For the content analyst, textual data are extraordinarily rich and varied, reflecting ideas, attitudes, and styles partly unique to the individual from whom the words emanate and partly derived from his or her particular cultural milieu. The question, however, is how an infinite variety of words, phrases, sentences, and styles can be converted into a basis for social scientific inference. When analyzing texts qualitatively or without the assistance of a computer, we typically use a cultural standard acquired from past experience to make sense of sentences like "It was the same old story." But while impressionistic conclusions may satisfy the needs of day-to-day living, they do not usually constitute a reliable method for research, especially when we deal with vast quantities of text. Social scientists have developed a procedure known as "content analysis" to explicate such judgmental processes more clearly, so that a uniform set of rules is used to extract meaning from vast quantities of text.

Content analysis is the method of classifying, and thereby compressing, the words of a text into a list of content categories based on explicit rules of coding.[53] For instance, a "religiosity" category, which registers a percentage of the total number of words in a text that referred to "God," "deity," the names of biblical prophets, and other like references made explicit in a coding rule, can explicate the religious tenor of a text in a fairly objective measure. Although there will remain a residually interpretive component to the inferential process in the construction of relevant categories, the computer has removed a principal methodological pitfall of earlier attempts at content analysis by ensuring perfect intertemporal and intercoder reliability. That is, with the computer, we ensure that the same text coded by different human operators at different times will yield the same results. More recently, advances in technology have broadened the scope of content analysis so that it is now also used to specify a fairly objective range of textual characteristics, such as grade readability or repetitiousness, which equip researchers to infer some aspect of external reality presumed to be latently encapsulated within each text, which cannot be discerned by the unaided human eye.[54]

Because all presidential words, not just those of the selectively "great," hold analytic potential, I examine rhetoric from every president, thus spanning over two centuries of presidential rhetoric in this book.[55] The computer may miss some insights that close human coding could yield, but I am interested here in discerning macroscopic patterns that require quantitative (large N) analysis. Indeed, a larger swath allows the computer to help us "read between the lines" in a different way, by discerning patterns across large quantities of text across time that will not be immediately apparent to the unaided human eye. Because, as James Fallows, a former speechwriter, reminds us, "a large and alarming percentage of the time the cause for a speech is the Scheduling Office,"[56] quantitative analysis allows us to examine macroscopic rhetorical patterns that have been consciously and often inadvertently transmitted from the White House, which has become a prolific prose production factory. The American presidency, in particular, lends itself to quantitative content analysis because there is probably no other public office in the world for which we have managed to keep a more comprehensive rhetorical record. As Woodrow Wilson put it, "There is no trouble now about getting the president's speeches printed and read, every word."[57] The systematic recording of presidential rhetoric presents a more comprehensive account of presidential history than even the sum of public opinion polls, which only began in the 1940s.[58] It is one of the very few ways by which we can generate a longitudinal data set that covers the entire span of presidential history, with minimal selection bias.

Now, there are theoretical objections to content analysis. Is my focus on rhetoric merely a romantic preoccupation with the poetry of history but tells us little about real life? Perhaps, but only if my database of presidential rhetoric systematically selects for the speeches of "great presidents." The data for this book were constructed from over 12,000 documents produced by all 43 presidents of the United States. This is a considerable increase compared to previous treatments of presidential communication, where the predominant use of a relatively small number of cases has offered limited analytic traction. Another related objection is that rhetoric is epiphenomenal, so observations at the rhetorical dimension cannot be reliably extrapolated to enhance our understanding of the presidency. My reply is that it is itself internal and relevant to our inquiry how rhetoric has become "mere rhetoric." The subject of our inquiry, after all, has been called the *rhetorical* presidency, and presidential loquaciousness has become the defining quality examined in an entire subfield of presidential studies. If anything, presidential rhetoric should be the first thing we study to understand the institution and not, as the objection implies, the last. If historians turn to speeches and rhetoric as primary sources with which they reconstruct the past, if politicians in a democratic republic are held accountable, assessed, and remembered for what they say (as the engraved walls of the presidential monuments in Washington amply reveal), and if the president of the United States is a public figure who "monopolizes the public space," then it is fair to assume that rhetoric is more than epiphenomenal.[59]

Rhetoric, of course, does not tell us everything. Technically, speeches and presidential statements cannot be anti-intellectual (or emotional, or inspirational, or so forth). Only persons can. So when we say that a speech has a certain quality, say, that it is anti-intellectual, we really mean to say that its speaker is anti-intellectual, and his anti-intellectual sentiments are conveyed in his speech. These sentiments may or may not be subjectively or internally felt (the speaker may not, in fact, be anti-intellectual), but that does not mean that the speaker and the content conveyed by his speech cannot be objectively or externally perceived to be anti-intellectual. And that is all that I am interested in here. Why not probe deeper? Because politics is external reality, and anti-intellectualism, in particular, is a potent political phenomenon only when it is a public stance. The content of politics is not infused with unspoken sentiments but is defined by our leaders' public words, and these words are all we have as a basis for information acquisition, deliberation, and political accountability.

Interviews with Speechwriters

While political scientists worry that the qualitative approach of rhetorical criticism is too often inescapably subjective, rhetorical scholars worry that the quantitative approach misses the nuances detectable only by the trained human eye and ear. To supplement the quantitative analysis of the kind described above, I interviewed 42 former and present speechwriters from the Truman administration (before which there are no surviving speechwriters) through the current Bush administration to elicit their views of presidential rhetoric. Selection was determined by membership in the exclusive Judson Welliver Society, named after the first full-time presidential speechwriter, of former White House speechwriters. The society was founded by former Nixon administration speechwriter William Safire in April 1987.[60] Throughout the book, but especially in chapter 3, I register the views of almost two-thirds of the membership of the Judson Welliver Society. I also consulted oral histories to elicit the views of 12 more speechwriters whom I was unable to personally interview and to elaborate on the views of some speechwriters whom I had already interviewed.[61] The oral histories provided closely contemporaneous accounts of the earlier administrations and supplemented what some of my interviewees were unable to recall several years after the fact. These primary accounts were further supplemented by memoirs and books written by other former speechwriters in order to register as many views as possible from the speechwriting community. In all, I was able to elicit the views of 63 men and women who helped to write the major speeches of every president from Harry S Truman to George W. Bush. As "eyewitness(es) to power" and the actual (co)authors of presidential rhetoric, these speechwriters are uniquely qualified to shed light on presidential rhetoric.[62] The interviews will corroborate that the conclusions drawn in this book are not just artifacts of the quantitative analysis. They recover the human texture of the process and institution of rhetorical invention, which we cannot fully capture just with quantitative analysis.

Chapter Synopses

The argument of this book proceeds in seven chapters. I present, in chapter 2, evidence of the relentless linguistic (syntactic and semantic) simplification of presidential rhetoric that occurred between 1789 and 2006. In chapter 3,

I reverse the prior chapter's direction of inquiry to examine the source, rather than the output, of presidential rhetoric. I show that presidents' and speech-writers' exceptionless and deliberate drive to simplify presidential rhetoric since the mid-twentieth century has been the linguistic underpinning of the anti-intellectual presidency.

In chapter 4, I supplement the evidence of linguistic simplification pre-sented in chapter 2 with evidence of substantive anti-intellectualism. I chart the relative demise of argument and explanation against the corresponding surge of applause-rendering platitudes, partisan punch lines, and emotional and human interest appeals in contemporary presidential rhetoric—all of which have contributed to the impoverishment of our public deliberative sphere.

In chapter 5, I step back from the data again to examine the evolu-tion of the White House speechwriting office and the institutional appara-tus of the anti-intellectual presidency. I track the institutional changes that have accompanied and reinforced the rise of the anti-intellectual presidency, namely, the creation and expansion of the speechwriting function and office, the legitimization of delegated speechwriting, and President Nixon's separa-tion of speechwriting from the policymaking function in 1969. Insofar as there was a precise birth date of the anti-intellectual presidency, it was 1969.

I evaluate the findings of the preceding chapters with an explicitly nor-mative lens in chapter 6 by tackling and ultimately refuting a cluster of argu-ments deployed to justify anti-intellectualism. I call the phenomenon what it is in this chapter and show why presidential anti-intellectualism is a threat to our democracy.

I conclude, in chapter 7, with a solution to the problem of presiden-tial anti-intellectualism by articulating the pedagogical purpose of rhetoric as theorized and practiced by the founding rhetorical presidents, Theodore Roosevelt, Woodrow Wilson, and Franklin Roosevelt, and as implied in scholarly criticisms of the contemporary presidency. I offer the model of a presidential pedagogue as the solution to the problem of presidential anti-intellectualism.

The Linguistic Simplification
of Presidential Rhetoric

In this chapter, I propose anti-intellectualism as *the* unifying critique of the contemporary presidency and begin a debate on how we might redirect our attention toward the quality, rather than just the quantity, of presidential rhetoric. Here, I present evidence of the transformed—syntactically truncated and semantically shortened—*structure* of presidential rhetoric, which militates against meaningful argument and deliberation, leaving a more focused account of the *substantive* impoverishment of presidential rhetoric to chapter 4 and the political-philosophical arguments about whether or not anti-intellectualism threatens the health of democracy to chapter 6. Here, I take off from the less ambitious proposition that there can be no plausible case for a thoroughgoing anti-intellectualism, which I will operationally define for this chapter as the relentless semantic and syntactic simplification of presidential rhetoric, because at some point simplification becomes oversimplification, and the drastically truncated structure of such language will fail to convey the minimum amount of information required as the basis for competent civic judgments.

Defining and Operationalizing Presidential Anti-Intellectualism

I begin with conceptual groundwork that will clear the way toward an operational definition of anti-intellectualism, my preferred term for a phenomenon more generally known as "dumbing down."[1] Anti-intellectualism is often alloyed to (and easily disguised by) disapprobative attitudes toward elitism, sophistry, effeminacy, and artifice and approbative attitudes toward sincerity, modesty, accessibility, and democracy, making it a potent political stance and weapon, but at the same time a difficult phenomenon to define. Yet it is important to note that the connections between anti-intellectualism and other disapprobative attitudes are constructed rather than necessary, and we must not mistake one part of an alloy with its essence. Take elitism, for example. It is only a historically contingent fact that American intellectuals have typically and derogatorily been labeled as elites. The connection between intellectuals and the elite is more complex in Europe, where anti-intellectualism was allied with the forces of conservatism and the establishment for significant periods of history. Unlike in America, many European intellectuals in the nineteenth century *were* the anti-elites: visionary outcasts advocating for social revolution. According to Voltaire, intellectuals neither "argufied on the benches of the universities nor said things by halves in the academies."[2] For Condorcet, intellectuals were iconoclasts who applied themselves to "the tracking down of prejudices in the hiding places where the priests, the schools, the governments and all long-established institutions had gathered and protected them."[3] And so, while the connection between anti-intellectualism and anti-elitism may go some way in explaining how anti-intellectualism developed strong roots in America, we must not confuse a historically contingent explanation of a phenomenon's history, or an associated concept, with its definition.

The classic treatment of American anti-intellectualism, from whence I derive my own definition, is Richard Hofstadter's *Anti-Intellectualism in American Life*. Hofstadter defined anti-intellectualism as a "resentment and suspicion of the life of the mind and of those who are considered to represent it; and a disposition constantly to minimize the value of that life."[4] Later in the book, Hofstadter clarified what he meant by a hostility to the "life of the mind" by articulating the common prejudicial distinction between "intelligence" and "intellect." The distinction is insightful because it highlights the political potency of a stance that rejects the latter in a way that simultaneously valorizes the former. Hofstadter wrote:

> Intellect... is the critical, creative, and contemplative side of mind.
> Whereas intelligence seeks to grasp, manipulate, re-order, adjust,
> intellect examines, ponders, wonders, theorizes, criticizes, imagines.
> Intelligence will seize the immediate meaning in a situation and
> evaluate it. Intellect evaluates evaluations.... Intelligence can be praised

as a quality in animals; intellect, being a unique manifestation of human dignity, is both praised and assailed as a quality in men.[5]

The operations of the intelligence are the functional, everyday workings of the mind. Their range is "narrow, immediate, and predictable," and their focus is "unfailingly practical."[6] Because intelligence can be found even in animals, the operations of the intelligence are deemed simple, innate, uncomplicated, and down-to-earth. Common parlance endorses Hofstadter's distinction. The possessor of intelligence, it may be said, is happily endowed with "common sense," unencumbered by the debilitating operations of the intellect. Because intelligence is something that almost all humans possess—Hofstadter believed that "the man of intelligence is always praised"[7]—there is little, if any, political gain that could be obtained from an anti-*intelligence* stance. Indeed, many anti-intellectuals can be identified by their frequent advocacy of common sense, a strategy I examine more closely in chapter 4.

Intellect, on the other hand, involves not the first-order operations of the mind with which intelligence is concerned, but the activities of the mind's eye on itself. Such activities as criticizing, examining, and theorizing are the second-order mental operations that are the life and trade of intellectuals and those who live the life of the mind. These mental operations are derided by the anti-intellectual as too complex, recondite, and sophistic. Again, common parlance captures the distinction aptly. The operations of the intellect are likened to "rocket science" constructed in an "ivory tower." They are deemed "highfalutin," out of touch with reality and common sense, and even occlusive of "practical" intelligence. Anti-intellectuals reject not intelligence—indeed, they valorize it in themselves—but the needlessly complex processes and products of the intellect.

This distinction between intellect and intelligence helps us to make sense of one of the best remembered episodes of anti-intellectualism in recent history: President Bush's commencement address at Yale University in 2001. Here are some of his remarks:

> And to the C students, I say, you, too, can be president of the United States....
>
> So now we know: If you graduate from Yale, you become president. If you drop out, you get to be vice president....
>
> If you're like me, you won't remember everything you did here. That can be a good thing....
>
> We both put a lot of time in at the Sterling Library, in the reading room, where they have those big leather couches. We had a mutual

understanding—Dick [Richard Brodhead, now president of Duke University] wouldn't read aloud, and I wouldn't snore.…

My critics don't realize I don't make verbal gaffes. I'm speaking in the perfect forms and rhythms of ancient haiku.[8]

The intended message of these remarks was that because—and not in spite of the fact that—he coasted through Yale on a C average, Bush was an intelligent guy who made the right choices in life. He had a whale of a time at Yale, forgot all attempts made to hone his intellect, and still became president. Verbal gaffes are everyday and down-to-earth, nothing like the convoluted constructions of poetry. His choices in college may not have led to the best grades, but as time would reveal, they were eminently intelligent. And so, on each of his seemingly artless anti-intellectual stabs, it was always the complex processes of (someone else's) intellect that were denigrated and the simple, commonsensical choices of (his) intelligence that were elevated.

Anti-intellectualism, then, is usually less benign than it initially appears. Distilled to its essence, it is a hostile stance toward the ostensibly complex processes and products of the mind (intellect), often accompanied by a celebration of its supposedly simple and everyday functions (intelligence). Since presidential anti-intellectualism is politically salient only at the public, rhetorical level, this leads us to an operationalized definition: presidential anti-intellectualism is detectable in terms of its rejection of rhetorical or linguistic complexity and in its valorization, in practice and by example, of linguistic simplicity.

Crucially, the Bush example reminds us of the suppressed correlative of the anti-intellectual stance. There is method to this seeming foolery. It is usually true in politics that, in order to be anti-X, one must also be pro-Y (where X and Y do not have to exist in a logically complementary relationship, though they often do) because in the political realm, almost all repudiative stances are also constructive efforts for a cherished alternative. Thus, when one is antiwar or antiestablishment, one is almost invariably also pro–something else, such as, respectively, a peace activist or a Burkean conservative. What then is the often unspoken correlative of the anti-intellectualist stance? It is a fetishization of simplicity. Anti-intellectuals aim not only to denigrate their intellectual adversaries and their ideas by mocking their manner of speech, but also to endear themselves and their ideas to their interlocutors by adopting and imitating their locution. They do this by rejecting the arguments of others as sophistic and abstruse with language that insinuates their own as the simple, unadorned, and therefore incontrovertible pearls of folk wisdom. Thus, anti-intellectualism is not only about the rejection of sophisticates and their verbosity, but it is also detectable in the conspicuous valorization of the common citizen and the mimicry of his or her simple locution. Anti-intellectualism thus operationalized is therefore measurable.

Measuring Anti-Intellectualism by Tracking Readability

Presidential rhetorical simplification is not the sole reason for the perceived degeneration of presidential rhetoric, but it is a major one and a phenomenon that we can attempt to quantify. Beginning after World War I, a developing science of measuring the simplicity, or the ease of readability, of texts gave us various formulas for computing textual readability. Readability is a judgment of how easy a text is to understand, where comprehension is a function of both linguistic (semantic and syntactic) form and the content being communicated.[9] I adopt the most widely used of extant readability formulas, the Flesch Readability formula, which measures readability as a function of sentence and word length.[10] The formula has been used in various studies in political science and other disciplines, as well as by the U.S. government in specifying the readability of texts.[11]

The formula is calculated as such:

$$\text{Flesch Readability} = 206.835 - (1.015 \times \text{ASL}) - (84.6 \times \text{ASW}),$$

where ASL = average sentence length (the number of words divided by the number of sentences), and ASW = average number of syllables per word (the number of syllables divided by the number of words). The scores normally range on a 100-point scale (although this is not mathematically necessary), with a higher score indicating greater readability or simplicity.[12]

To be sure, readability is not merely a function of the semantic and syntactic simplicity of a text. Critics of reading formulas rightly contend that these formulas only measure the "surface features" of a text and ignore other features, like a reader's level of preparedness and the organizational coherence of the text.[13] Is it not possible, it may be asked, for a text filled with short sentences and monosyllabic words to nevertheless convey complex meaning? I avoid such objections by applying a different set of measures for quantifying substantive simplicity in chapter 4. But for now, the force of these objections can be tested. To do this, I applied the Flesch test across 13 genres of texts for which we expect a broad variance in substantive simplicity and complexity.[14] The results are depicted in figure 2.1, with the different genres of text (transcribed if originally in aural form) arranged in increasing order of readability ease from left to right. The left-hand side shows that academic writing, such as social scientific and humanities scholarship, which our pretheoretical expectations tell us tend to be substantively complex, obtained very low Flesch scores and are correspondingly also the most difficult to read. The right-hand side shows that television drama and comedy, which we expect will tend to be substantively simple, are the most easy to read. Thus, as we observe a broad range of Flesch scores pegged to their respective textual genres, we have prima facie evidence that readability is correlated to substantive simplicity. Perhaps it is merely a stylistic predilection that scholars and academics write with multisyllabic words and long sentences, but it is less than plausible that that is *all* the Flesch score tells us and that this complex linguistic structure does not also predict the substantive complexity of the texts analyzed. That there is a structural limit to expressing complex thoughts with monosyllabic words and short sentences is indicated by the fact that even the how-to *Dummies* series is written at the 10th-grade level and up.[15] At ever regressing levels, the semantic and syntactic structure of language invariably constrains the complexity of ideas being expressed.

One may, however, quarrel with the seemingly nonintuitive findings that philosophical essays appear to be more substantively simple, in figure 2.1, than social scientific scholarship, and that celebrity reporting is more complex than, say, television comedies.[16] So, rather than pit intuition against intuition, we can test the relationship between rhetorical/linguistic simplicity (as measured by the Flesch scores) and substantive simplicity more systematically by first deploying some content analytic categories that help us to capture the substantive sense of these texts. In deciding on which of these categories to use, I assumed that words are articulated thoughts, and, among other

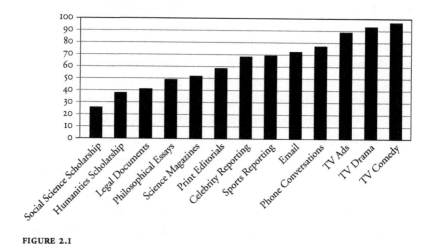

FIGURE 2.1

Flesch Scores for Various Genres of Text

discriminating criteria, substantively complex texts contain more thoughts per page than do simple texts. Substantive simplicity-complexity can therefore be measured by counting the references to and, correspondingly, the amount of intellectual processing—such as analyzing, comparing, contrasting, deducing, inferring, and so forth—that occurred in our sample of texts. Two categories from the Harvard IV-4 dictionary suggested themselves here. Using the *General Inquirer* program, I tracked the amount of intellectual processing in our textual samples with the categories *Know* and *Think*.[17] Figures 2.2 and 2.3 indicate the scores achieved for our 13 genres of texts for these two categories. As expected, substantively complex texts (e.g., social science scholarship) tend to involve and therefore rhetorically invoke significant levels of cognitive processing, while substantively simple texts involve less processing. I found a statistically significant relationship between the Flesch scores and each of these Harvard IV-4 categories, suggesting that there is a relationship between linguistic simplicity and substantive simplicity.[18]

So, for now, I make the assumption that, in tracking readability or linguistic simplicity, the Flesch formula also tracks—not perfectly but at least generally—the substantive simplicity (or complexity) of a text. The Flesch score is useful because it provides a temporally insensitive metric of rhetorical simplicity based on an austere formula that shows no bias toward phraseology or manner of expression, the principal modulators of language across time. To be sure, its relatively austere formula holds both its promise and its limitations. The formula holds promise because words, phrases, and sentences can be deployed and arranged in an almost infinite number of meaningful ways, and any

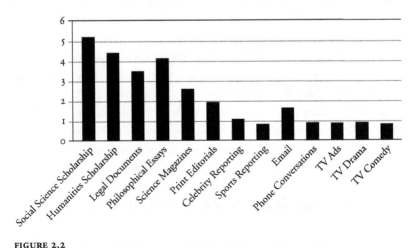

FIGURE 2.2

Percentage Occurrence of *Know* for Various Genres of Text

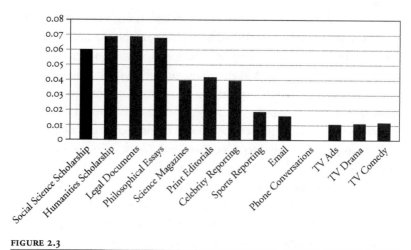

FIGURE 2.3

Percentage Occurrence of *Think* for Various Genres of Text

formula that attempts to measure readability ease by tracking such occurrences and permutations will likely become unworkably encumbered. However, the consensus remains that until these other linguistic features can be unambiguously operationalized and reliably measured, these surface features remain the best predictors of text difficulty as measured by comprehension tests.[19] Susan Kemper argues that "sentence length and word familiarity do contribute to the comprehension of these passages...[and] these two different approaches to measuring the grade level difficulty of texts are equivalent in predictive power."[20] Many linguists, once critical of readability formulas, have come around to admit that "these formulas are correlated with the conceptual properties of the text" and that word and sentence length are the strongest predictors of difficulty.[21]

Nevertheless, I tread carefully. I will use the Flesch formula to make relative claims about the readability trends of presidential rhetoric across time, not to make absolute claims about the exact levels of readability at any particular time. Conclusions of the latter kind require stricter standards for construct validity whereas those of the former only require that the same formula be applied against texts in order to provide a meaningful ranking of which texts are more or less simple.

The Waxing and Waxing (?) of Anti-Intellectualism

Hofstadter observed, "Anti-intellectualism is, in fact, older than our national identity, and has a long historical background."[22] On this point, there is little disagreement. While the possession of an intellect has not excluded persons from the presidential office, such credentials have not, in general, been sufficient for garnering significant political support. Indeed, as the cases of Hoover and Carter—both of whom were trained engineers—reveal, intellectual credentials alone have little intrinsic political value. As one commentator tartly (and anti-intellectually) observed, "Ronald Reagan never pretended to be an intellectual and never bothered to read much political philosophy. Yet his ideas probably changed the world as much as those of any other political leader in the late twentieth century."[23] The suggestion, of course, was that the intellectual ruminations of political philosophy were at best tangential to, and at worst an obstacle to, grasping the elemental ideas that helped President Reagan to transform our world. An intellectual bent was not politically injurious and even advantageous only if a president also displayed an aptitude for other, nonintellectual pursuits—a combination Theodore Roosevelt assiduously finessed.

On closer examination, however, Hofstadter believed that anti-intellectualism in American life exhibited cyclical tendencies, although this was never a thesis he set out to demonstrate. He observed, "Regard for intellectuals in the United States has not moved steadily downward and has not gone into sudden, recent decline, but is subject to cyclical fluctuations."[24] What follows is a brief historical survey indicating why we may have reason to doubt this hypothesis, and hence reason to test it empirically.

There were at least two intellectual high points in American history, which would seem to support the cyclical thesis. As was the case with the revolutionary generations in France, Russia, and China, America's founding fathers were intellectuals in various guises: ministers, scientists, philosophers, and men of cultural refinement. In this period, the ideal of an enlightened philosopher-king tolerated and even venerated intellect as a virtue relevant for office. It was necessary, according to Samuel Adams, to "cultivate the natural genius, elevate the soul, excite laudable emulation to excel in knowledge, piety, and benevolence; and finally it will reward its patrons and benefactors by shedding its benign influence on the public mind."[25] The relationship between power and intellect in the patrician period was symbiotic, but with important caveats. The intellectuals who founded our nation rejected the "ancient prejudices and manners" of the Old World.[26] As Europeans saw the American colonials as intellectually inferior and culturally unrefined, some American intellectuals celebrated the wisdom of the unschooled and untainted mind, preferring to see Europe as a declining Rome looking jealously at Athens. Even Thomas Jefferson, an undisputed man of letters, would profess in 1787: "State a moral case to a ploughman and a professor. The former will decide it well, and often better than the latter, because he has not been led astray by artificial rules."[27] Ironically, Jefferson would later become the victim of possibly the first sustained political anti-intellectual attack in the years leading up to the election of 1800.[28]

A second exception was the Progressive era, during which the country turned to its intellectuals for ideas, explanations, technical solutions, and justifications for governmental action in the context of great social and economic changes in the country and its place in the world. Once again, men who were comfortable with and committed to the intellectual enterprise were able to ascend in the political arena: Theodore Roosevelt, prolific writer and erstwhile president of the American Historical Association; Henry Cabot Lodge, who was a lecturer in American history at Harvard; Woodrow Wilson, former professor and president of Princeton; Robert La Follette, whose use of experts from the University of Wisconsin during his gubernatorial term became the prototype (the "Wisconsin idea") for FDR's "Brains Trust."[29] It was also during this time that public intellectuals and academics alike—individuals like Walter Lippmann, Herbert Croly, and John Dewey—were able to attain a level of prominence and public rapprochement that their predecessors rarely achieved. But again, while there were fewer visible signs of anti-intellectualism in this period, facets of the phenomenon remained latent. Theodore Roosevelt was no enemy of reflection, but his first priority was action. In a speech he delivered in Paris, he noted that "it is not the critic who counts; not the man who points out how the strong man stumbles....The credit belongs to the man who is actually in the arena, whose face is marred by dust and sweat and blood."[30] Even Woodrow Wilson, the scholar-president, did not fully reinstate intellectuals to the place they had occupied during the patrician period. He said in his 1912 campaign:

> What I fear is a government of experts. God forbid that in a democratic country we should resign the task and give the government over to experts. What are we for if we are to be scientifically taken care of by a small number of gentlemen who are the only men who understand the job?[31]

If New Deal politics were an extension of the Progressive era, so were its attitudes toward intellectuals. The rising fortunes of intellectuals during the Progressive era eventually culminated in the famous Brains Trust, a team of close advisors whom Franklin Roosevelt gathered mostly from the academic community to write New Deal policies. But even then, it was not clear, given the purposes to which intellectuals were put, if this truly constituted a renaissance of their fortunes. As Bertrand Russell noted, it was not so much the intellectual, but "the technician...[who was] the really big man in the modern world."[32] Certainly, the marriage of power and intellect in this period was radically different from the symbiosis of the patrician period. Intellectuals were co-opted not only because their ideas were intrinsically valued, but because they were useful for reasons other than their contribution to policy, such as serving in ambassadorial functions to the intellectual community, as ideational scapegoats, and as policy legitimators. Thus, Tevi Troy observes that the best use of intellectuals in the White House was not as advisors, or even technicians, but as ambassadors to a community that had to be courted like any other special interest group.[33] Equally tellingly, even Roosevelt's Brains Trust soon generated a brains distrust. The co-optation of experts and intellectuals into the machinery of government also made them the objects of jealousy and fulmination by those they supplanted and others who disagreed with their prescriptions, finally culminating in the anti-intellectual backlash of the McCarthy years.

And so, even the two periods of intellectual revival contained within them latent manifestations of anti-intellectualism that would at least qualify the cyclical thesis, suggesting that the germ of anti-intellectualism existed as early as at the founding of the republic. Writing during the interstice between the McCarthy years and the intellectual renaissance of the Kennedy years, there was reason enough for Hofstadter's sanguinity. But even his confidence was qualified. Hofstadter observed that, with the election of John Kennedy and the rehabilitation of intellectuals within the White House, their only gain was "the legitimacy of a special interest," a point reiterated in Troy's discussion of the place of intellectuals in the White House.[34]

The observation of cyclicity, if plausible in 1963, seems off the mark with the benefit of hindsight. In the mid-1960s, student protests around the nation fueled a new round of anti-intellectualism among politicians. In California, Ronald Reagan based his political emergence on anti-intellectualism in part by exploiting the gulf between the university community and the general public by calling faculty and students troublemakers and "self-indulgent snobs,"[35] condemning universities for "subsidizing intellectual curiosity," and threatening to dismiss university chancellors if they failed to control campus unrest.[36] In the White House, aides in the Johnson administration found themselves actually, and not just publicly, suspicious of intellectuals, no doubt as a result of intellectuals' involvement in the radicalization of the Left. One cautiously observed: "Intellectuals—men who in their own fields resisted loose reasoning and specious analogies—began to accept the most extreme assessments of the country and those who governed it. The more savage the analysis, the more appropriate they found it; the more violent the proposed response, the more condign."[37] Nixon co-opted intellectuals in his cabinet, but he also appointed a vice president, Spiro Agnew, who called the media "nattering nabobs of negativism" (and who was also a fitting foil for Democratic presidential candidate George Wallace, who had been leading a campaign against "pointy-headed bureaucrats"). For his part, Nixon's successful mobilization of a "silent majority" against an articulate minority pitted folk wisdom against the wisdom of the "chattering classes," a strategy that would flower into a recurring anti-intellectual strategy practiced by presidents since. Hofstadter's book also presaged the "credibility gap" that emerged after Vietnam and Watergate, which further discredited Beltway experts and necessitated a new imperative for presidential plain talking and the new champions of anti-intellectualism since the 1980s, numbering among them Ronald Reagan, whose sentimental anecdotes often displayed a tenuous relationship with properly researched facts; the elder President Bush, who taunted Clinton for his association with Oxford; and Newt Gingrich, who led an assault against "the cognitive elite" in 1995. In more recent times, the Bush campaign of 2000 and the nature of his administration's justifications for war in Iraq resurrected fears of an increasing anti-intellectualism in the White House, suggesting that even if we have underestimated the trough length of the anti-intellectual cycle, we are nowhere near a point of inflexion.[38] In the 2000 presidential campaign, Bush's witting and unwitting stabs at the intellect became political assets:

> What Bush understands, and the pundits do not, is that he is a brilliant candidate not despite his anti-intellectualism but because of it. He has stumbled upon a fortuitous moment in which the political culture, tired of wonks and pointy-heads and ideologues, yearns instead for a candidate unburdened by, or even hostile to, ideas.[39]

That a Harvard- and Yale-educated president should find himself so publicly arrayed against intellect and intellectuals—unlike similarly credentialed presidents like FDR and Kennedy, who courted them—suggests that presidential anti-intellectualism may not be in retreat, but may possibly be advancing. The germ of anti-intellectualism, barely detectable during the founding era, appears to have become a virulent force in our time.

Charting the Anti-Intellectual Presidency

So, is the anti-intellectual presidency waxing and only waxing? I turn to the public record of presidential words to answer this question. I look at the annual messages first because they allow me to generate an annual time series, and changes can be observed across constant intervals of time within and across presidencies.[40]

Figure 2.4 is a scatter plot of the Flesch Readability scores of all 216 annual messages delivered between 1790 and 2006 fitted on a lowess curve connecting 50 percent of the data points and showing the relentless simplification of the annual message.[41] Note that the annual message should be the genre least susceptible to the pressures of simplification. It is a formal, constitutionally mandated genre, as well as the one speech that presidents today can be assured will have uninterrupted prime-time coverage on all major television networks so that presidents are relatively free from the pressure to abbreviate and sloganize. As "a marching order for the bureaucracy" intended to communicate all of the major policy initiatives of an administration for the next legislative year, it is just about the most important speech that a president delivers.[42]

Yet, the simplification of the State of the Union address is unmistakable. Whereas the annual messages were pitched at a college reading level (a score of about 30–50) through most of the eighteenth and nineteenth centuries, they have now come down to an eighth-grade reading level (a score of about 60–70).

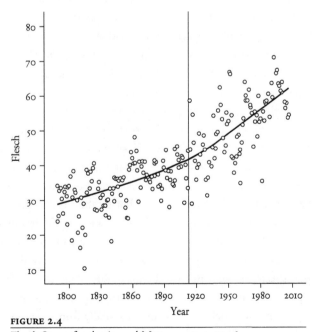

FIGURE 2.4

Flesch Scores for the Annual Messages, 1790–2006

Theodore Roosevelt (whose messages averaged at 42.4) and Woodrow Wilson (at 43.6) were part of a pattern of rhetorical simplification that has occurred across two centuries, but they were not anti-intellectual presidents (unless one were to make the implausible case that *any* simplification is anti-intellectual). These data belie the sharp modern-traditional divide entrenched in presidential studies.[43] Rhetorical simplification started well before Theodore Roosevelt and Woodrow Wilson, and it continued apace after these founding rhetorical presidents. However, it was only deep into the twentieth century that the culmination of years of benign, even commendable, linguistic simplification (which facilitated popular access) culminated in the anti-intellectual presidency.

There was a discernible upward movement in the Flesch scores as a result of Woodrow Wilson returning to the pre-Jeffersonian tradition of delivering the annual message in person to the congress in 1913, marked by the vertical line inserted in figure 2.4. As would be expected, 1913 serves as a fairly neat dividing point between two periods. Fitting two linear functions to the two periods reveals a clearer picture of the effect of the change in 1913. The first, from 1790 to 1912, shows an annual rate of increase of the Flesch score (β_1) of 0.10; and the second, from 1913 to 2006, shows a rate of increase of 0.21.[44] However, Wilson's appearance before the congress in 1913 did not inaugurate the simplifying trend in presidential rhetoric; it merely intensified it. The existence of only a single point of inflexion in figure 2.4 suggests that no other event was sufficient to create another discernible kink in this trend: not when the annual message was first broadcast on the radio in 1923 or via television in 1947 or on the Web in 2000. Whatever the engine of presidential rhetorical simplification, it spans a more impressive temporal spectrum than the individual effects of radio, television, or any other accoutrement or happenstance of modernity.

The kink observed in 1913 suggests that the Flesch score is possibly sensitive to mode of delivery, but the case has been overstated. Ceaser et al. were only partly correct to note that "the written word formerly provided a partial screen or check against the most simplistic argumentations."[45] The annual messages before those delivered by Wilson *were* also orally delivered, just not by the president of the United States, but by the clerk of the House of Representatives, who read aloud the written message of the president. This is an often-missed fact that alters the conventional causal narrative. It is true that the annual message changed from a written letter (read aloud by a clerk) to an actual speech in 1913. But it was not orality alone that supplied the simplifying pressure in presidential rhetoric after 1913. It was the fact that it was the *president* who delivered the message orally from 1913 onward that exacerbated the readability trends. It was not so much the mode of delivery or indeed the frequency of speechmaking (as quantitative critics may argue) that altered the language of the annual messages as it was the altered relationship among the president, the congress, and the people. Those who have argued that rhetorical simplification has occurred because of the onset of the aural culture in the first few decades of the twentieth century (or the popularization of television at midcentury) cannot explain the continued trajectory of rhetorical simplification in the decades since Wilson's innovation, an observation that points to larger patterns in American democracy as well as the endogenous, self-reinforcing tendency of anti-intellectualism, which I will discuss in the next chapter.[46]

Figure 2.5 depicts the same analysis performed on every inaugural address delivered between 1789 and 2005, showing that the pattern observed in figure 2.4 is not genre specific. It also tells us that the simplification of presidential rhetoric has been driven by something other than the mode of delivery, since the inaugural address is and (unlike the annual message) has always been a spoken genre.[47] Note also that inaugural addresses are quadrennially delivered, so there has been no surfeit of speech to hasten the degeneration of their quality. The "inferior art form" of the inaugural addresses evolved independently of the pressures from oral delivery and excessive speechmaking.[48]

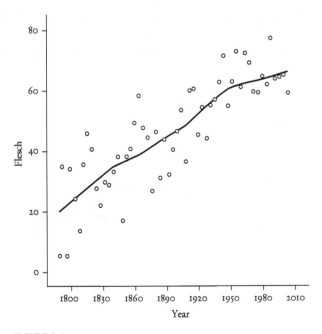

FIGURE 2.5

Flesch Scores for the Inaugural Addresses, 1789–2005

The Flesch formula can be broken down further into its component parts in order to understand the linguistic structure of presidential anti-intellectualism. Figure 2.6 shows the downward trajectory of the average sentence length in the annual message, which has done most of the work of driving the Flesch scores upward. The average sentence length of the annual message has fallen from 35.2 words before 1913 to 22 words after. That is why observers have noticed that State of the Union addresses have increasingly become a "laundry list" of sound bites punctuated by pause and applause, exemplifying the "primer style" of presidential rhetoric.[49]

A similar trend can be observed in the inaugural addresses. Figure 2.7 indicates that a similar shortening of the sentences in the inaugural addresses has occurred across the 200-year history of the presidency. The data are consistent with the finding that the average presidential sound bite shrank from 42 seconds in 1968 to 7 seconds in 2000, about the time required to say the 15 to 20 words in an average presidential sentence today.[50]

A larger question remains. Are these changes in presidential rhetoric only reflections of across-the-board linguistic changes in society? Obviously, we cannot rule out a feedback loop between presidents and their audiences. And evidence does suggest the simplification of the American language at around the turn of the twentieth century. Scholars have argued that these linguistic changes began with the turn to the aural culture as the telephone, phonograph, and then radio came into common use in the final decades of the nineteenth century and the first few decades of the twentieth century.[51]

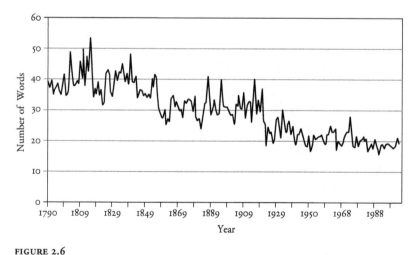

FIGURE 2.6

Average Sentence Length of Annual Messages, 1790–2006

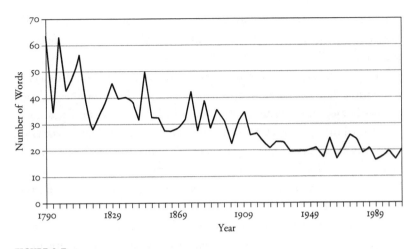

FIGURE 2.7

Average Sentence Length of Inaugural Addresses, 1789–2005

It was also at this time that Mencken wrote his monumental *The American Language*, which was a seminal treatment of the differences between American and British English, and he became the first unabashed champion of American English. Of the effort to impose British English on the American tongue, he had this to say:

> Such grammar, so-called, as is taught in our schools and colleges, is a grammar standing four-legged upon the theorizings and false inferences of English Latinists of a past generation, eager only to break the wild tongue of Shakespeare to a rule; and its frank aim is to create in us a high respect for a book language which few of us ever actually speak and not many of us even learn to write.[52]

Mencken's fight with the traditional grammarians was continued by his fellow linguists, so that by the 1960s, it was clear that a linguistic revolution had taken place. (Indeed, contemporary scholars decrying the degeneration of the American language put the start of that degeneration in the 1960s, though it is more likely, given my data, that it was around this time that the culmination of long-term trends became *evident*.)[53] In 1961, the magnitude of this perceived linguistic revolution was dramatized by the publication of and the reaction to the unabridged *Webster's Third New International Dictionary*.[54] This edition included 100,000 new words never before found in the unabridged dictionary and was marked by a conspicuous effort not to make a distinction between "right" and "wrong" and between "colloquial" and "formal" usages.[55]

Insofar as the distinction ever existed, the third edition of *Webster's*, still the most recently published edition even today, brought the status of colloquial (American) English on a par with that of formal (British) English.

In part because of the pioneering efforts of Mencken and others to legitimize colloquial usage, simplicity has become the recommended best practice in modern communication.[56] Admittedly then, the simplification of presidential rhetoric reflects a larger pattern in American language writ large, which has become increasingly permissive of simplicity. This does not mean, however, that presidents do not possess a margin of rhetorical autonomy. But how much are presidents themselves contributing to the simplification of their rhetoric?

Presidents are not mere slaves to larger linguistic trends. We only need to look at the Flesch scores of other nonpresidential genres of rhetoric to see this. The contemporary cross-sectional data in figure 2.1 above show that whatever societal linguistic trends there have been that have brought us to where we are, they have not affected every genre of rhetoric to the same degree. Social scientific scholarship, for instance, remains pitched at college reading level, while television advertisements are now pitched at a fifth-grade reading level. Figure 2.1 shows that, if societal linguistic trends assuredly exist, they are *not* deterministic.

Time series data, though admittedly limited here, take us to the same conclusion as the cross-sectional data above. Figure 2.8 compares the changes in readability of four presidential campaign rhetorical genres between 1948 and 2000 (so that, in each year, content and context across genres are held

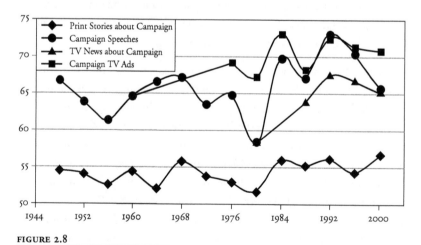

FIGURE 2.8

Flesch Scores for Four Rhetorical Genres, 1948–2000

constant), where the data are available.[57] The three oral genres pitched to the widest audiences (campaign speeches, television news about the campaign, and television advertisements) remained consistently more readable than the one textual genre (print stories about the campaign), which did not experience a significant increase in readability ease in more than 50 years. Note, again, that mode of delivery (whether or not a genre is oral or textual) does not fully account for the differences in readability. Even among the oral genres, presidential campaign speeches have tended to be significantly more readable than television news reports of the campaigns; indeed, in some years, campaign speeches have almost attained the same readability level as campaign television advertisements, the prototypical genre of sound bites. These uneven trajectories blunt the force of the claim that changes in presidential rhetoric are *merely* changes in across-the-board societal linguistics, at least since 1948. Instead, it is likely that presidential candidates have exerted some independent discretion in simplifying their messages for the public. This is a point I will deal with frontally in chapter 3.

Figure 2.9 looks at presidential language writ large via the totality of presidential documents—both written and spoken, formal and informal—recorded in the *Public Papers* of each president in his first full year in office from Herbert Hoover to George W. Bush. Each president's *Papers* constitute the full public record of his rhetoric in office, so the *Papers* lend themselves

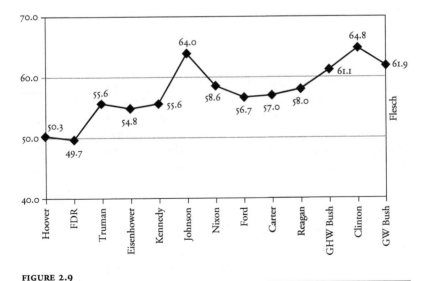

FIGURE 2.9

Flesch Scores of the *Public Papers* of Presidents Hoover to G. W. Bush to meaningful comparisons among the rhetorical modes of different presidents.[58] By looking at the full spectrum of presidential rhetoric, we avoid Mel Laracey's charge that "modern scholars have almost automatically equated 'going public' with speechmaking" and provide evidence that rhetorical simplification has occurred across the board in presidential rhetoric.[59]

Figure 2.9 shows that the upward trend of the Flesch scores from 1929 to 2001 is, again, unmistakable.[60] In this brief span of less than 80 years, the readability of presidential rhetoric has transformed from college level to the eighth-grade level. (And we have reason to think that present trends will continue. As of 2003, just under half [43 percent] of the adult [≥ 16 years old] U.S. population struggled to read prose at or below the fourth-grade level, which, in the language of the U.S. Census, makes them just shy of being "functionally literate."[61] This figure has not changed much since 1992, when the figure was 42 percent.) The demand for presidential anti-intellectualism appears high, and there has been no evidence that presidents have hesitated in supplying it.

Certainly, these results are partially reflective of changes in the relative composition of each of the *Public Papers*, as some informal rhetorical genres prone to rhetorical simplification have become increasingly represented. Table 2.1 shows that the proportion of items labeled "address," "remark," and "toast" (usually to a visiting dignitary) in the *Public Papers* has increased across time. However, these observations are endogenous to the interpretation made here: the changing composition of the *Papers* is itself indicative of the changing conceptions and prioritizations of the presidential rhetorical role, which have encouraged the simplification of rhetoric.

TABLE 2.1

Addresses, Remarks, and Toasts of Presidents Hoover through Ford

	Addresses (A)	Remarks (R)	Toasts (T)	(A)+(R)+ (T) = (1)	Total number of items in *Public Papers* (2)	(1) as % of (2)
Hoover	82	84	0	166	1699	.10
Roosevelt	274	186	10	470	2137	.22
Truman	247	392	15	654	2325	.28
Eisenhower	134	529	57	720	2563	.28
Kennedy	59	579	57	695	1560	.44
Johnson	28	1382	105	1515	3424	.44
Nixon	804	88	106	998	2468	.40
Ford	41	980	74	1095	2166	.51

If we accept that, however constituted, each president's *Papers* nevertheless represent the full rhetorical record of his presidency, figure 2.9 tells us that Presidents Herbert Hoover and Franklin Roosevelt belonged to a different era where simplicity (or the reliance on simple rhetorical genres) was not the first priority of presidential rhetoric. These scores indicate that Roosevelt's presidential rhetoric was less partial to the demands of readability than conventional wisdom would have us expect. Indeed, Roosevelt, remembered as among the most "eloquent" of the last 12 presidents, was also the most rhetorically complex. In contrast, it will not be an overinterpretation of the data to say that *government*, and not just the speeches delivered in the first year of the Clinton administration, was conducted in the language of eighth- and ninth-graders, the grade equivalent of a Flesch score of 64.8.

Further discussion of the implications of these figures will be postponed until I have examined in chapter 3 the individual decisions that have driven these cumulative outcomes. For now, I conclude that (1) presidential rhetorical simplification across the last two centuries is real and demonstrable, and (2) we cannot endorse the virtue of rhetorical simplicity indefinitely, because at some point simplification becomes oversimplification. While the marginal return to society of rhetorical simplification remains positive as long as it increases accessibility to the population without sacrificing substance, presidential rhetoric is either already well past this rewarding threshold or getting there. As Einstein put it best: "Everything should be made as simple as possible, but no simpler."[62] As we shall see in the next chapter, presidents have observed Einstein's injunction *without* his caveat.

3

The Anti-Intellectual Speechwriters

Although presidents respond to voters and context, they retain the preroga-
tive to decide to whom to speak, when, and, most important, how. In order to
understand the logic that has inspired the anti-intellectual presidency, we need to
unlatch the black box of presidential speechwriting to discover the motivations of
those who helped to pen the words of our presidents. I examine opinions extracted
from personal interviews with 42 former and present speechwriters, going back
to the Truman administration, and their published accounts to understand the
efforts and struggles of these men and women and their responses to the editorial
demands of their principals. These speechwriters speak directly to the findings in
the previous chapter, since they wrote most of the presidential speeches, including all of the State of the Union messages and inaugural addresses of the last half
century. They not only take us as close as we can get to the rhetorical intentions
of presidents themselves, but their views are independently significant because
they enjoy significant discretion in the crafting of presidential rhetoric.

In this chapter, I demonstrate the unanimity of opinion among speechwriters that simplicity is always preferred to complexity and justify the operationalized link between a cult of rhetorical simplicity and anti-intellectualism
operationalized in the previous chapter. This is an important extension of the
previous chapter's findings: if we observe the products of presidents' valorization of simplicity in their public speeches, then we observe, behind the
scenes, the intense disdain for verbal complexity shared by speechwriters and

presidents alike. If rhetorical practices constitute, as Tulis argued, "reflections and elaborations of underlying doctrines of governance," then we should not underestimate the impact of the uniform application of these practices.[1] While a preference for simplicity appears to be a benign precept of good writing, the across-the-board preference for simplicity among speechwriters has been one of the principal motors of presidential anti-intellectualism.[2] I will conclude this chapter by modeling the accumulation of several discrete decisions to go anti-intellectual as a classic tyranny of small decisions. In doing so, I offer an explanation to the puzzle of how such a radical institutional transformation as the anti-intellectual presidency crept up on us.

Servicing the Anti-Intellectual Presidency

If presidents have become more anti-intellectual, it is in part because they have lieutenants who endorse and execute their programs. Three key propositions emerge from my interviews with 42 former speechwriters: (1) rhetorical construction in the contemporary White House is a deliberate enterprise; (2) presidents have been trenchantly against complex and ornate "rhetoric"; and (3) this has been accompanied by an exceptionless preference for rhetorical simplicity. The combination of a deliberate rejection of "rhetoric" and an immoderate preference for simplicity are the drivers of presidential anti-intellectualism. The unanimity of opinion depicted here points to a tyrannical decisional logic with cumulative consequences unforeseen by individual presidents going anti-intellectual.

Deliberate Rhetorical Construction

The deliberateness of speech crafting matters because, otherwise, presidential anti-intellectualism would only be a reflection of larger sociolinguistic changes impinging on the presidency. To be sure, these forces exist, but the principled anti-intellectualism of contemporary presidents suggests as much leading as following. Rhetorical simplification in and by itself is only proof of *un*intellectualism, the product of an unwitting simpleton. It is only when simplification is deliberately and immoderately pursued that unintellectualism becomes *anti*-intellectualism. And it is the latter that properly explains the impoverished state of presidential rhetoric.

Rhetorical construction in the era of the packaged presidency is a deliberate process because of the observed distinction between what speechwriters would write for themselves and what they produce for presidents, and because of the parallel distinction between private and public presidential utterances. Most speechwriters are "very sophisticated, knowledgeable, clever people who probably would write very different speeches for themselves than they would for the people they work for."[3] Many admit a built-in antagonism between their inclinations as writers and the instructions they received from presidents. One complains that "what you do, most of the time, is serve up the same kind of pap."[4] Another observes:

> We all have [Ted] Sorensen in mind, we have the words of Lincoln ringing in our inner ears. And so we all have the secret ambition to write the words that can be carved in granite in some national monument somewhere. And so there's always the aspiration to higher rhetoric. And it was frustrating often for all of us that Clinton eschewed that sort of thing.[5]

Other speechwriters have expressed discomfort with the increasing demands for manufactured extemporaneity, as opposed to a speech that would sound like it had been coherently thought out. The former director of speechwriting for George W. Bush describes his challenge:

> In some ways, ever since [I was] young, I've felt like a fossil in this profession, because I felt like almost all of the time, it was a failure to have any element of coherence or preparation. Spontaneity is the only thing that matters. There are a lot of people in American public life that way.[6]

The fact, then, that speechwriters have had to act in opposition to their natural literary inclinations tells us that these choices were made at least in partial response to contrary directions from above. Paralleling the tensions that they experienced in the practice of their craft, speechwriters in turn have observed a Janus-like quality in their bosses, who are articulate, formal, and sophisticated in private, but decidedly casual and simplistic in public. According to his personal secretary, Ann Whitman, Eisenhower was "deathly afraid of being considered highbrow."[7] His speechwriter, however, observed characteristics that could have branded him as such:

> The general public thinks of him as a grandfatherly old man who had no concept of the English language, no interest in it, no feeling for the precision of words, no capacity for determining when a sentence ended and when it began, no knowledge of paragraphing or of organization. And yet in all of these things he had a greater capacity than anybody I've ever known....Absolute pedant with the English language. Insufferable.[8]

Another former Eisenhower speechwriter similarly notes a contrast between the public and private president, observing that his boss was "a very serious editor, strangely, because of his reputation as somebody who mangled syntax."[9]

Although Johnson is usually unfavorably compared to his predecessor, Kennedy, in terms of his public performance, his counsel recalls the surprising formalism of Johnson's private speech:

> What struck me very strongly is that Johnson . . . finished every sentence. All the sentences were parsed. The verb tenses were correct. It didn't sound very elegant, and it didn't sound grand or thrilling at all. But it was certainly . . . quite correct.[10]

Nixon, according to one of his speechwriters, was "an intellectual who pretended not to be."[11] Another speechwriter observes:

> He [Nixon] would often choose language that was simple and direct. He liked slogans to the point of almost sloganizing some things, and even, I think, he sometimes disguised his intelligence. I think he's a much more sophisticated and intelligent person than some of his language indicated.[12]

Reagan continued in this tradition. According to Chris Matthews:

> When Reagan [spoke] . . . he was positioning himself with enormous science, establishing himself in the public mind not as an aloof head of government but as the man next door. Where his predecessors identified themselves with the attainment of government power, Reagan posed as a visiting citizen.[13]

A former speechwriter observed that President George W. Bush, who continues to suffer and enjoy the epithet of a rhetorical philistine, possesses a hunger for detail and subtlety that belies his public rhetorical style. The former speechwriter wrote:

> Bush was an exacting editor. . . . *Bush seldom cited statistics when he talked. But he demanded that they be included on the page.* A sentence such as "We're increasing federal support for teacher training" would provoke the marking pen into paroxysms of exasperation. BY HOW MUCH? FROM WHAT? TO WHAT? (my italics)[14]

The Jekyll and Hyde faces of the contemporary presidency reveal the disingenuousness of anti-intellectualism. Intelligent men and women are hired to craft speeches that shield, rather than reflect, the true rhetorical identity of presidents from their audiences. This Janus-like quality helps explain why, as government has become more complex, as more expert advice is sought, and as more intellectuals have been co-opted into the machinery of government, the public face of the contemporary presidency remains so stubbornly and increasingly anti-intellectual. It puts the deliberate "anti" in presidential anti-intellectualism, because the guilelessness that presidents project is calculated; their rhetorical artlessness is a honed art and, as Chris Matthews explained above, an "enormous science."

Anti-Rhetoric

It is in their trenchant opposition to "rhetoric," "oratory," and their corresponding celebration of rhetorical simplicity that presidents have been most explicitly anti-intellectual. Here, the link between rhetorical simplicity and anti-intellectualism that was operationalized in the Flesch scores discussed in the previous chapter is manifest. President Eisenhower's definition of an intellectual displays this link: "the intellectual...[is] a man who takes more words than are necessary to tell more than he knows," he once proposed.[15] A Nixon speechwriter echoes this sentiment when he observes: "the people who are most eloquent are often the least wise."[16] As a Reagan speechwriter observes, "One of the great myths of the modern age in particular is that great speeches and effective leadership [are] about speaking cleverly."[17]

Originally referring to all forms of verbal and written communication and to an art form to which Aristotle devoted three eponymous books, "rhetoric" in contemporary usage has come to describe artificial and excessive verbal ornamentation. Embracing this derogatory sense of the word, former speechwriters and presidents have exhibited a distinct anti-rhetoricalism. (They would also fervently refuse the appellation of a "rhetorical presidency" thus understood.) For modern speechwriters, plain, conversational language, not ornate oration, is the key to effective presidential communication; and their anti-intellectualism is embedded within their prescriptions for simple rhetoric. As one speechwriter reflects:

> I think there's a certain democratic bias that ought to put us on the side of plain speaking....I don't think that's a bad thing at all, I don't think the president has to be the poet laureate.[18]

Richard Neustadt, too, has added his voice to this chorus, championing "simple eloquence" and diagnosing the cause of Truman's rhetorical problems in this way:

> With his set addresses, in his formal speeches, he was conferring with text that had far too much Latin in them for his comfort. They were

all written by people with academic degrees, and academic degrees are ruinous for the use of Anglo-Saxon sentence structures.[19]

Even in their praise of presidents, speechwriters take special care to define eloquence as anything but oratory. As one speechwriter notes, "Roosevelt was pompous, Churchill was pompous. Their pomposity was well timed, but they were orating rather than speaking."[20] Another speechwriter gladly concedes that Kennedy was "not a great orator," but his gift resided in his ability to "make each person in the audience feel that he was talking to them."[21] Jack Valenti observed similarly of Lyndon Johnson: "Johnson loved eloquent prose," but, he continued, "not ornate prose, but prose that soared in its passion and its reach."[22] It is a sign of our times that Reagan was not called the great orator, but the great communicator, whose eloquence was "conversational rather than oratorical."[23]

These opinions may or may not have been independently formed by speechwriters, but we do know from them that they also emanated from specific instructions from their bosses. As his speechwriter observed, Eisenhower "was often rebuffing his speechwriters and drafters for trying to put in too much and being too complicated and too sophisticated."[24] According to Emmet Hughes, Eisenhower possessed "more than a healthy scorn for the contrived and effortful. It extended to a distrust of eloquence."[25] Even presidents who were comfortable with intellectuals and the intellect guarded the parameters of their public rhetoric. President Kennedy, according to Ted Sorensen, "disliked verbosity and pomposity in his own remarks as much as he disliked them in others."[26] When Arthur Schlesinger, Jr., who used to write for Adlai Stevenson, first started writing for Kennedy, his boss would hand his drafts back to him, saying, "Adlai Stevenson was comfortable with this, but it's too complex and literary for me."[27] President Gerald Ford was known to be "suspicious of anything that smacks of being grandiose."[28] Clinton, too, was stridently "arhetorical." According to his chief speechwriter, "he's skeptical of that kind of talk.... He would take the flowery stuff and discard it."[29] Clearly, these speechwriters were not at will to elevate the quality of presidential rhetoric even if they wanted to.

All of this is in striking contrast to the oratorical style of the nineteenth and early twentieth centuries, a contrast that highlights the differences between the rhetorical and anti-intellectual presidencies. The modern president's and speechwriter's call for simplicity is not a neutral prescription for good writing and speaking, but a deliberate repudiation of an earlier mode of rhetoric. The speechwriters quoted above were in fact rejecting the oratory exemplified by the founding rhetorical presidents—Theodore Roosevelt and Woodrow Wilson, whose presidencies are more precisely described as "oratorical" rather than "anti-intellectual." Presidential rhetoric at the turn of the twentieth century belonged to a completely different genre, one captured by Theodore Roosevelt's metaphor of the bully pulpit. TR's metaphor assumed a demarcation of authority and wisdom between the two sides of the pulpit, in stark contrast to modern presidents, who have crossed this divide to enter into our living rooms via the television. Roosevelt's metaphor was inspired by the Jeremiad preacher, the religious analogue of the presidential preacher, who was the wise and anointed seer of things to come.[30] The preacher stood apart from his church both physically and spiritually, because of his special anointment. His job was to articulate a message from God, often harsh and unpalatable, as a warning or plan for things to come. In the early twentieth century, Theodore Roosevelt used the bully pulpit in precisely this way, which led him to make the analogy. For him, part of the job of the president was to champion sometimes unpopular choices, even to "muckrake" for the greater good of society. Theodore Roosevelt pontificated from the bully pulpit, and not, as Bill Clinton did, on the television stage of the *Arsenio Hall Show*. His *oration* was qualitatively distinct from Bill Clinton's *conversation*.[31] The pulpit analogy no longer describes the relationship between the president and his audience, though it continues to be misleadingly and interchangeably used to describe the rhetorical presidency.

Similarly, Woodrow Wilson's vision of a great leader was the eloquent orator, not the casual conversationalist that recent presidents have become. As our speechwriters have been at pains to distinguish, orators are conspicuously eloquent. They are rhetoricians, not everyday conversationalists. Wilson's heroes were Daniel Webster, John C. Calhoun, and Henry Clay, orators of the most ornate order. These are not orators in the modern speechwriter's hall of fame. Whether or not we agree with Wilson's assessments, his praise of William Pitt, Sir Robert Peel, and William Gladstone indicate that he was a fan of the Oxford Union style of oratory, not the prose of the contemporary White House.[32] Contemporary presidents have descended from the pulpit and entered into our living rooms via television like traveling salesmen. We are none the wiser for these visitations, and Theodore Roosevelt and Woodrow Wilson had little to do with these choices. Once we recognize that the bully pulpit has gone out of fashion, we will realize that the anti-intellectual presidency is a very different beast than the rhetorical presidency that TR and Wilson inaugurated a century ago.

The Cult of Simplicity

The flip side of contemporary presidents' anti-rhetorical posture is their enthusiastic advocacy of simplicity. We often think the latter to be benign because we fail to tease out the former and the undercurrent of anti-intellectualism accompanying it. Yet presidents have done more than ask for unadorned language; they have aggressively sought colloquial language. Truman, for instance, sought a "down home" touch to his speeches; Nixon asked for "truck drivers' language"; Reagan, for "muscular workaday prose"; and Clinton's constant direction to his speechwriters was to "make it more talky."[33] These instructions—direct from the presidents' mouths—are not lukewarm requests for plain language; they are insistent instructions for an assiduously colloquial way of speaking. The call for "truck drivers' language" and "muscular workaday prose" indicates not only the rejection of ornate language but also a veritable cult of simplicity.

Peggy Noonan articulates the groupthink behind contemporary speech craft: "It is simplicity that gives the speech its power.... And we pick the signal up because *we have gained a sense in our lives that true things are usually said straight and plain and direct*" (original emphasis).[34] But simplicity does not guarantee the truth, only the semblance of sincerity. Paradoxically, in heeding Noonan's advice, presidents have to be untruthful or duplicitous—altering their innate speech patterns—in order to appear truthful.

Speechwriters in the last half century have, by their own accounts, killed oratory. Eloquence, today, has become a function of simplicity. "I don't see eloquence as the other end of the spectrum from simplicity," notes Ray Price. "I see eloquence as being a symptom of simplicity."[35] When posed the question of the tension between including policy details in a speech and its communicability, one speechwriter says: "I don't think one is exclusive of the other. I think you can be very lyrical, I think you can be even poetic with some of the simplest of words." What is striking about this observation is that this speechwriter understood the tension to be between simplicity and lyricism, rather than between simplicity and complexity or policy detail. The principal goal for this speechwriter was to divine the quotable quote: to find a wording that was "very simple, very understandable, and yet puts [a point across] in a way that continues to ring and is quoted."[36]

We observe in these interviews a global rejection of rhetorical complexity, with no qualification as to the limits of simplification or the dangers of oversimplification, much less any concern about the potential duplicity of simplifying language not for the sake of the transmission of truth but for its semblance. Indeed, presidential instructions for "workaday prose" are obviously an effort to push the frontiers of simplification. As is the case with any intemperate position, there is something troubling about this. Education experts tell us that, in order to maximize learning, there is an optimal readability level that should be set above, not at or below, the reader's present level of ability. Using books that are at or below a reader's level may increase reading fluency and rate, but not comprehension.[37] Judging by the cult of simplicity that presidents have promoted, it would appear that they have been less concerned with educating members of the public than with wooing them. The cult of simplicity endorsed by presidents and speechwriters is anti-intellectualism with a demagogic smile; it is a seductive justification of anti-intellectualism that has blinded us to the gradual rot of our public deliberative sphere.

The Tyranny of Anti-Intellectualism

The valorization of rhetorical simplicity, commonplace and endemic, is one of the principal motors of presidential anti-intellectualism. We have been slow to cry foul about it, because individual instances appear benign, even advantageous to the president. What could be wrong with a "down-home" speech? If anything, it gives a president a personal touch and it signals his honesty, as Peggy Noonan suggests. But that is exactly where the problem lies. Presidential rhetoric has suffered from a repeated rejection of complexity akin to a classic tyranny of small decisions: each individual presidential decision to go anti-intellectual is strategically rewarding with diffused and unacknowledged costs to the polity; yet the accretion of these small, isolated decisions generates a significant, unintended, and deleterious post hoc decision.[38] Indeed, that speechwriters lament the degeneration of presidential rhetoric while contributing to its degeneration reveals the dangerous clash of individual and collective rationalities.

The manmade teleology of presidential anti-intellectualism stems from the perceived benefit of going anti-intellectual, which is nearly universally felt, as my interviews have shown. I say "perceived," because there is no reason to think that these calculations are objectively true; we know only that presidents and speechwriters appear to believe them to be true. As each president and his team of speechwriters seek to simplify his public rhetoric even further, the effect of a succession of such efforts is cumulatively felt even if each administration does not feel individually responsible. We model this argument by specifying the individual president's perceived payoff distribution of going anti-intellectual in figure 3.1 and the tyrannical outcome in figure 3.2.

At the individual level, presidents and speechwriters perceive going anti-intellectual (AI) to be a rewarding strategy at all times. In a two-player game,

		Opponent	
		AI	NAI
President	AI	1, 1	2, −1
	NAI	−1, 2	0, 0

FIGURE 3.1

The Individual Logic to Go Anti-Intellectual

when neither a president nor his opponent adopts the strategy (NAI), it follows that no one gains (0, 0).[39] When both the president and opponent go anti-intellectual, both (assuming that both exercise the strategy with more or less equal political finesse) share the gains (1, 1), because the game is not perceived to be zero-sum. For example, if both go anti-intellectual, both will appear to be "in touch" with the people.

Now, it may be expected that, if one party goes anti-intellectual, he gains (1, ?), and when the other party does not go anti-intellectual, he does not gain (?, 0); so when the anti-intellectual strategy is asymmetrically applied, this would result in a payoff of (1, 0). However, this payoff does not appear to capture the strong preference that presidents and speechwriters appear to have for going anti-intellectual, since it implies that the actor who goes anti-intellectual gains as much when his opponent also goes anti-intellectual (1, 1) as when he does not (1, 0). This does not appear to capture the negative, repudiative power of the anti-intellectual stance against one's opponent. The anti-intellectual strategy is both self- and other-referential, as I observed in chapter 2. It makes an actor look good (humble, truthful) while making his opponent look bad (aloof, equivocal).

Instead, it is more likely that presidents and speechwriters believe that when anti-intellectualism is asymmetrically applied, the party that does not go anti-intellectual not only fails to obtain the gains of going anti-intellectual, but also suffers the consequences of his opponent's attack. It was probably this lesson that George W. Bush learned in his unsuccessful run for congress in 1978, after which he "vowed never to get out-countried [*sic*] again."[40] The risks of not going anti-intellectual are just too high. Therefore, in this asymmetrical situation, the ordinary result of (1, 0) is more accurately adjusted to (2, −1) to better capture the perceived magnitude of the asymmetrical payoff. Hence, individual gains are deemed to be absolutely and relatively highest (2, −1) when the opponent is not going anti-intellectual, and the president is able to deploy the "plowman-versus-professor" strategy against his opponent (for instance Jackson versus John Quincy Adams, Eisenhower versus

Stevenson, Bush versus Gore). Conversely, the losses are absolutely and relatively highest (–1, 2) when the strategy is effectively deployed against the president himself. Going anti-intellectual is not only the dominant outcome, but it emerges without dilemma (which would have been depicted by an inversion of the upper-left and lower-right quadrants), as my interviews suggest. Actors believe that, even if both parties go anti-intellectual, their individual gains will be more than if both choose not to go anti-intellectual.

The "inconsequentiality problem" facilitates the tyranny of small decisions. Some of the most powerful sociopolitical forces are those that are founded on seemingly benign premises. Those who adopt an anti-intellectual stance more often than not downplay the import of their actions because they genuinely believe that what I call anti-intellectualism actually promotes communication and democracy.[41] What, after all, could be wrong with extolling the virtues of the "language of the living room"?[42] Setting aside these normative questions until chapter 6, I will merely note here that because most if not all speechwriters have decried the quality of presidential rhetoric, and most if not all speechwriters have also endorsed the rule of simplicity, then there is likely to be a hidden and systematic relationship between lamentation and prescription that individual speechwriters have not noticed.

Figure 3.2 illustrates the cumulative and long-term consequences of a succession of anti-intellectual decisions. At the cumulative level, we do not see anti-intellectualism as a strategy by individual actors to gain political points in the immediate future, as in figure 3.1, but in terms of its accumulated costs in the long run. The payoff distribution in figure 3.2 is straightforward. Assuming that the country can ill afford perpetual rounds of anti-intellectualism, the deleterious long-term consequences to the polity are minimal (0) when neither party goes anti-intellectual, moderate (–1) when one party goes anti-intellectual, and maximal (–2) when both go anti-intellectual.

The cumulative costs of anti-intellectualism, depicted in figure 3.2, are easily missed because it is not in the nature of politicians to analyze trends over long periods of time, since incumbents have long passed out of office by

		Opponent	
		AI	NAI
President	AI	–2	–1
	NAI	–1	0

FIGURE 3.2

The Cumulative Consequences of Going
Anti-Intellectual

the time they are placed before the tribunal of posterity. But this short-term perspective has created a tyranny of small decisions and their cumulative consequences. I have introduced such a longitudinal perspective in order to call attention to the cumulative consequences of a succession of seemingly benign anti-intellectual stances. Figures 2.4, 2.5, and 2.9 painted a macroevolutionary story of the cumulative impact of these sequential choices. While presidential decisions to simplify might have appeared like a benign and constant refrain in (at least) the past half century, their rhetorical output has not. Indeed, the unbroken monotonicity of these trends in spite of the exogenous shocks of history suggests that anti-intellectualism exhibits a self-reinforcing logic. Since to be anti-anything is to repudiate the status quo ante, each successive president who chooses to go anti-intellectual cannot simply imitate his predecessor (who has already repudiated the repudiated); he must go one step further in order to "out-country" him. The more presidents simplify, the further their successors must go. For the same reason, once inaugurated, a succession of anti-intellectual stances accumulates a repudiated backlog that becomes increasingly difficult to unhinge.

To depict this trajectory in more tangible terms: if the trend in figure 2.4 from chapter 2 continues unabated (and unaccelerated), in 121 years, the State of the Union address will reach a score of 90, which is to say that it will read like a comic strip or a fifth-grade textbook. Even if this were merely a matter of readability (and not also of substantive simplicity), this is likely not a level of discourse at which serious public deliberation could take place. These are especially serious observations because we have reason to believe that the monotonic drive toward the oversimplification of presidential rhetoric will persist because of the enormous momentum resulting from the institutional and infrastructural context of the permanent campaign: the decline of political parties as campaign machines, the rise of the personal campaign, and the growth of media and opinion technologies to support these trends.

In anticipation of a solution I will sketch in chapter 7, it is worth noting that presidents are individually responsible for this tyranny of anti-intellectualism. The tyranny of small decisions is different from "herd behavior"—even if some pressure to conform does exist—in that it is a scenario consisting of a sequence of individually rational decisions that produces an escalating outcome with the increasing numbers of endorsing adopters.[43] The choice to go anti-intellectual does not usually emerge from a president's decision to abide by a general (herd) pattern of presidential speechmaking, but from an individual, local decision. Truman and Johnson, for instance, did not choose plain talk over high rhetoric because they recognized a pattern that presidents following oratorical greats should not try to outperform their predecessors. Instead, their decisions emerged from local considerations. Truman's response to FDR's oratorical shadow, according to Clark Clifford, was to develop "a short, punch[y] style, one that came to reflect accurately his own homespun Missouri personality and values, in contrast to the very different phrasing and style of FDR."[44] Dick Goodwin, Johnson's speechwriter, describes Johnson's "deeply founded fear that his own unpolished expression would draw contempt from the educated and worldly elite, and stimulate unfavorable comparisons with his predecessor."[45] Johnson's decision, like Truman's, was to not even try. Hence, although all presidents have felt the incentive to go anti-intellectual, at any moment in time, each president is a herd leader and a precedent setter (and because every president is a herd leader, there is in effect no herd leader), each making the decision to go anti-intellectual from a decisional calculus outside of the pattern that he also happens to be driving.

The Incremental Morphology of Presidential Anti-Intellectualism

We are accustomed to a view of institutional change that is intermittently gradual or sudden, but not simultaneously both. While anti-intellectualism is a central organizing criticism in much of presidential scholarship, what also connects an even wider body of scholarship—including not only the "personal presidency," the "public presidency," the "symbolic presidency," and the "rhetorical presidency," but also the "administrative presidency," the "legislative presidency," and the "imperial presidency"—is a view of institutional evolution premised on a view of institutional change that is guided by the notion of punctuated equilibrium. This is the idea that institutional change is an imperceptibly gradual evolutionary process punctuated by periods of sudden morphology.[46] Scholars have examined the contexts and reasons behind the emergence of a qualitatively different kind of institution during different points of the twentieth century, relying on either a modern-traditional or some other epochal divide to designate critical developmental junctures. The anti-intellectual presidency, however, has exhibited a different evolutionary history. Figures 2.4, 2.5, and 2.9 indicate that the urge to simplify has been a rare constant in the 200-year history of the presidency. Simplification has persisted in spite of the different personalities and ideologies of the 42 men who have held the office, the several institutional adaptations of the presidency in secular time, and even the radically differing tectonics of political time that different incumbents have confronted.[47] There have been no distinctly morphological periods even though the cumulative effect of subtle changes across the two centuries has been dramatic. The development of the anti-intellectual presidency was not a sudden institutional speciation but followed an incremental morphology, absent of both bursts of regnancy and periods of dormancy.[48]

This is very possibly why we have been slow or reluctant to cry foul at it. Focused on immediate history as presidents and speechwriters have been, it has been easy to overlook the incremental morphology of the anti-intellectual presidency. When change is incremental, legitimating mores of what constitutes good speaking and writing catch up so that the change becomes imperceptible. Indeed, linguistic simplification is often advocated in modern-day best practice in communication, as accessible language has become an article of faith in our democratic era.[49] Yet we cannot afford to accept without challenge the taken-for-granted axioms of good speaking and writing endorsed by presidents and speechwriters: that every complex thought can be represented in simple language; compound thoughts can be parsed in simple language; and there is nothing lost in splitting up an elaborate sentence. Rhetorical simplification may help a president to communicate a message more clearly, but it potentially also robs the message of nuance and changes its meaning. Anti-intellectual presidents and their speechwriters have demonstrated no regard for this darker side of simplicity.

4

The Substantive Impoverishment of Presidential Rhetoric

Presidential anti-intellectualism is more than a matter of linguistic simplification. If that were all, we would have less reason to worry for it is possible, if improbable, that little of substance is lost when a message is drastically simplified. Having addressed linguistic simplification as a principal manifestation of presidential anti-intellectualism in its output and at its source in chapters 2 and 3, I turn now to specifically examine the substantive impoverishment of presidential rhetoric. As presidents have taken the rhetorical path of least resistance by serving up simplistic sentences to citizens, they have correspondingly offered an easily digestible substantive menu devoid of argument and infused with inspirational platitudes, partisan punch lines, and emotional and human interest appeals.

The Demise of Logos

The substantive hollowing out of presidential rhetoric can be examined by the fate of the three Aristotelian "proofs" of rhetoric. Aristotle recognized that effective rhetoric combines elements of *logos*, or the weighing and judging of reasons for a particular course of action; *ethos*, the credibility of the speaker; and *pathos*, emotional appeal.[1] In this chapter, I will show that presidential rhetoric today is short on logos, disingenuous on ethos, and long on pathos.

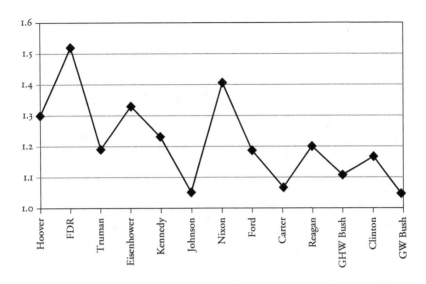

FIGURE 4.1

Occurrence of *Causal* in the *Public Papers* of Presidents Hoover to Bush

In recognizing the value of ethos and pathos, Aristotle had a more balanced view of the proofs of rhetoric than, say, Plato, who wanted the rhetorician to be a logician and for whom only truth and the best argument mattered; or Emerson, who saw the rhetorician as stylist and poet; or Cicero, who placed utmost emphasis on pathos or emotion. While there is a place for personal and emotional rhetorical appeals, we expect the language of democratic political leaders to prioritize logos, the weighing and judging of reasons for a particular course of action.[2] Democratic political leaders have a special obligation to submit their governing ideas to citizens in a form that can be subjected to public rational disputation, so that only the best can pass legitimately into legislation or governmental action. In monarchies and autocracies, political speeches serve ceremonial and propagandistic functions. There is no urgent need for logos in such regimes, because the people do not rule. Democratic political speech will allow the people to govern, keep leaders accountable, and promote the best public policies, only if it is infused with logos. Whereas logos can be deliberated on, ethos and pathos are persuasive strategies that are largely nonfalsifiable, offering very little additional value to the deliberative purposes of democratic political speech.

This conception of rhetorical leadership and public deliberation is captured in John Rawls's ideal of "public reason," which is "realized or satisfied whenever judges, legislators, chief executives, and other government

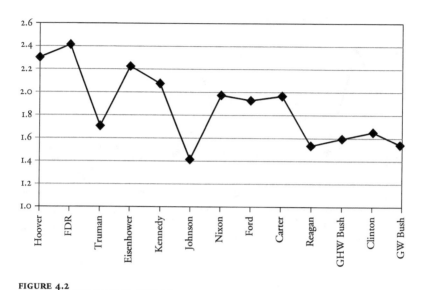

FIGURE 4.2

Occurrence of *Know* in the *Public Papers* of Presidents Hoover to Bush

officials…act from and follow the idea of public reason and explain to other citizens their reasons for supporting fundamental political positions in terms of the political conception of justice they regard as the most reasonable."[3] Much presidential rhetoric today fails the Rawlsian test of public reason. To obtain a sense of the amount of weighing and judging of reasons going on in presidential rhetoric, I applied the *Causal* and *Know* categories of the *General Inquirer*[4] to the texts of the *Public Papers* of each president from Herbert Hoover to George W. Bush in their first full year in office.[5] Figures 4.1 and 4.2 suggest the attenuation of logos, or the weighing or judging of reasons, in the *Public Papers*.

To see more precisely how recent anti-intellectual presidents have disregarded the weighing and judging of reasons, we need to look more closely at their words and to observe the increasing recourse to rhetorical tactics that are antithetical to deliberation: applause-rendering platitudes and partisan punch lines, personal persuasion (ethos), and emotional seduction (pathos). I elaborate on each of these in the following pages.

Inspirational Platitudes and Anti-Intellectualism

Instead of bringing arguments to the public deliberative sphere, presidents are increasingly inclined to declare and assert, offering us a predictable inventory of inspirational platitudes and partisan punch lines. I turn first to George W. Bush and his use of inspirational platitudes as an instance of argument by declaration, then to Bill Clinton and his use of partisan punch lines as an instance of argument by assertion.[6] It may appear at first glance that these two anti-intellectual strategies are polar opposites of each other. Platitudes articulate the obvious and are therefore assumed to be universal, while partisan punch lines are strategically one-sided and therefore particular. Both however, are united by their rejection of the weighing and judging of reasons. Both are proffered as foundational beliefs that cannot be argued for or against. Self-evident truths can be declared without justification, just like partisan punch lines are asserted strategically to preempt consideration of the other side. Both paradoxically transmit ambiguous meaning in categorical language. Indeed, that is why partisan punch lines are often dressed up in the ambiguous language of platitudes. Phrases such as "liberty," "support our troops," and "freedom in Iraq" are often deployed as coded conservative punch lines delivered as creedal platitudes that cannot be denied, while "fairness," "universal health care," and "equal employment opportunity" are the liberal analogues of projects that are self-evidently unobjectionable. All of these coded punch lines appear universally unobjectionable until we begin to address the competing priorities that the pursuit of each will entail. (To be sure, *within* the liberal and conservative camps, these punch lines are nearly universally approved platitudes.) Neither conservatives nor liberals have a monopoly on anti-intellectualism, though each camp is quick to characterize the other as such when its opposition deploys partisan punch lines with impunity.

The attenuation of logos, and in particular its substitution with inspirational platitudes, can be sharply exemplified in a comparative context. The arguments and appeals made in support of the war in Iraq in 2003 presented an opportunity to do this, as both the U.K. and U.S. governments attempted to convince their publics and the world of a similar mission at the same time. Here, I examine the last, and therefore most urgent, acts of justification for war in the form of the final speeches that Prime Minister Tony Blair and President George W. Bush gave before hostilities began.[7] In a speech to the House of Commons on March 18, 2003, Blair supplied seven reasons in his thesis-making paragraph:

> Why does it matter so much? Because the outcome of this issue will now determine more than the fate of the Iraqi regime and more than the future of the Iraqi people, for so long brutalized by Saddam. It will determine the way Britain and the world confront the central security threat of the 21st century; the development of the UN; the relationship

between Europe and the US; the relations within the EU and the way the US engages with the rest of the world. It will determine the pattern of international politics for the next generation.

Bush's explanation for the urgency of war adopted a narrower and more categorical justificatory perspective:

> We are now acting because the risks of inaction would be far greater. In one year, or five years, the power of Iraq to inflict harm on all free nations would be multiplied many times over. With these capabilities, Saddam Hussein and his terrorist allies could choose the moment of deadly conflict when they are strongest. We choose to meet that threat now, where it arises, before it can appear suddenly in our skies and cities.

Here, only one reason prevailed, less an argument than a platitudinous appeal through fear—of that which "can appear suddenly in our skies and cities"—even if the Bush administration probably shared the other strategic, if less popularly persuasive, arguments that Blair articulated in his speech. Of course, we have to deal with that which "can appear suddenly in our skies and cities." The undefended assumption was that there was something coming our way. With the benefit of hindsight, it is clear which of these paragraphs is more likely to stand the test of history. Blair's paragraph was not prolix, as some presidential speechwriters might assess, but it was not simple either. Blair supplied five strategic reasons in one long sentence; Bush offered one reason in a series of shorter sentences. While Blair's reasons were specific and manifold, Bush's reason was vague and implied: the "risks of inaction" and the threat of that which "can appear suddenly in our skies and cities" is argument by speculation. As it turns out, the Bush administration has since fallen back on precisely those reasons that Blair adduced years ago, because Saddam's alleged weapons of mass destruction were nowhere to be found. At least in this case, the world turned out to be more complex than Bush's simple, singular explanation allowed.

Bush's speech was probably effective at the time it was delivered. Passionate, assertive, and inspirational rhetoric moves the audience, and that was probably all that mattered. But that is why anti-intellectual rhetoric, in eschewing reasons and arguments that would serve as the basis of deliberation and rational disputation, is dangerous. "We choose to meet that threat now, where it arises, before it can appear suddenly in our skies and cities" is just the sort of sentence that could raise the stubborn hairs on the back of even the most cynical rhetorical scholar, but many Americans have lived to regret their susceptibility to such chest thumping. We were susceptible because we were not invited to think, but to feel and to agree.

The perorations to both speeches, as all perorations tend to go, ended on a lyrical note. But even there, Blair took the opportunity to squeeze in four more reasons for why war was necessary, three of which retained a specificity pertaining to the mission at hand. His reasons may have been right or wrong, but at least they were presented for public assessment and disputation. Like his previous paragraph, this one would probably score low on the Flesch test of readability:

> To retreat now, I believe, would put at hazard all that we hold dearest, turn the UN back into a talking shop, stifle the first steps of progress in the Middle East; leave the Iraqi people to the mercy of events on which we would have relinquished all power to influence for the better.

While Blair tried to argue via specific reasons (plausible or not), Bush tried to inspire via abstract generalization in short, powerful sentences practically devoid of specific arguments. President Bush's words zoomed in on abstract, creedal passions that served not so much an argumentative, but an inspirational purpose:

> The United States, with other countries, will work to advance liberty and peace in that region. Our goal will not be achieved overnight, but it can come over time. The power and appeal of human liberty is felt in every life and every land. And the greatest power of freedom is to overcome hatred and violence, and turn the creative gifts of men and women to the pursuits of peace.

Bush's words likely sent an electric charge through a large proportion of his audience. But deciphering the basis for this internal applause identifies the problem of inspirational platitudes devoid of argument. Inspirational language, while it might have unifying, epideictic purposes, tends to discourage dialogue and debate. Indeed, inspirational platitudes are asserted precisely because they are allegedly so self-evident that they need not be argued for. Rhetorical "spaciousness" is rewarding precisely because it obscures differences by focusing on a "rhetoric of assent."[8] As seen in the excerpts above, not one clause in Bush's peroration contained a specific reference to the mission in Iraq. The paragraph could have concluded practically any foreign policy speech that any president in the last century could have given. If a president's words are platitudinous and ambiguous, his speeches are substitutable from one occasion to another and so, apparently, would he. Leadership would then become no more than national cheerleading.

Bush's words were assuredly poetic and powerful—inspirational platitudes that passed for what some have deemed "brilliance, power and intellectual seriousness"—but if we were moved by the peroration, we were persuaded not by specific facts or precise arguments, but by stoked emotions and psychic urges.[9] We were not asked to deliberate on the urgent issue of war at hand, but merely to join in the president's war cry. In effect, our assent to a specific policy was craftily borrowed from our consensus on creedal beliefs. (Who isn't a fan of liberty?) Because persuasion through inspiration and assertion, as opposed to deliberation through justification, assumes the conclusion for which the inspiration is intended, argument is unnecessary. Rather, credibility or strength of personality becomes preeminent (ethos, as we shall see below), and Bush's speech delivered this meta-message effectively with assertive and categorical language.

Why did two leaders with so much ideological and policy agreement, speaking to their publics on the same issue and at the same time, end up making such distinct appeals? The explanation may lie in the demographic differences between the American and British audiences as a function of the presidential and parliamentary systems in which they are embedded. Prime Minister Blair was speaking in front of the British House of Commons to party backbenchers; President Bush, via television, was speaking to U.S. citizens sitting in their family living rooms. And the task of convincing parliamentary members is very different from convincing a television audience. Figure 4.3, which compares the readability of the State of the Union addresses with the British Queen's Speeches for 18 years, beginning in 1988, offers some evidence

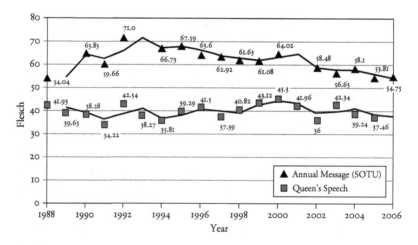

FIGURE 4.3

Flesch Scores of the SOTU and the Queen's Speech, 1988–2006

for this hypothesis.[10] Like Blair, the queen addresses her speech principally to members of Parliament (even though her speech is also televised); whereas State of the Union addresses have become rhetorical fanfares addressed to television audiences. Figure 4.3 shows us that the State of the Union messages have been consistently simpler than the Queen's Speeches between 1988 and 2006.[11]

A rare opportunity to test this hypothesis still further came in 2003, when Blair and Bush exchanged places and made state visits to the United States and United Kingdom, respectively, and addressed public audiences. Prime Minister Blair's speech on July 17, though nominally addressed to congress as a president's State of the Union address is, had, compared to his usual utterances, an unusually high Flesch score of 64.8, because he knew that he was also speaking to the American public. Conversely, President Bush's speech at Whitehall Palace on November 19 was intellectually pumped up, at 59.9. The "real" Bush emerged at a joint press conference with Blair the next day. Relieved somewhat from the contextual restraint of the day before, his contributed remarks attained a score of 70.6, compared to Blair's 62.9.

Partisan Punch Lines and Anti-Intellectualism

It is easy to confuse inspirational platitudes with intellectual rhetoric. Here is how Reagan's communications director explains the president's winning style:

> Woven into almost every speech Reagan gave, especially on memorable occasions, was an evocation of what America had been and could be again. Liberty, heroism, honor, a love of country, a love of God. Those were notions that sophisticates tend to dismiss as platitudes, or worse. But they went deep with Reagan, and as he had discovered from years on the speaking circuit, they went deep with most Americans.[12]

There is nothing wrong with inspirational platitudes, and there are certainly times that call for a unifying rhetoric of assent, such as ceremonial occasions. But they should not recur with such frequency that they crowd out argument or the weighing and judging of reasons. More important, if we look closely enough, many if not most inspirational platitudes turn out to be partisan punch lines. Reagan's inspirational appeal to "liberty, heroism, honor, a love of country, a love of God" deploys partisan code words vague enough so as not to galvanize opposition, but pointed enough to stroke partisan emotions. It is unclear that Reagan's ideals, properly unpacked and juxtaposed against competing priorities, "went deep with most Americans." They probably went deeper with conservative Americans than they did with liberal Americans. As with inspirational platitudes, anti-intellectual presidents use partisan punch lines to oversimplify the world and to preempt competing visions in order to persuade their audiences. Consider the equivalent strategy that Bill Clinton deployed in his last State of the Union address in 2000:

> To 21st century America, let us pledge these things: Every child will begin school ready to learn and graduate ready to succeed. (Applause.) Every family will be able to succeed at home and at work, and no child will be raised in poverty. (Applause.) We will meet the challenge of the aging of America. We will assure quality, affordable health care, at last, for all Americans. (Applause.)[13]

Clinton's aim, presumably, was to declare a partisan list of Christmas goodies dressed up in the language of commonsensical platitudes. But his words betray a blissful assumption that no one could be against universal education, welfare, and health care. And there are few things more infuriating to an audience—and more preemptive of deliberation—than a presumptuously partisan assertion of commonsensical platitudes. Instead of arguments and nuanced accounts of public policies, we are increasingly coaxed with a stream of sloganistic punch lines that have created many problems even as they have adhered to the speech-writer's rule of simplicity and memorability. These catchy slogans do not merely advertise public policies, but bleed into the very nature and structure of the policies themselves. The recent history of public policy in our country is full of examples of flawed policies, such as Bill Clinton's "Don't Ask, Don't Tell" and George W. Bush's "No Child Left Behind," which have delivered far less than their bold and catchy slogans would have us expect. According to Sharkansky, Richard Nixon's "War on Drugs" continues to guide U.S. policy on illicit drugs by framing the debate with these fateful words, focusing the federal govern-ment's effort on the problem of production and trafficking, and predisposing it to allocate less resources to demand-side solutions like treating habitual users.[14] According to Tulis, Lyndon Johnson's "War on Poverty" concealed the nuances of social welfare policies by characterizing poverty as an external enemy to be vanquished by the federal government, and not also a problem of personal responsibility. This occurred because Johnson crafted the rhetorical pitch for his program before working out its technicalities, focusing on the publicity of the policy rather than on its merit.[15] In each of these cases, simplistic slogans discouraged contemplation of the full complexity or scope of a problem and encouraged policymakers to deliver a partial response. As Orwell warned, "The slovenliness of our language makes it easier for us to have foolish thoughts."[16]

Applause and the Anti-Intellectual Presidency

Platitudes and partisan punch lines have become the coin of the presidential rhetorical realm because they are applause-rendering, and it is applause, rather than deliberation or contemplation, that is the intended effect of most presidential speeches today. This trend dates at least to the late 1940s. Clark Clifford wrote that he initially thought that the "Truman Doctrine" speech was a failure because "there were no interruptions for applause until more than half-way through the forty-minute speech."[17] Perhaps it was a good thing that the speech was not written specifically for applause. The soundness of a policy cannot be measured by the enthusiasm of the applause received on its enunciation. Speechwriters in the post-Nixon White House, however, have become dedicated wordsmiths, and they work by different imperatives from those of the policymaker. As I will examine in chapter 5, Nixon separated the speechwriting and policy-advising function and in so doing institutionalized a model of presidential rhetoric measured by the number of quotable quotes and nurtured by applause, imperatives that call for the short and sweet sentences tracked in presidential speeches in chapter 2, as well as for the platitudes and partisan punch lines discussed above. Nixon is said to have tutored his speechwriter David Gergen thus:

> "Let's try this exercise," he suggested. "Each time you send me a final draft, underline the three sentences in the speech that you think the press will quote. We will check the television networks and the papers to see whether they quote those same sentences."

Over time, Gergen recalled, "I came to understand what 'breaks through,' the line that not only snaps but advances the story."[18] Commenting on the drafting of President Ford's nomination acceptance address in 1976, Patrick Butler observes: "We tried as hard as we could to make almost every sentence end with a burst of applause."[19] Most strikingly, we can observe in an internal memorandum by Dan McGroarty, deputy director of speechwriting in the second Bush's administration, the rhetorical ethic of the modern White House:

> The President, Mrs. Bush and senior staff continue to measure the success of a speech by the number of applause lines. The President interprets long stretches of silence as a failure on his part to connect. From the podium, nodding heads may be nodding off. Let's face it, applause lines are a kind of currency.[20]

Figure 4.4 gives us a rough measure of how important applause has become in our own time. The first time applause was registered (parenthetically) in

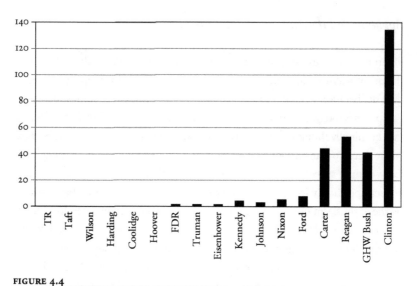

FIGURE 4.4

Average Number of Speeches with "Applause" by President

the presidential papers was in Franklin Roosevelt's. Before that, the word "applause" appeared in the *Messages and Papers* of the presidents just 18 times.[21] From FDR through Clinton, the word "applause" has occurred in the *Public Papers* of the presidents 1,939 times, 97 percent of the references occurring in the *Papers* of Nixon through Clinton. Applause has become, as McGroarty mentioned, the currency of presidential rhetoric, a litmus test of presidential accomplishment that successive White House press offices have deemed important enough to record for posterity.

The same rhetorical ethic appears to exist in the second Bush's White House. There was an average of 71 applause breaks per speech among the seven State of the Union addresses President Bush delivered between 2001 and 2007. That is a lot of clapping for a phenomenon we have come to call the *rhetorical* presidency. Figure 4.5 gives us a sense of the duration of these applause breaks in comparison to the actual time that Bush spent talking. On average, the nation was treated to 29 seconds of congressional applause for every minute of President Bush's speech. It seems more apt to characterize Bush here as an "applause-rendering" president rather than as a rhetorical president; after all, a third of the time in his most important rhetorical act as president was spent generating, and then basking in, applause. The label "rhetorical presidency" in highlighting presidential loquaciousness does not convey this defining rhetorical ethic of the anti-intellectual president.

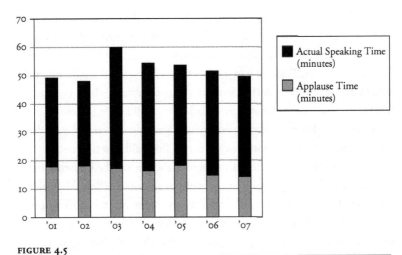

FIGURE 4.5

Actual Speaking and Applause Times for G. W. Bush's SOTU Addresses, 2001–2007

Let us consider another excerpt from Clinton's last State of the Union address, which was interrupted some 120 times with applause, to observe the dangerous futility of a rhetorical ethic premised on it:

> Again, I ask you to pass a real patients' bill of rights. [Applause.] I ask you to pass common sense gun safety legislation. [Applause.] I ask you to pass campaign finance reform. [Applause.] I ask you to vote up or down on judicial nominations and other important appointees. [Applause.] And, again I ask you—I implore you—to raise the minimum wage. [Applause.]

There were five applause breaks in this paragraph, one at the end of every sentence. The actual talking time was about 30 seconds, and about a minute and a half was dedicated to applause. By most speechwriters' standards, this would have been a canonically successful portion of the speech. It was successful at that moment perhaps. But if Clinton succeeded in earning congressional validation as he delivered his speech, he was less successful in educating or rallying the congress into legislative action—not surprisingly, because he was jam-packing his speech with partisan punch lines. The 106th Congress did not deliver anything in the way of a "real" patients' bill of rights (whatever "real" meant), "common sense" gun safety legislation (whatever "common sense" meant), campaign finance reform, an agreement on an up-or-down vote for judicial nominations, or raising the minimum wage. The 107th Congress did pass the Bipartisan Campaign Reform (McCain-Feingold) Act in 2002, and the 110th Congress did pass the Fair Labor Standards Act to raise the minimum wage much later in 2007, but it is difficult to say that Clinton had a hand in the former and nearly impossible to say that he had one in the latter. It is fair to observe that the raucously partisan applause that Clinton generated in 2000 did little to help his causes or our nation. Even by the institutionally partisan criteria of presidential persuasiveness, Clinton's applause-rendering lines did *him* no good.

Our era of intense partisanship among and within the branches of government is itself a symptom, if not a result, of an anti-intellectual presidency that has failed to infuse our public sphere with reasons and explanations for rational adjudication. No amount of applause will convince errant representatives and senators from the other side of the aisle into agreement. In fact, declaring the allegedly obvious or delivering punch lines to fellow partisans only serves to infuriate members of the other party. Only a painstaking discussion of the issues and the differences preempting consensus will take the debate constructively forward, even if this may make for a bad speech with no applause lines. Perhaps an effective speech should be greeted on its conclusion by silence rather than applause as it invites contemplation and a consideration of matters hitherto unexamined among partisan audiences. At best, the partisan applause that greeted Clinton's sentences represented a transient show of support predicated only on (and possibly as a result of) the deliberate ambiguity and partisanship of his proposals. Clinton probably skipped over the vexing specifics and deeper philosophical disagreements in order to elicit the applause, but in so doing he confused a moment's gratification with the nation's edification.

Clinton's rhetorical facility, related to his capacity for rendering applause, is worth exploring some more. According to one former speechwriter, he was "the most gifted extemporaneous speaker of our era."[22] (This facility was famously and successfully put to the test when the teleprompter failed in the middle of his first State of the Union message, and Clinton proceeded seamlessly until the teleprompter was restored.)[23] Speechwriters across party lines, however, agree that there was something paradoxical about Clinton's rhetoric:

> I don't think you can name a single Clinton speech that is memorable or changed people's thinking.[24]

> Clinton is a great mystery. There is no one who is more easily articulate in my memory and I can't remember a thing he said.[25]

> An extraordinarily effective communicator who never said anything memorable.[26]

Peggy Noonan takes us closer to the answer to the Clinton paradox:

> Never tongue-tied and never eloquent—six years into his presidency, his only candidates for Bartlett's are "I didn't inhale" and "The era of big government is over"—his easy facility is a two-edged sword. While it suggests a certain command, it also highlights Clinton's prime perceptual problem: that he is too fluid, too smooth, like a real estate salesman talking to a walk-in with a Rolex.[27]

The Clinton paradox tells us that a successful presidential rhetorical endeavor is not just about being articulate or rhetorically quick on the feet. As "Slick Willy" found out, while punch lines and pathos may generate applause and an emotional connection with the audience, they cannot perform the democratic functions of logos. Even though we often valorize the ability to extemporize—which is really just the ability to fill up a communicative space—we do care about the substance of what is offered to fill these spaces. Clinton was glib but unmemorable probably because he was a smooth-operating anti-intellectual rhetorician. Here was a president who was by all accounts as bright as presidents come, yet he dedicated his intellectual resources to selling—some would say seducing—rather than educating the public. His was the "campaign style of governing."[28]

Clinton's anti-intellectual presidency exemplifies the contemporary paradigm of presidential rhetoric motivated and measured by the currency of applause. When applause becomes the yardstick for rhetorical success—indeed, when it becomes the currency of rhetoric itself—it sets up the speaker as a performer before a crowd ever ready to be pleased. It sets up a mutually congratulatory and collectively self-deceptive dynamic in which seduced auditors fail to see the vacuousness of the applause lines. No wonder we have been slow to decry the anti-intellectual presidency: too often, "applause drowns into a bottomless pit."[29] While applause-rendering speech, whether inspirational or partisan, is rhetorically appealing, it is a masquerade for logos because it enunciates platitudes or punch lines that presuppose the merit of the policy at hand and forecloses deliberation. Universally or partisanly endorsed slogans are an excuse not to express our differences in an effort to reconcile them. Because they preempt rather than encourage debate, they are the tools of the demagogue and a threat to democracy.

The Subversion of Ethos

Aristotle believed that a person of good character is more credible, and there-fore more compelling, than one who is not. Ethos, for him, was a rhetori-cal proof that reinforces the moral excellence and intellectual competence of a rhetor in order to establish trustworthiness and the veracity of what is said. Our founders and the patrician presidents adopted the same paradigm, advocating a model of leadership that emphasized virtuous statesmanship.[30] Woodrow Wilson, a founding rhetorical, but not anti-intellectual, president advocated this original meaning of ethos. Praising his oratorical heroes, he said, "Webster, Clay, and Calhoun, whose hearts seem to have been lighted with some of the heroism of the Revolution, devoted their lives to implant-ing principles which they represented and died the idols of the people."[31]

Ethos has increasingly supplanted logos in modern presidential rhet-oric, but it is not ethos in the Aristotelian sense, because anti-intellectual presidents are not concerned with signaling the excellence of their char-acters. They have opted for a quicker and easier way of engendering trust with partisan punch lines (a signal to audiences that the speaker is a fellow partisan) and assertive language (a signal to audiences that the speaker is a bold and confident leader).[32] But the real innovation of the anti-intellec-tual presidency in terms of ethos lies in linguistic mimicry. Anti-intellectual presidents insinuate their trustworthiness not so much by cataloging in their rhetoric a lifetime of virtuous public service and hence their right to speak authoritatively, but by imitating the language of the people. Anti-intellectual presidents believe that if they sound like the people, then they demonstrate that they are of the people and therefore for the people. Their competence to speak authoritatively to citizens is not argued for; it is merely linguisti-cally implied. This reconceptualization of ethos is exemplified in how anti-intellectual presidents have strategically deployed "common sense." Whereas all of the presidents through Woodrow Wilson appealed to "common sense" just 11 times in their recorded *Papers*, presidents since Wilson have done so more than 1,600 times. Figure 4.6 depicts the growing popularity of "common sense" in presidential rhetoric, even as (or perhaps because) the common sense has become increasingly divided in our polarized times.[33] By borrowing the locution of the people, anti-intellectual presidents purport to speak for them.

Credibility, up to as late as Nixon's presidency, had to be earned and argued for, rather than just linguistically insinuated. Consider how even Woodrow Wilson, the father of the idea that the president is the national spokesperson and interpreter of public opinion, was at pains to demonstrate

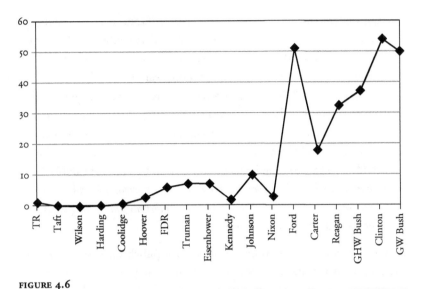

FIGURE 4.6

Speeches with References to "Common Sense" and "Commonsense" in the *Public Papers*, Averaged per Year by President

his faithful representation of it. In one of his swings around the circle to sell the Treaty of Versailles and his "Fourteen Points," he entreated:

> Don't you remember that we laid down fourteen points which should contain the principles of the settlement? They were not my points. In every one of them I was conscientiously trying to read the thought of the people of the United States. And, after I uttered those points, I had every assurance given me that could be given me that they did speak the moral judgment of the United States and not my single judgment.[34]

This rhetorical president abstained from the rhetorical tricks of the anti-intellectual presidents. Contrast Wilson to Bill Clinton and George Bush, who liberally interpreted the contents of U.S. citizens' common sense more than 50 times a year, such that practically every policy statement proceeded as a surefire proposition of common sense. Observe, for instance, the almost cavalier appropriation of common sense by Bill Clinton in a speech to the Democratic Congressional Campaign Committee, as if he alone held the key to deciphering public opinion and as if his interpretation were incontestable. In this speech, he addressed no less controversial a topic than welfare, purporting to speak *for* the people because he spoke *like* the people:

On welfare, the debate was structured as: "All these people on welfare, they don't want to work, and we're tough. We're going to make them work." And the other side, our side, was, "Well, that's probably right, but we feel so bad about the kids we don't want to do it." ...

So we said, "Okay, make people who are able-bodied go to work, but get them the education and training, and let's don't hurt their children because their most important job is raising their children. Provide the child care for the children. Provide the medical care for the children. Then you can be tough on work and good to the kids." *Guess what? It worked. Why? Not because it was rocket science. It was common sense, mainstream values, thinking about tomorrow, and getting away from the hot air.* (my emphasis)[35]

As was the case with Clinton's use of partisan punch lines, the casual and presumptuous rendition of common sense here swept under the carpet the nuances of contested and competing priorities, which may have had the paradoxical effect of polarizing Clinton's audience rather than expressing consensual opinion. Here we see another example of simplistic rhetoric that also oversimplified reality. Those who opposed welfare may not just have wanted to be "tough," and those who supported welfare may have believed that the state has a responsibility to all of its citizens, and not just its children. If politics were so easy and common sense so incontestable, Clinton's move to "end welfare as we know it" would have been more successful and less controversial. More insidiously, for all of Clinton's talk of common sense, Steven Teles has argued persuasively that the controversial policies of Aid for Families with Dependent Children (AFDC) were dominated and created by the posturing of opposing ideological elites who had little regard for the public's preferences.[36]

The anti-intellectual president's credibility is simply insinuated by his enunciation of common sense. But that which is attributed to common sense is often just a president's intuition or partisan opinion, rather than considered public judgment. It is an alleged truism that does not need to be mined from the diversity of the nation's population.

From Pathos to Bathos

Pathos plays an important function in persuasive speech, but its excessive deployment—bathos—is also a key ingredient of anti-intellectual speech. Cicero was among the first to recognize the mass psychological power of pathos: "men's judgments are more often formed under the influence of hatred, love, desire, anger, grief, joy, hope, fear, misconception or some other emotion, than by truth and ordinance, the principles of justice, the procedure of the courts or the laws."[37] The American founders probably recognized the danger behind this insight, and they created a set of institutions and electoral procedures that prioritized logos over pathos in the language of government. As James Madison argued in the *Federalist* No. 49, "it is the reason, alone, of the public, that ought to control and regulate the government. The passions ought to be controlled and regulated by the government." Even Richard Nixon, the president who hired speechwriter William Gavin specifically to craft words that appealed to the "heart," knew this:

> Clear words are the great servant of reason. Intemperate words are the great enemy of reason. The cute slogan, the glib headline, the clever retort, the appeal to passion—these are not the way to truth or to good public policy.[38]

Revealingly, Nixon sent these words in a separate 15,000-word message to congress on the same day that he delivered a shortened, television audience–tailored State of the Union address to the nation. Nixon's words suggest that he understood that the "appeal to passion" may serve a persuasive or epideictic function, but it is often also "the great enemy of reason" and of "good public policy." Presidential rhetoric does have persuasive and nation-unifying functions, which pathos ideally facilitates, but these purposes should not be the be-all and end-all of presidential rhetoric. After all, where the constitution does sanction presidential rhetoric, Article 2 mandates the president to "give to the congress *information* of the state of the union" (my emphasis).

The last 13 presidents have sought increasingly to share their affections freely in their public rhetoric (*AffGain*), as can be seen in figure 4.7. When emotions are increasingly shared in the absence of argument, when sentimentality is gratuitously injected into speeches in place of reason, pathos turns to bathos. Nixon's famous comeback "Checkers" speech, which he delivered on television in 1952 (as the vice presidential candidate of the Republican Party) in response to charges that he had received illegal campaign donations, is a case in point. Nixon's conspicuous play on emotion to the exclusion of argument in the speech reveals the strategic value of bathos. According to one commentator, "It was the well-honed Nixon appeal: resentful, emotional, square. If the sophisticates thought it mawkish or corny, it mattered little. He was talking to all the people out in the country who had to struggle,

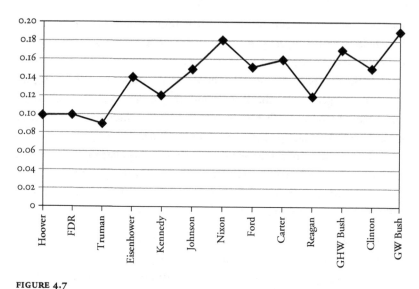

FIGURE 4.7

Occurrence of *AffGain* in the *Public Papers* of Presidents Hoover to Bush

who were tired of being talked down to by the elite New Dealers. And he got to them."[39] No wonder Nixon remembered this lesson, and when he later became president, he hired a speechwriter (the "staff poet," as Nixon designated him) specifically to provide him with "heart" in his rhetoric.[40] Yet it was this same writer who later recognized the flaw in Nixon's rhetorical priorities:

> I have come completely 180 degrees from the view I had earlier. While I believe if you take any president's output as a whole, [it] has to have grace notes, humanizing anecdotes, I believe that the best thing that a president or a politician could do, is to put out the arguments....The whole question of argument is something that has been totally lost in American rhetoric.[41]

Bathos is also especially evident in presidents' unsparing talk of families (*Kin@*) and children (*Nonadlt*), as shown in figure 4.8, when discussing practically any public policy issue. Indeed, well over half of all references to children in State of the Union addresses since 1790 were uttered by our last five presidents. In his second State of the Union address, Bill Clinton made 19 of these references, including, "You know, tonight, this is the first State of the Union Address ever delivered since the beginning of the cold war when not a single Russian missile is pointed at the children of America."[42]

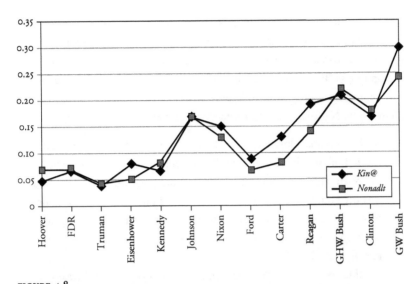

FIGURE 4.8

Occurrence of *Kin@* and *Nonadlt* in the *Public Papers* of Presidents Hoover to Bush

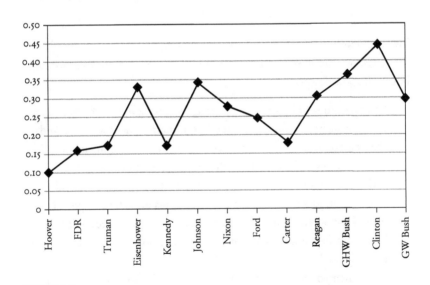

FIGURE 4.9

Occurrence of *Say* in the *Public Papers* of Presidents Hoover to Bush

Presidents have also sought to establish an emotional rapport with the audience via rhetorical conversationalism, as can be measured by the increase in words referencing direct verbal communication (*Say*), as shown in figure 4.9. President Clinton, in particular, made regular use of the storytelling technique in his frequent delivery of bathos. In a speech to the Democratic National Committee in 1999, he waxed poetic:

> And let me just close with this story. I want to tell you a story that I thought about that I told the folks at home when I went to dedicate my birthplace. Last year I had a 91-year-old great uncle who died. He was my grandmother's brother. And I loved him very much, and he helped to raise me when my mother was widowed and went off to study so she could be a nurse anesthetist, and my grandparents were raising me....
>
> He and his wife were married for over 50 years, and she came down with Alzheimer's. And they had one of these old-fashioned houses with gas stoves, so they had to take her to the local nursing facility that was tied to our nursing home in this little town because they were afraid she'd turn on the stove and forget about it and blow the house up. We can laugh—we all laughed about it.

Two paragraphs, 224 words, and a lot of laughter later, Clinton was still at his story, with no end in sight. I cite the rest of the speech not for its significance but for its pointlessness:

> So I went to see him one night, about 10 years ago, after his wife went into this nursing home. And they'd been married over 50 years. And the first 20 or 30 minutes we talked, all he did was tell me jokes and tell me stories and think about the old days. And I was walking out and for the only time in our life, he grabbed me by the arm. And I looked around and he had big old tears in his eyes. And I said, "This is really hard on you, isn't it." And he said this, he said, "Yes, it is." "But," he said, "you know, I signed on for the whole load, and most of it was pretty good."
>
> When you were up there singing "Stand By Me" tonight and I thought about how the American people have stood by me through thick and thin, I would just like to say to all of you, when I talk about community, that's what I mean. [Applause] Now, wait a minute. You don't have to sit down, because I'm nearly through. [Laughter] Don't sit down. Don't sit down. I'm nearly through. Here's the point I want

to make: The reason I wanted you to come here tonight, the reason I'm thankful for your contributions, the reason I'm thankful for what you do is, this country has got to get over believing that our political life is about beating each other up and hurting people, instead of lifting people up and bringing them together. That is what I've tried to do. That is what we stand for. And if we remember that, we're going to do just fine in the 21st century.

Thank you, and God bless you.[43]

The stated purpose of Clinton's story was that we should stop bickering and start loving. Never mind that his conclusion was trivially true, but the story meandered so aimlessly toward it that we are left to surmise that his purpose was only to tell a feel-good story as the end in itself. So, the conventional criticism that Clinton rambled on is only half right. The problem is that he went on about nothing, and he did so precisely with the storytelling technique for which his admirers have praised his ability to connect with his audience. Such was the "talk show" presidency of Bill Clinton.[44] But the cost of bathos must be measured not only in the crowding out of substantive argument but, more important, in how it substitutes genuine responsiveness to the "folks at home" in terms of tangible public policies with a feigned emotional connection. In his second State of the Union address, Clinton said:

> When the last congress killed political reform last year, it was reported in the press that the lobbyists actually stood in the Halls of this sacred building and cheered. This year, let's give the folks at home something to cheer about.[45]

The hypocrisy of this applause line was revealed when, in 1997, the folks at home learned of allegations that China and China-backing lobbyists had given money to the Democratic National Committee for the 1996 election campaign, and worse still, a Senate investigation concluded that the Clinton-Gore campaign was deeply implicated in the Democratic Party's fundraising activities.[46] Rhetorical chattiness and emotional connection is one thing; being actually responsive to the political needs of the country is another. Bathos produces in auditors a false comfort in leaders who are able to tug at our hearts but who may have no intention whatsoever to genuinely address our hearts' desires.

Finally, the case of Hillary Clinton is worth briefly discussing in light of the potential contrast with Bill Clinton. Here, we have an intellectual heavyweight, a candidate who graduated in the top 5 percent of her high school class and was a valedictorian at Wellesley. But this pedigree appeared to work against her as she was criticized during her husband's campaign for her rhetorical stiffness and her failure to deliver the winning conversational bathos of Bill Clinton. According to one observer, "Bill Clinton sounds intimate and conversational when he's discussing energy policy. Hillary Clinton sounds like a policy wonk when she talks about her mother's childhood struggles."[47] But Hillary Clinton made a concerted effort to change rhetorical course, and her contrivance in her campaign for president has been noticed:

> In Mrs. Clinton's campaign now, her operative conceit is "the conversation." It is impossible to attend a Hillary-for-president event and forget you are joining a "conversation," instead of hearing a conventional political speech. Mrs. Clinton relentlessly repeats the catchword, and for those who missed it, there are huge "Let the Conversation Begin" signs on the wall.[48]

Similarly, Dana Milbank of the *Washington Post* observed, "More than any other candidate, Clinton has brought the sensibility of Hallmark greeting cards to the 2008 presidential race."[49] Hillary Clinton was an initial exception who has learned and proved our rule. Like her husband and others before her, she is clearly campaigning for the anti-intellectual presidency.

5

Institutionalizing the Anti-Intellectual Presidency

Presidential rhetoric today is linguistically simplistic, short on logos, disingenuous on ethos, and long on pathos because the White House speechwriting office was created and evolved in a way that facilitated the rise of the anti-intellectual presidency. In this chapter, I examine the evolution of the White House speechwriting function to show how the institutionalization of speechwriting has altered its output. I examine the developmental trajectory of the White House speechwriting office from a one-man operation to a specialized and legitimate institution within the White House as a double-edged adaptation that partially ameliorated the demands of the rhetorical presidency but augmented the anti-intellectual presidency.

The Specialization of the White House Speechwriting Function

Surrogate or delegated speechwriting is not a new practice. For instance, George Washington's farewell address was penned by Alexander Hamilton, James Madison, and John Jay. However, the delegation of the speechwriting responsibility was secret, ad hoc, and indistinguishable from the policy-advising process for most of presidential history. The formal institutionalization and specialization of the White House speechwriting function is a relatively recent innovation and a reaction to the increasing demands for presidential speechifying that occurred in three phases during the twentieth century: the early ghostwriters, who served with a "passion for anonymity" from 1921 to 1932, were succeeded by influential speechwriting policy advisors from 1933 to 1968, and then by contemporary speechwriters in the post-Nixon years, who were divested of their policy-advising function.

Early Ghostwriters: 1921–1932

Until Franklin Roosevelt, most presidents did not rely heavily on their speechwriters. Although it was Theodore Roosevelt who coined the term "bully pulpit" and who was a founder of the rhetorical presidency, he never employed a speechwriter. Like Roosevelt, William Howard Taft and Woodrow Wilson wrote their own speeches and scarcely contemplated the possibility of leadership divorced from the authentic authorship of their own words. The founding rhetorical presidencies of Roosevelt and Wilson, then, were in this important regard radically different from the rhetorical (and anti-intellectual) presidencies that followed. This change began during the Harding administration with Judson C. Welliver, the first person placed on the White House payroll whose primary job was to write speeches. Welliver, who was inherited by the Coolidge administration and served until November 1, 1925, was succeeded by Stuart Crawford.[1] Presidential rhetoric became simultaneously more and less important as a result of these hires: presidential words were important enough to justify the employment of dedicated persons to craft them, but they were not so important that a president had to author them all. And so began the troubled history of delegated speechwriting.

The fledging speechwriting apparatus in the White House took a hiatus during the Hoover administration. For the most part, President Hoover did not rely on others to write his speeches. He "did a good deal of his drafting in longhand."[2] Even when he could not afford the time, Hoover would dictate his thoughts to a stenographer as they came to him, cut the speech up into paragraphs, and then arrange them on the train on his way to a speaking event.[3] The closest that Hoover ever came to having a speechwriter was his "administrative assistant," French Strother, who helped to research material for his speeches.[4] Strother was succeeded by George Hastings, who stayed with Hoover until February 1932.[5]

Two characteristics distinguished the early speechwriters for Presidents Harding and Coolidge from contemporary (post-Nixon) speechwriters.

First and most important, the early speechwriters operated anonymously, as ghostwriters. William Safire defined a *ghostwriter* as "one who surreptitiously prepares written and oral messages for public figures below the highest levels." A *speechwriter*, by contrast, is "a ghost who operates out in the open."[6] Ghost-writing emerged during a time when increasing presidential responsibilities necessitated a creative amanuensis to secretly help the president to draft his speeches, but political ethical norms had not caught up with the speechify-ing demands of the modern presidency. By Safire's definition, only Harding's, Coolidge's, and Hoover's speechwriters, Judson Welliver, Stuart Crawford, French Strother, and George Hastings, were ghostwriters. These were rela-tively unknown men who did not take public credit for what they wrote. But-tressing this practice were entrenched political ethical norms disparaging both credit-claiming writers for their egotism and principals for their duplicity.

A *Dictionary of Americanisms on Historical Principles* reports that the term "ghostwriting" first appeared in print in 1928, no doubt to describe the "passion for anonymity" shared by the earliest generation of writers.[7] President Hoover distrusted ghostwriters so much that he once said: "Ghost writers…are the bane of our existence!"[8] Consider also Henry L. Mencken's attack on FDR: "I think it's hooey. I don't believe Roosevelt writes his fireside speeches,"[9] a claim that would only make sense in a world in which delegated speechwriting was a disdained practice. Writing in the early twentieth cen-tury, Walter Lippmann also expressed the prevailing opinion of his time:

> A public man can and needs to be supplied with material advice and criti-cism in preparing an important address. But no one can write an authen-tic speech for another man; it is as impossible as writing his love letters for him or saying his prayers for him.…Those who cannot speak for themselves are, with very few exceptions, not very sure of what they are doing and of what they mean. The sooner they are found out, the better.[10]

A second distinguishing characteristic of the early ghostwriters compared to today's speechwriters is that the former were not prominent members of the White House. Because the White House had not yet become a "high-speed prose factory," ghostwriters typically functioned alone, without deputies.[11] In fact, because of their minimal workload, the duties of the ghostwriters in this period extended significantly beyond speechwriting, as was the case for the midcentury policy-advising speechwriters. Although Welliver's (and his successor, Crawford's) primary responsibility was speechwriting, his formal title was "chief clerk," and he was expected to perform other duties, such as responding to the White House mail.[12]

The cavalier attitude toward the ghostwriting (or early speechwriting) profession is revealed by the way in which the ghostwriters' salaries were legally appropriated: "here, there, and everywhere." At one point, speechwriters were paid from the fund for the payment of chauffeurs and the upkeep of the White House garage.[13] Indeed, another indication of Judson Welliver's dispensability was that, when he left the Coolidge White House in 1925 to accept the position of public relations director of the American Petroleum Institute, it took over a month for the White House to appoint his successor.[14]

Speechwriting Policy Makers at Midcentury: 1933–1968

It was during the FDR administration that speechwriters assumed the role of more than just the chief clerk and became presidential advisors with policymaking responsibilities. The number of speechwriters in the White House exploded during FDR's tenure, though this number is somewhat inflated precisely because many of his speechwriters were also his advisors, including Raymond Moley, Sam Rosenman, Thomas Corcoran, Harry Hopkins, Benjamin Cohen, Robert Sherwood, and Archibald MacLeish. As the number of people involved in speechwriting increased, it spawned new innovations. Because it became a challenge to keep the president's public and rhetorical persona consistent amid the multitude of speechwriting personnel, Raymond Moley (and later, Sam Rosenman) emerged as the principal speechwriter who vetted almost every word that the president spoke in order to ensure a consistency of style and content in all of his utterances. Moley became what would in later years be called a "chief speechwriter" because he was in Roosevelt's inner circle and possessed an uncanny ability to divine what his boss wanted to say and how to say it. Most subsequent administrations inherited this practice and also employed a final arbiter of the president's words, as was the case with Ted Sorensen for John Kennedy, Dick Goodwin for Lyndon Johnson, Bob Hartmann for Gerald Ford, Rick Hertzberg for Jimmy Carter, Aram Bakshian for Ronald Reagan, and Mike Gerson for George W. Bush. The chief speechwriter remained as the final arbiter of the president's speeches even when the speechwriting and policy-advising functions were separated during the Nixon administration.

Although Roosevelt vastly increased the number of White House speechwriters, there was a single exception to the new institutional rule. We are accustomed to the view that the modern and rhetorical presidency was in irreversible ascendance by midcentury, but as late as 1960, it was still possible for a president who did not place particular emphasis on speechifying,

Dwight Eisenhower, to have relied on only two speechwriters, Malcolm Moos and Stephen Hess. According to Hess, "the workload was not particularly heavy.... We were not terribly busy. In fact, Moos and I managed to write a book at the same time that we were doing this."[15] Indeed, Roderick Hart has showed that President Eisenhower was the least talkative of any president since Franklin Roosevelt, giving an average of just 9.6 speeches a month.[16] It is worth nothing, then, that the expansion of the White House speechwriting operation was to some degree a matter of presidential choice. To the extent that President Eisenhower (and some might include the case of George H. W. Bush) succeeded in resisting the rhetorical presidency but succumbing to the anti-intellectual presidency, it is likely that the forces driving the rhetorical and anti-intellectual presidencies are quite distinct.

Contemporary Speechwriters in the Post-Nixon Years: 1969–Present

In 1969, Nixon separated what FDR had put together, when the jobs of policy advising and speechwriting were divorced. Nixon created the Writing and Research Department, the first formally structured White House speechwriting office. Specialization did not necessarily make the speechwriting office more efficient. The speechwriting office was in relative disarray during the Ford and first Bush administrations.[17] Rather, it institutionalized the reification of style over policy substance in the speechwriting office and altered the content of what speechwriters produced henceforth. Insofar as there was a precise birth date of the anti-intellectual presidency, it was 1969.

Unlike their successors, the policy-advising speechwriters from the pre-Nixon administrations had little patience for matters of style. Richard Neustadt, who wrote for Truman, articulates this sentiment in strong terms:

> If they [speechwriting and policy advising] tended to be separated [in the post-Nixon White House] it's only because of a notion ... that there's some magic in words, some mystique in words that they need people who are experts in words to give you good words. And if those people then turn around and try to make themselves into a profession, that's hubris and the gods are watching and will punish them all.[18]

"I don't believe I have any theory of speechwriting or speechmaking," George Elsey insists. "The work I did on his [Truman's] staff was very practical. My ideas were purely pragmatic."[19] In this period, according to Milton Kayle, speechwriters *were* the "substantive issue men":

> When I joined the staff, I found that there were two main groups,
> if I can put it that way. There was the intellectual group—the
> speechwriting, substantive issue men—which were Murphy and his
> people....Then, as another group you had Matt Connelly and Joe
> Feeney and those people who were very important in the daily running
> of the White House.[20]

Ted Sorensen, who wrote for John Kennedy, believed that speeches were successful "only if the *ideas* they conveyed were forceful" (my emphasis).[21] As the White House transitioned toward the Nixon era, Richard Goodwin resigned from his speechwriting job precisely because he saw his job as "trivia[l]" and "mostly image-making."[22] Clearly, the instinct to be more than just a word technician was a shared sentiment among this earlier generation of speechwriters. When asked the question "what makes a great speech?" less than one-third of the speechwriters (12 of 42) I interviewed indicated substantive content, and those who did were disproportionately from pre-Nixon administrations. Nixon's specialization of the speechwriting function officially inverted this ethic and institutionalized a divide between the speechwriters and the policy advisors in the White House so that speechwriters were now concerned primarily with style and the advisors with policy substance. One former speechwriter put it starkly: "The speechwriter today is more beautician than brain truster."[23]

This division of labor was part of a series of organizational changes in the White House that reflected the president's heightened concern for image and packaging.[24] Nixon also created the Office of Communications, the public relations arm of the White House, and the Office of Public Liaison, which fed the nation's local and regional news organizations with news from the administration. The speechwriting team at the Nixon White House was the largest in White House history until then, with "a speechwriter for every Nixon there was."[25] Some have argued that this newfound preoccupation with public relations was sparked by Nixon's ignominious defeat in his debates with John Kennedy and his subsequent recognition of the power of prime-time television.[26]

The Legitimization of Delegated Speechwriting

I will turn to the dramatic consequences of these institutional developments in the next section. Before that, there is a parallel story at the normative level accompanying these institutional changes that is often missed, but must be told. The specialization of the speechwriting job was possible only because of an accompanying development in political ethics, the *legitimization* of the practice of delegated speechwriting, without which the White House speechwriting office could not have become the anti-intellectual fiefdom it has become. Only after presidents retreated from the speechwriting process and delegated speechwriting became legitimate practice over the twentieth century did speechwriters become influential members of the White House empowered to execute their specialized mission as wordsmiths.

The legitimization of the speechwriting profession occurred in inverse relationship to the expiration of ghostwriters' passion for anonymity, the standard to which Louis Brownlow had held those who served under the president. Ghostwriters were able to emerge unabashedly from the woodwork during Roosevelt's administration because they were policy-advising brain trusters who also happened to help the president draft his speeches. Their stature as speechwriters was elevated, perhaps exonerated, by the fact that they were also policy advisors who understood the details of policy and were in intimate contact with the president and his decision-making calculus. Contrast this to Judson Welliver—"the patron saint of the unquotables"— and his contemporaries, whose passion for anonymity was partly a function of their relative obscurity in the White Houses in which they served.[27] This became all but impossible with the advent of the speechwriting brains truster. Moley's contempt for the term "ghostwriting" is exemplary:

> I have always resented the characterization of my service to Roosevelt as that of a "speech writer." Even more odious is the expression "ghost writer." For there is suggested by such expressions something fictitious, phony, shabby—even dishonest—when a man in high authority and vested with great responsibility delegates to someone else the writing of the expressions he presents to the public as his own.[28]

While it was easier for Welliver to remain anonymous, it was difficult for Raymond Moley, who was appointed to be the assistant secretary of state (and who by Safire's definition was the first presidential *speechwriter*), to have remained so even if he had wanted to.[29] It was arguably also unnecessary, since as an advisor and policymaker in his own right, he was a legitimate contributor to presidential rhetoric. Moley and his generation of policy-advising speechwriters, then, were a critical transitional generation without which we could not explain the about-turn in perceptions of the speechwriting profession exemplified by Judson Welliver's obscurity and Peggy Noonan's celebrity. Today, not only is the stigma gone from speechwriting, the profession has become an ideal launching pad for successful careers in journalism and public life. Among speechwriters who achieved celebrity status since leaving the White House are William Safire, Chris Matthews, and Peggy Noonan. Others who started out as speechwriters and then transitioned to important political positions are Pat Buchanan, David Gergen, and Mike Gerson. Although today's speechwriters have shed their policy-advising functions, they have benefited from the pathbreaking generation of Raymond Moley and others, whose service to the nation helped, without their realizing it, to legitimize a profession that had hitherto been held in disdain. With the passion for anonymity now fully expired, contemporary speechwriters continue to enjoy the legitimacy that others earned for them even as they have been divested of the policy-advising responsibility out of which this legitimacy was first earned. Their job description has largely reverted back to the days of Judson Welliver, but now sans the ignominy. Now, they can be "beauticians" and be unabashed about it.

The process did not happen overnight, of course, and the expiration of the passion for anonymity also exhibited an inverse relationship with how heavily involved presidents were in the speechwriting process. The more legitimized the speechwriting profession, the more presidents withdrew from involvement in the speechwriting process from that of principal author in the case of the presidents before Harry Truman to occasional editor in the case of presidents after Richard Nixon. According to his speechwriters, FDR dictated or wrote whole drafts of many of his major speeches.[30] One scholar concluded that "the late president was the primary source of the ideas, the arguments, and the language of [his] speeches."[31] For example, in the middle of the Second World War and unsatisfied with the first draft of his eighteenth Fireside Chat (on the progress of the war, February 23, 1942), Franklin Roosevelt actually took the time to handwrite an entire second draft of his speech.[32] The same can be said of Harry Truman's heavy involvement in speechwriting. Clark Clifford, who wrote for President Truman, remarked, "I can't recall ever writing a speech for the president and having it escape unscathed and go to the public in the original form. He always had his own ideas that went into it."[33]

Roosevelt's and Truman's heavy involvement in the speechwriting process in the middle of World War II and the Cold War tells us that the practice of delegating speechwriting has less to do with increasing presidential work or speech loads than sympathetic accounts in the public presidency scholarship may imply, and more to do with political-ethical norms. The new practice of delegated speechwriting is not a result of increasing speech loads, since we know that Roosevelt gave more speeches in an average year in office than either Eisenhower or Ford.[34] And FDR did not fail to delegate for lack of resources either, since he possessed a large and distinguished speechwriting and policy-advising staff. Roosevelt and Truman adopted a hands-on approach to rhetorical leadership. They were reluctant to overdelegate a job that existing political-ethical norms determined to be a significant presidential responsibility. That is why, during the Roosevelt administration, speechwriters were still residual "ghosts" in their meticulous adherence to the custom of attributing every speech they wrote to the president. To keep up appearances, even Raymond Moley dutifully tossed his own draft of Franklin Roosevelt's first inaugural address into the fireplace at Hyde Park, and provided the yellow legal paper on which Roosevelt reproduced the draft of the address in his own hand so that the myth of authenticity would be preserved for posterity in the FDR Library.[35]

However, it did not take very long for Moley's example to be forgotten. In March 1948, *Time* ran no less than a cover story on Clark Clifford, Truman's principal advisor and speechwriter, reporting:

> When [the president] opened his mouth to deliver one of the messages
> prepared by Clifford, the president talked like a New Dealer. And
> adviser Clifford was kept busy scribbling. He wrote the tax vetoes;
> the Taft-Hartley veto; the October 1947 call for a special session; the
> State of the Union message last January; this year's Jackson Day dinner
> speech and the civil-rights message.

The passion for anonymity was temporarily revived during the Eisenhower administration, when speechwriters agreed that "it would be very poor form if our name got in the paper. Very poor form, and we knew that."[36] But it was lost when Ted Sorensen became Kennedy's advisor and chief speechwriter, and it was an open secret that "the Camelot speeches of JFK manifested more of Sorensen's taste than Kennedy's."[37] Not surprisingly, it soon became a matter of conventional wisdom that the president's time was better spent elsewhere than in laboring on his speeches. In examining John Kennedy's involvement in the speechwriting process, James Golden found that he "served [primarily] as *outliner* who suggested guidelines which an assistant used in writing a first draft...and *editor* and *collaborator* who tuned up thoughts" (original emphasis).[38] During the Johnson administration, the code of anonymity was somewhat respected, but under pressure. According to Johnson's special counsel, Harry McPherson, "A knowing shrug [acknowledging authorship] was permissible, but only just."[39]

By the 1970s, scholarly discussions of the ethical implications of delegated speechwriting, once popular a few decades earlier, fell off research agendas.[40] At this time, as Ford's chief speechwriter, Robert Hartmann, noted, presidents "abandoned even the pretense of handcrafting their own public utterances."[41] Just as speechwriters were fully out of the closet, presidents retreated from the speechwriting environment. It was acknowledged, even by his chief speechwriter, that President Carter "never worked in any consistent way or directly with the people who wrote his speeches."[42] For example, Jimmy Carter's contribution to perhaps the most important speech of his presidency, his "malaise" speech to the nation on July 15, 1979, was minimal. His main contribution was a series of quotations from political and civic leaders that appeared at the beginning of the final version of the speech, and a partial draft of just 500 words (in a speech that eventually took 3,600 words) on the "crisis of confidence" portion of the speech.[43]

While some contemporary speechwriters will still credit their bosses as the principal author of their words, it will now take the most naïve Washingtonian to take these token attributions at face value.[44] FDR and Carter possessed different conceptions of rhetorical authorship that reflected the changing ethical mores regarding delegated speechwriting. For Carter, who had a legitimized speechwriting operation at his service, it was an obvious if not a tautologous conclusion that the job of speechwriting was that of the speechwriters, and not that of the president.

The Consequences of Institutionalized Speechwriting

The evolution of a specialized and legitimized speechwriting office unapologetically charged to craft the public communications of the president was a significant milestone of the anti-intellectual presidency. First, it contributed to the reification of style over substance in the crafting of presidential rhetoric. Second, it redefined the meaning of authorial responsibility and necessitated a reconfiguration of the manner in which the "authenticity" of presidential rhetoric was insinuated. Third, a specialized and legitimized speechwriting office reinforced both of these consequences by strengthening the speechwriters' control, and therefore their priorities, over the nature of presidential rhetoric.

The Reification of Style over Substance

Institutionalization both alleviated and exacerbated the speechifying pressure on the president. Because it is now understood that a president has a coterie of men and women crafting his words, it is expected that he should have something to say about everything, almost anytime. So although their number has grown, today's speechwriters face a daily production battle against time that has altered the product of their pens. A heavy production load does not necessarily predispose speechwriters to produce clumsily worded speeches, but it does incline them to be on the constant prowl for catchy phrases that will stand out amid the deluge of words. There has been a parallel effect on presidents, who have little time to consider the impact of a speech other than the instantly gratifying measure of applause because the next speaking engagement is already looming on the horizon. The punch line has become the bottom line in this rhetorical frenzy. One speechwriter dramatizes the peak writing periods and their effect on policymaking:

> Words, words, words—faster, faster, faster—write, edit, stencil,
> telegraph: there was no place, here, for the verb "to think." Coin that
> epigram, edit that peroration, sharpen that retort, catch that head-
> line: they were, and remain, the crude imperatives. Policy meant one
> thing: produce speeches in number to match scheduled engagements.
> Strategy gave its crisp corollary: do it faster. There was one solace. There
> remained no leisure time for reflecting, sagely or sadly, whether this was
> a responsible way for a great democracy to make its great decisions.[45]

The specialization of the speechwriting function in the post-Nixon White House encouraged speechwriters, who were now relieved of the responsibility of considering matters of policy, to devote what little time they had for each speech to matters of style. It is worth noting that the transitional Nixon White House recognized and grappled seriously with the competing demands of the rhetoric of interbranch deliberation and governance versus the rhetoric of public communication and persuasion. As we saw in chapter 4, on January 20, 1972, Nixon delivered a televised "Address on the State of the Union" before a joint session of congress, which was really tailored to a national audience, while separately submitting a differently worded "Annual Message to the Congress on the State of the Union" to the speaker of the House and the president of the Senate after his public address.[46] Even though Nixon separated the speechwriting and policy-advising functions, he understood the distinction between the rhetoric of deliberation and the rhetoric of persuasion and did not purvey one to the exclusion of the other, at least when it came to the most important speech that a president delivers each year. Subsequent White Houses inherited Nixon's institutional reform but not his balanced rhetorical priorities. Contemporary speechwriting offices have either not perceived or not conceded a difference between the rhetoric of deliberation and the rhetoric of persuasion and have discontinued Nixon's practice. The speechwriting office is today concerned, almost exclusively, with the rhetoric of public communication and persuasion.

To be sure, bureaucrats and policy advisors are also involved in the speechwriting process, but because speechwriters remain the gatekeepers of presidential rhetoric, the imperatives of style have taken center stage. Indeed, the division of labor between policymakers and wordsmiths has only exacerbated the differences between the two and made wordsmiths even more furious champions of style. Today, the negotiation between substance and style that used to be worked out within each individual now has to be worked out among several people with very different job descriptions and priorities. A process known as "staffing," in which draft speeches are sent to bureaucrats in the relevant executive branch to be vetted before speechwriters complete the final draft, was introduced to rationalize this elaborate process. But staffing does not bring together what the institutional division of labor has pulled asunder. It intensifies the turf battles between the speechwriters and the policy advisors, exacerbating the speechwriter's disdain for the bureaucrat's pedantry and the policy advisor's contempt for the wordsmith's rhetorical flights. The sharp style-substance chasm unintentionally created by Nixon can be observed in contemporary speechwriters' universal disdain for "bureaucratese."[47] The greatest challenge that Tony Dolan faced as a speechwriter was "getting [speeches] through the bureaucracy."[48] Said Ben Wattenberg, "Stuff that comes over from the State Department—speeches—are usually so absurdly bad...I sometimes just end up tossing them in the waste paper basket and just starting afresh."[49] Another speechwriter describes staffing as "an enervating, infuriating, and bureaucratically Byzantine process."[50] The disdain, of course, works in both directions, and many bureaucrats view the speechwriting office as "a black hole from which no sophisticated thought could escape."[51] Bureaucrats have been particularly wary of speechwriters who occasionally back-channeled speech drafts to their bosses to sidestep departmental censorship, as was the case in Anthony Dolan's dramatic word choice in Reagan's "evil empire" speech.[52]

The end result of all this has been the reification of style to the detriment of substance or policy specificity, otherwise read as bureaucratese. If speechwriters before were nonchalant about their speech suggestions—if only because their claims of utility to the president could come also in the form of policy advice—the specialization of their job function has made them fiercely protective of their words. Indeed, it has even become unclear whether presidents or their speechwriters are the gatekeepers of presidential rhetoric. In 1991, the president of the United States handwrote a note to the principal author of the 1991 State of the Union address, saying, "Dear Mark, It's not easy to do work and then watch edit after edit. You did all that and came out with a product that went over quite well. Many many thanks."[53] Courtesy gesture aside, here was a president who felt obliged to offer an apologetic note to his speechwriter for editing the content of a speech that he, not the speechwriter, delivered and for which he would take public responsibility. Bush appeared to acknowledge the writers' ethic that authors do not take kindly to edits, even though this writer was employed specifically to pen *his* words.

The reification of style over policy substance, institutionalized by Nixon's division of labor between policy advisors and speechwriters, has been reinforced by a return to the pre-FDR norm of hiring journalists as speechwriters. In the early years, speechwriters were recruited from the journalistic profession. Judson Welliver had been a "widely known newspaper man"; Stuart Crawford had been a writer for the *Sun*, the *New York Tribune*, and the *Herald*; and French Strother had been an editor at the *World's Work* magazine.[54] However, a deviation from this earlier practice occurred in the interregnum administrations of Roosevelt, Truman, Kennedy, and Johnson. With the exception of the Eisenhower years, the principal speechwriters from the midcentury administrations were almost all legally or academically trained. Sam Rosenman, Clark Clifford, George Elsey, Ted Sorensen, Myer Feldman, and Harry McPherson were lawyers. Raymond Moley, Richard Neustadt, and Arthur Schlesinger were professors. Unsurprisingly, these men were also heavily involved in policy advising.

The professional background for post-Nixon presidential speechwriters has reverted back to the pre-Rooseveltian norm to reflect the now-specialized function of presidential speechwriters as stylists. An overwhelming majority of speechwriters since the 1970s have been recruited from the journalistic profession. The selection of speechwriters on the basis of writing ability has reinforced the function of speechwriters as literary stylists and not policy experts writing to a general audience. Further, because the essential credential that the post-Nixon speechwriters needed was evidence of good writing ability, many were recruited in their 20s and 30s (while they were still prime candidates for a stressful job that requires the mass production of prose at a grueling rate), well before they had any chance of acquiring any experience in the policy world. Among former chief speechwriters, Raymond Price (Nixon) had been a reporter for the *New York Herald*; Robert Hartmann (Ford) had been a reporter, then Washington bureau chief of the *Los Angeles*

Times; Rick Hertzberg (Carter) started off as the San Francisco correspondent for *Newsweek* magazine and became the editorial director of the *New Yorker*; Tony Dolan was a reporter for the *Stamford Advocate* and winner of the 1978 Pulitzer Prize for investigative reporting. The present director of speechwriting, William McGurn, was a writer for the *Wall Street Journal*, and his predecessor, Mike Gerson, was formerly a reporter for *U.S. News & World Report*. Professionally trained and experienced journalists, then, have taken their particular facility with words and their generalist knowledge of politics into the White House.

It is important to note that there are different consequences to today's norm of hiring journalists as speechwriters from the norm that selected Judson Welliver and the first generation of ghostwriters. Welliver, like today's speechwriters, was recruited from the journalistic profession. But while Welliver was an unknown and marginal entity in the White House, today's speechwriters are powerful staffers. Indeed, a notable exception to the post-Nixon rule which separates the speechwriting from the policy-advising function illuminates this difference. Mike Gerson, President Bush's former chief speechwriter, had been recruited from the journalism profession, like Judson Welliver and like most other contemporary speechwriters. But Gerson also ascended very quickly to occupy a policy-advising position in the Bush White House. Whereas Welliver was only an obscure chief clerk, Gerson became assistant to the president for speechwriting *and* policy advisor. Here was the revenge of one wordsmith: his rhetorical contributions to the Bush presidency were so esteemed that he transitioned into the role of full-fledged policy advisor, which says as much about the word-styling talent of Gerson as the priorities of the Bush White House.[55] Gerson's career progression can be contrasted to Clark Clifford's. Sam Rosenman, FDR's chief speechwriter, did not prize writing ability over other abilities when selecting his successor in the Truman administration. Clark Clifford observed: "I did not consider myself to have any special gift as a writer.... even though he had suggested me as his successor, Rosenman himself understood my limitations in this area."[56] While Clifford was a policy advisor turned speechwriter, Gerson was a speechwriter turned policy advisor. Gerson's career progression does not indicate that the speechwriting function is cycling back either to the golden era of Clifford in the middle of the twentieth century or to the ghostwriting era of Welliver. Instead, his career is a telling example of how the speechwriting function has possibly engulfed the policy-advising function in the contemporary era, so that style and substance are increasingly indistinguishable, with the imperatives of the former encroaching on the latter.

Redefining Authenticity, Reconfiguring Rhetoric

As presidents began to delegate the speechwriting responsibility, the degree to which the president was involved in the speechwriting process automatically became a matter of concern for reasons of democratic accountability: only elected officials, democratic theory tells us, ought to make decisions and promulgate them. In this regard, President Warren Harding exemplified perhaps the most troubling relationship a president could have with his speeches when he apparently said after a speech: "Well, I never saw this before. I didn't write this speech and I don't believe what I just said."[57] Contemporary presidents share this sentiment more often than we would think. With the expiration of the passion for anonymity, today's speechwriters do not deny that they author presidential words, but to preserve the legitimacy of their profession, they are still at pains to affirm that they produce what a president would have written for himself. Said one speechwriter, "My understanding of my role as a speechwriter...was not to put words in someone's mouth, but simply to do what a busy, important and highly capable man would have done for himself if he had had time to do it for himself."[58] But how is this possible, in a context where speechwriters are no longer advisors acquainted with policy details and have limited access to the president? The answer to this question suggests another consequence of legitimized delegated speechwriting: the emergence of new rhetorical strategies to project the "authenticity" of presidential speeches.

The White House staff, relatively small at the turn of the twentieth century, was housed in the West Wing. In 1934, Franklin Roosevelt renovated and expanded the West Wing to make more room for his expanding staff, and speechwriters were comfortably housed in it until the Johnson administration. During these decades, even the most junior speechwriter had access to senior members of the staff, if not the president. Milton Kayle, special assistant to President Truman, recalls this felicitous arrangement: "We were intimate, we knew everything....There's no way that this huge staff that's involved in the White House today can have the intimacy that we had when we were on the Truman staff."[59]

During the Johnson administration, speechwriters were moved out to a suite of offices in the Old Executive Office Building (now the Eisenhower Executive Office Building), and speechwriters began to experience reduced access to the president.[60] This physical separation was reinforced with intellectual separation when speechwriters were divested of their policy-advising functions, and there was even less reason for them to be within easy and constant access to the president. With the institutional separation of the policy advisors, the purveyors of policy substance, from the speechwriters, the purveyors of style, the need-to-know operational norm of the White House meant that most speechwriters from and after the Nixon administration were no longer given access to substantive information about the issues they were writing about. That is why Patrick Butler observes, "The greatest frustration we had on President Ford's speechwriting staff was that we didn't get the kind of regular access to the president that speechwriters in previous White Houses had taken as routine."[61] At the height of his responsibilities as the chief speechwriter, Butler met with Ford only once a week. According to David Gergen, President Reagan, the "Great Communicator," probably did not know "more than one or two of his writers by sight."[62]

Speechwriters' reduced access to the president spawned a pathological coping tactic. Since speechwriters no longer possessed unlimited access to the president to ascertain his specific views on any particular topic, the authenticity of presidential words had to be demonstrated in other ways. As we saw in chapter 3, speechwriters achieved this by eschewing elements of rhetoric that would betray a coordinated strategy of persuasion. As Harry Truman once said, "It takes special talent to be a speaker, but everybody can tell whether a man is sincere or knows what he's talking about without his having to have that special talent and that's what counts."[63] As speechwriters moved further and further away from the president's inner circle, simplistic, unrhetorical rhetoric has become the standard to which contemporary speechwriters aspire.

Further, because speechwriters can no longer replicate the substantive policy details circulating in the president's mind and among his advisors, they have been left to reproduce the president's rhetorical style and his world view at an abstract level. Inspirational platitudes became the rhetorical strategy of choice because they can be used to convey a serious message without saying anything specific at all. The recourse to platitudes and partisan slogans discussed in the previous chapter arose in part because speechwriters without sufficient access to the president and his deliberations have been left to devise stylish sentences that still appear to ring true. This is exactly what the Nixon and Reagan speechwriters did. Indeed, it is a little-discussed fact that the Nixon and Reagan speechwriters, celebrated for what they achieved for their principals, had very little contact with their principals. Housed across the street from the White House at the Executive Office Building, the Nixon speechwriters "were effectively cut off from direct contact with the president."[64] Similarly, a Reagan speechwriter observes, "Reagan was more distant than his warm image suggested.... Speechwriters were never sure he even knew their names."[65] The Nixon and Reagan speechwriters are remembered as great writers despite their limited access to the presidents they served because they were not expected to have that access, and they did not attempt to encumber presidential rhetoric with substantive details. Instead, they strove for simplistic, creedal slogans that summarized the thrust, but not the details, of their principals' policy positions.

In short, the content of presidential rhetoric changed because the meaning and purpose of speechwriting changed. Because speechwriters are now charged to address matters of style, because they now have limited access to the president, and because they nevertheless have to affirm the authenticity of the words they produce for their principals, presidential rhetoric has become increasingly devoid of policy substance, simplistic, and sloganistic. The post-Nixon speech-writing office has become an integral arm of the anti-intellectual presidency.

Because of the dire consequences of the legitimization and specialization of the speechwriting operation, many former speechwriters, mostly from the pre-Nixon era, have advocated a return to the golden age when speechwriters also played a central policy-advising role. Arthur Schlesinger, Jr., who made many an impassioned, but unheeded, plea for the reunion of both functions to fellow former speechwriters, was one such fierce opponent of specialization.[66] Although regarded by most speechwriters as the dean of their profession, Ted Sorensen, when invited to the White House to speak to Clinton's speechwriters, actually suggested the disbanding of the speechwriting office.[67] Schlesinger and Sorensen were exactly right in appreciating the deleterious consequences of specialization.

The Unexpected Influence of Wordsmiths

The contemporary presidential speechwriter performs a function that not too long ago was a distinctly presidential responsibility. For this reason, he or she is both a relatively insignificant member of the White House staff and a curiously empowered one. It is important that we understand this paradox, because speechwriters' reification of style over substance would not be significant but for the fact of their increasing influence in the White House. Their influence is displayed in their agenda-setting, situational, and gatekeeping powers.

Because staffing, or vetting, occurs only for major speeches, speechwriters practically instruct presidents as to what to say on most other occasions. As Bush's speechwriter recalls, "On many events, we don't get a whole lot of input" from the rest of the White House.[68] According to a speechwriter from the Reagan administration, "Eighty percent of what we write is spoken by the president without change."[69] A typical memorandum sent by speechwriters to President George H. W. Bush on the eve of an event-filled day provides a sense of the power that speechwriters yield:

> On Saturday, December 7 in Hawaii, you will give three speeches commemorating the 50th Anniversary of the Pearl Harbor attack....
>
> The speech at the cemetery (12 minutes, on cards) is meant as a remembrance and tribute to those who died.
>
> The speech on the Arizona Memorial (12 minutes, on cards) will be the emotional high point of the day and probably the most widely televised. For that reason, this speech is a rhetorical recreation of what happened that day in 1941, and what it means to us today.
>
> The third speech (15 minutes, on teleprompter) discusses the dangers of isolationism and the triumph of freedom over tyranny brought about by engagement. Near the end, as you reflect upon your war experiences, you look forward to the next 50 years.[70]

It is unclear if President Bush knew anything about these speeches before he delivered them, especially given the instructional tone of the memorandum one day before they were scheduled. The problem, of course, is that the White House often cannot distinguish, ahead of time, what is destined to be "rose-garden rubbish" and what may rise beyond that. But it assumes its capacity to do so anyway in selecting which speeches to provide speechwriters guidance for and which not to. Consider, for example, the remarkably free hand that Peter Robinson possessed in the construction of Reagan's speech at the Berlin Wall, where the president challenged his Soviet counterpart to "tear down this wall." Robinson recalls:

> In the Reagan White House we would often receive extremely scanty guidance from the senior staff. For example, the Berlin Wall speech. I was told he'll talk for forty minutes. He'll stand there and since he's speaking in Germany in front of the Berlin Wall he ought to say something about foreign policy. And this varies from White House to White House, but in the Reagan White House, quite often, the guidance was minimal. And it was up to the speechwriter not only to do, so to speak, the first draft writing but the first draft thinking for the president. If you were the president, what would you say in such a circumstance?[71]

When speechwriters end up writing something that resonates across several news cycles that was neither vetted nor planned, their standard defense of this enormous agenda-setting power is their ability (and faith in that ability) to accurately predict what a president would have wanted to say if he had written the speech himself. But the fact that speechwriters quarrel with the policy experts and advisors in the executive branch over bureaucratese (and indeed, in this particular case, over the wisdom of keeping the phrase "tear down this wall") is indication enough that the validity of their divination is often presumed rather than actual. Speechwriters' agenda-setting power resides precisely in their ability to act on this presumption. Another example in our own time is speechwriter David Frum's coinage of "axis of hatred," the child of the fateful "axis of evil" used to describe the rogue nations of Iraq, Iran, and Korea in President Bush's 2002 State of the Union address.[72] It is important to note, also, that speechwriters' agenda-setting power extends beyond speeches to executive orders, veto messages, and messages to the congress and the bureaucracy. As Raymond Price reminds us, White House speechwriters do a lot more than write speeches. Indeed, he referred to his office as "the writing group," because "most of our writing was not speeches."[73] The agenda-setting influence of White House speechwriters extends to the language of government.

Speechwriters also enjoy what may be called "situational" influence in their prevailing presumption that they alone hold the keys to an accurate representation of presidential thoughts. Although all power in the White House flows downward from the president, it does not follow the hierarchy of formal rank. Instead, speechwriters' influence is often an externality derived from the perceived importance of presidential rhetoric, especially when they are drafting a major speech. In these moments, access to the president is restored, and speechwriters enjoy a dispensation from the normal rules of the White House. Back in the Hoover administration, a former White House usher observed, "The regular secretaries seemed to resent the fact that, owing to the confidential nature of the work, the man holding this job had an entrée to the president which they themselves did not enjoy. He seemed always to be a separate part of the Executive Offices, under orders of no one but the president."[74] This perk to the speechwriter's job has remained. Decades later, President Bush's former speechwriter observed:

> The writing shop was recognized as an exception to all the normal rules
> governing the Bush White House. We were allowed to shut our doors
> and hit the "Do Not Disturb" buttons on our telephones—behavior
> that would have provoked a scandal just about anywhere else. The
> excuse "I'm writing" covered a lot of derelictions. Our shop was also a
> refuge for eccentrics and eggheads.[75]

Finally, and perhaps most significantly, speechwriters also possess gatekeeping influence as final arbiters in the staffing or major speech vetting process. Even though staffing was introduced to insert more points of input and verification into the speechwriting process, it has served mainly to strengthen the hand of speechwriters. This is because, as one writer acknowledges, "the speechwriter is basically the last domino before the president in terms of whatever speeches are given and whatever rhetoric comes out and whatever way policy is articulated because this is the person who has pieced together the words on that policy."[76] Describing the staffing process, the former chief speechwriter in the Bush White House admits that "we have a significant amount of discretion in the way we do this. When we don't take an edit at all, we get back to people and we tell them why."[77]

The speechwriters' agenda-setting, situational, and gatekeeping power means that, while they are no longer, formally, policy advisors, they are de facto policymakers. As Reagan's chief speechwriter put it, "You very often end up playing, just of necessity, a policy-making or policy-mediating role."[78] This can occur under a variety of circumstances. Sometimes, when an administration has not yet taken a position on a particular issue, the articulated position of the speechwriters becomes the de facto position.[79] As Gavin Williams recounts his assignment to write a Nixon campaign speech on conservation:

> In a presidential campaign, an apprentice speechwriter was given an assignment, almost as an afterthought, about a subject hardly anyone was interested in and about which he knew nothing. The topic eventually proved to be among the most important domestic politic[al] issues for the rest of the country.[80]

At other times, the speechwriting process also serves to clarify the position of the administration on a particular issue, or "to organize their thoughts."[81] According to Peter Robinson, "a big speech was a discipline whereby the administration would pull itself together, sort through policy initiatives, consider the alternatives in terms of politics and policy, and produce a coherent conclusion."[82] According to another speechwriter, "In the Reagan administration, speeches were policy. . . . Once a speech was written, it was Reagan's policy."[83]

All of this sounds innocuous until we recall that speechwriters in the post-Nixon era are wordsmiths, not policy advisors, who are nevertheless in a privileged position to commandeer the entire speechwriting process. An example of where this can go wrong in general, and the spectacular failure of staffing in particular, was observed in the debacle of President George W. Bush's 2003 State of the Union address, in which misleading claims about

Iraq obtaining uranium from Niger passed uncensored through the staffing process. As it turned out, the evidence that Iraq had made such acquisitions was unreliable, and further, the administration appeared to be aware of it at the time at which the speech was delivered. Acknowledging this, the administration deflected criticisms of the speech by blaming CIA director George Tenet for failing to do his part in the staffing process. In a press gaggle (a free-wheeling, on-record press conference sans videography) aboard *Air Force One* on July 11, 2003, Secretary of State Condoleezza Rice repeatedly reminded the press that the speech had been "cleared":

> The CIA cleared on it. There was even some discussion on that specific sentence, so that it reflected better what the CIA thought. And the speech was cleared.
>
> Now, I can tell you, if the CIA, the Director of Central Intelligence, had said, take this out of the speech, it would have been gone, without question....
>
> We don't make the President his own fact witness, we have a high standard for them. That's why we send them out for clearance. And had we heard from the DCI or the Agency that they didn't want that sentence in the speech, it would not have been in the speech.[84]

Rice was, at best, deflecting blame generally on staffing and, at worst, pointing an accusatory finger specifically at Tenet for failing to do his part in the speech vetting process. By hammering home the point that the CIA had "cleared" the speech, and that the CIA had veto power on what appeared in the president's speech, she was effectively saying that whatever factual errors that remained redounded to the CIA and the director of Central Intelligence. This would be like saying that the peer reviewers of this book had a veto power on what was printed here, and they alone must take responsibility for an error that passed unnoticed. Amazingly, this was the same position that the Senate Select Committee on Intelligence's report would later adopt, in the strong language of a "conclusion":

> Conclusion 22. The Director of Central Intelligence (DCI) should have taken the time to read the State of the Union speech and fact check it himself. Had he done so, he would have been able to alert the National Security Council (NSC) if he still had concerns about the use of the Iraq-Niger uranium reporting in a Presidential speech.[85]

George Tenet, for his part, adopted the same deflective strategy. In his testimony to congress, he alleged that he passed the speech draft to an assistant, who was supposed to have handed it to another senior CIA official, who apparently did not have the time to peruse the speech either.[86] The excuse of delegation worked for the president, but not for Tenet. He resigned from the CIA, citing "personal reasons," a year after the speech, in 2004, but he would later say in his book that he was forced out because he was used as a "deflection" of blame.[87] Washington was not impressed by his book, not because Tenet was necessarily lying, but because he waited three years to tell his side of the story.[88]

The standard narrative would end here, but there is more to be said. Where were the speechwriters when we needed them? If speechwriters are the "last domino" before a speech is sent to the teleprompter, then they are the actual if not the formal gatekeepers of presidential rhetoric. But, of course, the gatekeepers in this case could not do their job because they were not equipped to do so, as the final arbiters of presidential rhetoric are not policy advisors or experts. The narrative also does not end with Tenet's ignominious resignation because we have not said anything about presidential responsibility. Democrats have harped about how Bush allegedly misled the nation with his 2003 State of the Union address, but what is interesting for our purposes is *why* their criticisms have had little traction. Legitimate or not, contemporary presidents, operating in a thicker and delegated speechwriting environment, are no longer held fully responsible for their public utterances—not even for a misstatement in the most important speech a president gives every year. Thus, the merry-go-round of blame shifting allowed fellow partisans to dismiss Bush's infraction. House majority leader Tom DeLay (R-TX) described the misstatement as "one little flaw."[89] The error was trivial because it was a result of human error, not malicious intent. Senator James Inhofe (R-OK) described the issue as "nothing but an absurd, media-driven, diversionary tactic."[90] These partisan defenses of the president appeared plausible only because it is now public knowledge that presidential speeches are collaboratively drafted and the president cannot be wholly accountable for his public (mis)statements. The sheer scope of the contemporary White House speechwriting operation means that the rhetorical presidency is no longer a unitary agent but a collaborative institution, in which no single person, not even the president, takes full responsibility for the president's words.

Staffing and delegated speechwriting therefore have produced two related pathologies: those who are empowered to vet a speech are not equipped to, and those who should take responsibility for a speech are not held responsible. It is in the interest of both speechwriters and presidents to perpetuate this inefficient arrangement. Delegated speechwriting has benefited speech-writers by propelling them to prominence in the White House; and speech-writers have found willing allies in presidents, who have benefited from the diffusion of authorial responsibility for their public words. The only los-ers appear to be the American people, for whom presidential rhetoric has become "mere rhetoric."

6

Indicting the Anti-Intellectual Presidency

Because we have not taken systematic notice of the impoverished state of our public deliberative sphere, we have barely wrestled with the normative implications of the anti-intellectual presidency. But this theoretical gap may well be justified if there is nothing wrong with presidential anti-intellectualism. Perhaps, as Cicero once wrote, "the masses want it; custom permits it; humanity tolerates it," and, if so, this book is much ado about nothing.[1] In this chapter, I tackle the normative justifications of anti-intellectualism to explain its political seductiveness and, in rejecting them, explain why anti-intellectualism damages our democracy.

"Theories" of the Anti-Intellectual Presidency

If rhetorical practices constitute "reflections and elaborations of underlying doctrines of governance," then the rise of the anti-intellectual presidency indicates a transformation not only of the presidency, but of American democracy.[2] As Tulis argued, "By changing the meaning of policy, rhetoric alters policy itself and the meaning of politics in the future."[3] Just as a justificatory theory—in the form of an informal, second constitution—of the rhetorical presidency has risen alongside its practice, justifications for rhetorical simplicity constitute theories of the anti-intellectual presidency, which has altered the meaning of American democracy. I extract these justifications from interviews from the speechwriters reported in chapter 3, who may admittedly resist the notion that their rationales constitute justifications of anti-intellectualism. But this is exactly what the tyranny of small anti-intellectual decisions will predict. These justifications of anti-intellectualism constitute a politically seductive body of thought. They help to justify and perhaps mythologize a practice that would otherwise be described as cynical pandering.

The first two arguments I present below are active justifications: the argument against elitism and the argument for participation. The third and fourth arguments are passive defenses of anti-intellectualism: the argument of inconsequentialism and the argument from necessity. I have two goals here: first, to register, and second, to deconstruct, these related justifications/ defenses for the anti-intellectual presidency. I will present and dispense with the first two briefly and spend the rest of the chapter addressing the third and fourth defenses of anti-intellectualism.

Argument 1: Anti-Intellectualism Is Anti-Elitist

A familiar justification of presidential anti-intellectualism from the speech-writers is that it is an anti-elitist and appropriately modest stance. Their assumption is that intellectualism and its rhetorical corollary, "oratory," are particularly holier-than-thou instantiations of elitist behavior and that anti-intellectualism is the appropriately modest response. The truth may be closer to being the other way around. The anti-intellectualist assumes that his audience is not capable of understanding his native, unrevised rhetoric. Either he is irresponsible, because if his assumption is correct, he has opted to perpetuate if not exploit his auditors' ignorance rather than make an effort to educate them, or he is condescending, because his assumption is wrong, and he has underestimated his audience. Insofar as the anti-intellectualist deploying the anti-elitist justification recognizes the hypocrisy latent in the latter position, his motivation for going anti-intellectual cannot be modesty but instrumentality.

The intellectual does not have to be conceited or pretentious, though it tells us something about our political culture that these characteristics have become almost synonymous with non-anti-intellectualism. Yet the patroniz-ing self-effacement of the anti-intellectual is probably no less pretentious, and is certainly less sincere, than the pomposity of the intellectual. But at least we are reflexively wary of the latter, while we are frequently seduced by the former. Paradoxically, as I argued in chapter 4, the studied imperfection that is presidential anti-intellectualism, a rhetorical strategy ostensibly used to close the credibility gap in Washington, has served only to widen it.

The anti-elitist justification is also disingenuous in a second way. In other domains outside of the rhetorical, monarchical trappings of exaltation (the rendition of "Hail to the Chief" that heralds every formal presidential appearance) and privilege (the exclusive comforts of *Air Force One*) are all species of elitism that are not only broadly tolerated, but celebrated. Even if anti-intellectualism were a species of anti-elitism, presidents appear only to be sporadically committed to the latter, but single-mindedly devoted to the former. Some types of special treatment and behavior are legitimate (and hence not species of elitism), and others are not. Since these distinctions are culturally and arbitrarily drawn, we need to ask: "why don't we expect our presidents, leaders ostensibly of the free world, to speak at a different level from the rest of us?" The basis of this distinction has not yet been explained. The anti-elitist justification of anti-intellectualism is, at the very least, incomplete.

Argument 2: Anti-Intellectualism Increases Participation

A stronger justification of anti-intellectualism posits that speaking the language of the people increases democratic participation. Rhetorical simplification, so our speechwriters tell us, distills the complexity of government into a form that is digestible to the mass citizenry, thereby welcoming them into the public and deliberative square.

The intuitive appeal of this argument, premised on the virtue of participation, reveals the seductive tug of any argument that appropriates a democratic ideal. But we must unpack it. This argument appears to work, but only to a point, because the reductio ad absurdum of anti-intellectualism is a substantive black hole. There will come a time when simplification becomes oversimplification. Constrained as such, this justification for anti-intellectualism is riding on some other unbounded and therefore lexically superior justification other than the merits of increased democratic participation, namely, democratic deliberation.

The reason why we want to welcome more people into the public sphere is that we want to encourage more deliberation. More deliberation is only possible if more participants *and* more information are injected into the public sphere. A thoroughgoing anti-intellectualism might guarantee the former, but certainly not the latter. As the size of the mob that cheered to the demagogic exhortations of Hitler and Mussolini was no proof of democracy, more people in the agora does not mean more deliberation. Meaningful, nontrivial deliberation can only occur if citizens are adequately informed of the substance and complexity of public issues. Our failure to see that, at some point, rhetorical simplification drives the evaporation of substance has allowed presidential anti-intellectualism to chart its unfettered path. The argument that anti-intellectualism increases participation is countered by the argument that it will ultimately decrease deliberation.

Argument 3: Anti-Intellectualism Is Inconsequential

The third and fourth justifications for anti-intellectualism function more as defenses of the practice rather than as active justifications. The third defense acknowledges the potential ills of anti-intellectualism, but downplays the problem by distinguishing the president's public salesmanship from the serious deliberation that goes on in the White House. If decisions have already been deliberated by those in political power behind closed doors, so the argument goes, it does not really matter that public presidential rhetoric is oversimplified or sloganistic. The distinction between the selling and the making of policy behind the inconsequential argument would have us assume the soundness of the president's message so that a disagreement with the manner in which it is articulated becomes but a quibble. Paradoxically, this defense of anti-intellectualism trivializes the purpose of rhetoric in order to justify the trivialization of its content. At the very least, anti-intellectual presidents cannot publicly admit that "rhetoric is just rhetoric" because their sole justification for going over the heads of congress and short-circuiting the interbranch conversation is the alleged meaningfulness of their communication with the people.

The point of presidential rhetoric is to publicize and make transparent the democratic decision-making process and to hold leaders accountable for their decisions. Rhetoric fulfills these democratic functions only if it engenders a two-way public deliberation of the causes and means themselves. There is no point to presidential rhetoric if all it aims to do is sell a prepackaged cause and the means to achieve it to hapless citizens. While the persuasive task is important and legitimate, presidential rhetoric should articulate programs to citizens in a manner that solicits their support only if its wisdom passes muster. If we accept the inconsequentialist's argument that the sole job of presidential rhetoric is to sell, then anything goes, and facts and arguments matter only to the extent that either can be massaged for a political cause. The substance of presidential rhetoric will be constrained only by what an audience can be persuaded to believe. Presidential rhetoric would just be propaganda.

Even if we can accept this radically instrumental reasoning—that the anti-intellectual means justify the political ends—the argument assumes, perhaps too naively, that the White House is able and willing to separate selling from thinking. Has the White House really thought through everything so that we need not challenge its sales pitch? Even those who have worked inside the current White House express their reservations. According to a "senior White House official" in the Bush administration, "Domestic Policy Council meetings are a farce.... It's just kids on Big Wheels who talk politics and know nothing."[4] Rather than let policy determine its political presentation, we are told that the direction of causality often runs the other way. According to John J. Dilulio, Jr., former head of the White House Office of Faith-Based and Community Initiatives, "There were, truth be told, only a couple of people in the West Wing who worried at all about policy substance and analysis."[5] The focus, instead, was on matters of politics and presentation. Anti-intellectualism is not inconsequential. The language of political salesmanship can bleed into the language of policy-making, short-circuiting rather than edifying the substance of policy itself.

Argument 4: Anti-Intellectualism Is Necessary

We are left, then, with a fourth defense of anti-intellectualism that acknowledges its deleterious and nontrivial consequences but argues nonetheless that anti-intellectualism is unavoidable and therefore necessary. This defense adopts a transactional view of leadership. Leadership, so to speak, is not about standing above the anti-intellectual fray, but working with it. As one speechwriter put it, "speaking about ongoing realities in institutions that reflect them in terms of should and shouldn't isn't terribly relevant. Things will be what they are."[6] The argument from necessity contends that anti-intellectualism is a necessary corollary of democratic politics that presidents eschew at their own peril. This is less a defense of anti-intellectualism and more a matter-of-fact statement about the nature of political communication in a democracy. To be sure, different proponents of this view have defended their position with varying degrees of regret. A Clinton speechwriter wrestled with the dilemma of modern democratic public communication:

> We struggled not to be simplistic, to present as many sides of a case, problem, whatever it was, that we could. But remember what the job is here. The job is to convince people to go along with something, and sometimes to go along [with] something that they naturally wouldn't do.... You have to put things in bigger terms that people can relate to.

> Get out of the policy, and you have to use, in some cases, rhetorical
> appeals that involve values that are overly simplistic.[7]

A former Nixon speechwriter, who went on to become a state senator in
Colorado, expresses a similar experience:

> This is a perspective that I gained from having had to suppress my intel-
> lectual bent in order to serve in a legislative body. And I happen to be a
> leader in my legislative body now and when you have that responsibility
> you don't think much about "it shouldn't be like this or it's too bad it's like
> this or it didn't use[d] to be like this." You look at the realities that you face
> and you make the best of them and you deal with the cards in your hand.[8]

But Reagan's director for communications advances the argument from
political necessity more defiantly: "Reagan wasn't speaking for the history
books. He was interested in his audiences in the here and now; he would
leave history to others. He would stick to his television-style language."[9]

With or without regret, these expressions of the argument from necessity deflect the responsibility of presidential anti-intellectualism and return
it squarely to citizens' shoulders. If democracy makes followers of leaders,
we should blame citizens, not politicians. In effect, the argument proceeds
by switching the chicken and the egg. Presidential anti-intellectualism is a
matter of course only because citizens' anti-intellectualism is a matter of fact.
Henry Fairlie exemplifies this position:

> It is *we* who drive the politician to use jargon, words that evade and
> obscure the truth.... It is *we* who are afraid of the truth that politicians
> would tell us. We do not wish to be confronted. We do not wish to be
> challenged. We do not wish to be inspired.[10]

There is a powerful body of evidence that appears to validate the empirical
premise of the argument from necessity that we must address. Decades-old
research confirms that the American public is barely more politically informed
today than it was in the 1940s.[11] More important, we have learned that the
public is largely disinclined to do anything about its political ignorance.[12]
Correspondingly, scholars have shown that the "primer style" of presidential
rhetoric is well suited to an audience that is quick to fatigue and to a rhetorical
era that anticipates constant interruptions from applause.[13] Jeffrey Cohen has
even demonstrated the need to return to "substanceless" rhetoric, finding that
"the president does not have to convince the public that a policy problem is
important by offering substantive positions." In fact, he is better off replacing

substance with vague and ambiguous symbols: "Presidents can be responsive by employing these 'substanceless' symbols, reserving decisions about the substantive details of a policy to themselves and their advisors and allies."[14] Lawrence Jacobs and Robert Shapiro agree that politicians have learned anti-intellectualism, noting that they "rarely count on directly persuading the public of the merits of their position by grabbing the public's attention and walking it through detailed and complex reasoning. Their skepticism stems in part from their low regard for the public's capacity for reasoned and critical thought."[15]

The Paradox of Information Acquisition

The way to reject the argument from necessity is, ironically, to give the anti-intellectual president more credit than Jacobs and Shapiro grant, by properly characterizing the problem of political ignorance in the citizenry. If we assume that presidents have gone anti-intellectual with the best of intentions, then we can assume that they have not meanly estimated the public's *capacity* for reasoned thought, only their *motivation* to do so. Recalling our distinction between intelligence and intellect, the anti-intellectual president does not have to believe that his auditors are unintelligent, only that they are disinclined to challenge themselves intellectually. Indeed, this is exactly how scholars have characterized the problem of political ignorance—as one of motivation (the desire to acquire information), rather than capacity (the ability to be informed).[16] Citizens seeking political information face a collective action problem. It is collectively optimal for all citizens to be informed so that no politician, to adapt the familiar adage, will be able to fool all of the citizens all of the time, and with that, we hope, through maximal democratic reflective equilibrium, politicians will make the best possible public policy decisions at all times. But just like a participatory democracy in which the public good of a fully engaged (voting) citizenry is prey to the collective action problem of free-riding, so is the public good of an informed electorate.[17] Individual citizens do not feel inclined to pay the cost of acquiring political knowledge even if they know that they will enjoy the collective benefits of a fully informed electorate. The Downsian insight on the analogous paradox of voting reinforces this conclusion because it does not make sense, even for civic-minded citizens, to devote much time to acquiring political knowledge (or, as Downs analogously argued, to vote) because their efforts have only a vanishing probability of influencing policy directions (or electoral outcomes, in the case of a single individual's vote).[18] To be sure, it may be potentially rewarding for each individual citizen to acquire knowledge while everyone else is ignorant, but because her capacity to use this information to further her own ends is infinitesimally limited, she is still better off free-riding. Since each citizen will likely replicate this line of reasoning, the collective outcome is a thoroughly uninformed electorate.

There is an important implication from this characterization of the nature of political ignorance: it shifts the burden of blame from citizens back to presidents. Political ignorance does not stem from citizens' indolent refusal to do political homework, but is a condition that follows naturally when citizens weigh the costs of acquiring information and the realizable benefit of deploying this knowledge. Sure, citizens must bear some responsibility for the anti-intellectual presidency. But each citizen bears this responsibility diffusedly, no more than each individual herder takes responsibility for the "tragedy of the commons."[19] Compare this to the undiffused responsibility we must assign to presidents, who face no collective action conundrum analogous to the paradox of information acquisition which citizens face. Presidential anti-intellectualism takes advantage of the fact that it is not obviously in the individual citizen's self-interest to educate himself or herself about politics to dispense with the responsibility to look after the interests of a collectivity of uninformed (and admittedly free-riding) citizens. Rather than try to solve this collective action problem—which is the whole purpose of leadership—presidential anti-intellectualism exploits individual rationalities to perpetrate collective irrationalities. It is an abdication of leadership, a cheap ride on a free-ride.

We can now restore the chicken and the egg to their rightful order in the argument by necessity discussed before. The problem of political ignorance, then, is more than a demand-side problem of information acquisition, as proponents of our fourth argument would have us believe. It is also a supply-side problem of information provision, a result of the abdication of presidential leadership and the exploitation of the paradox of information acquisition. While politically ignorant, free-riding citizens may argue that they have delegated the task of doing their political homework to their elected representatives, it is disingenuous for politicians to then exploit their ignorance when they double back to seek public approval. This, in essence, is the reason that scholars have decried demagogy and pandering, of which anti-intellectualism is a species. J. S. Mill well understood the sociological moorings of democratic government, but he refrained from using it as an excuse for "mediocre government":

> In politics it is almost a triviality to say that public opinion now rules the world.... Their thinking is done for them by men much like

themselves, addressing them or speaking in their name, on the spur of the moment, through the newspapers. I am not complaining of all this. I do not assert that anything better is compatible, as a general rule, with the present low state of the human mind. *But that does not hinder the government of mediocrity from being mediocre government.* (my emphasis)[20]

Mill warned us that the danger of democracy lies not in the governed, but in governors who were unreflectively and excessively responsive to the opinion of the governed. For him, good government transcends the incentives to regress toward mediocrity. As William Galston has similarly argued, "Against desire the liberal leader must counterpose restraints; against the fantasy of the free lunch he or she must insist on the reality of the hard choice; against the lure of the immediate he or she must insist on the requirements of the long term."[21] The problem with anti-intellectualism is that voters are praised for and encouraged in their political ignorance. We would be blaming the victims if we insisted that presidents were merely responding to the fact of the political ignorance of American society, because we elected our presidents to be leaders, not panderers.

Informational Cues and Deliberation

So we cannot blame citizens for their political ignorance, at least not entirely. But the defender of anti-intellectualism has a final recourse, by reverting to our third argument from inconsequentialism. Perhaps we should not make too much of the problem of political ignorance, especially when there is no consensus on the optimal level of political knowledge that citizens should possess. Recent contributions to the political heuristics literature have set the minima in this regard. This literature advances the appealing claim that citizens, when supplied with informational and situational heuristics, or "cues," such as an estimation of the endorsements a politician receives, party affiliation, or even his personal appearance, can perform their civic tasks fairly well.[22] If citizens, armed with informational cues, are led to make the "correct" decisions, consistent with what they would have chosen had they been fully and substantively informed of the political issues at stake, then we need not worry about political ignorance or the quality of presidential rhetoric.

But we are far from a consensus that heuristics do the work of substantive political information. On the other side of the debate, scholars have found that the quality of information matters: "It is the *diagnostic value* of information that influences how well citizens are able to cope with policy choices. Information has high diagnostic value, in our terms, when it clearly and fully conveys the central considerations relevant to a decision or judgment task" (original emphasis).[23] Decisional errors do not cancel themselves out, especially when nonrandom errors are introduced; and heuristics increases the probability of "correct" decisions only for political experts and not for novices.[24] Even the heuristics literature acknowledges that "all things being equal, the more informed people are, the better able they are to perform as citizens."[25] As Richard Lau and David Redlawsk have argued, "The cognitive revolution will not allow us to get away from the importance of civic engagement and attention to politics in the mind of a successful citizen."[26] Political knowledge is important not only for competent decision making, but it is directly related to civic engagement.[27] In their analysis, Samuel Popkin and Michael Dimock indicate that "the dominant feature of nonvoting in America is lack of knowledge about government; not distrust of government, lack of interest in politics, lack of media exposure to politics, or feelings of inefficacy."[28] Even if citizens are successfully able to use informational cues to make the "correct" decisions, they do so at the cost of retreating from the public space.

Thus, recent advances in political psychology have not, and perhaps cannot, dislodge us from the cherished democratic axiom of civic deliberation and engagement. From the Greek polis to the Rousseauian general assembly, democratic theorists have valued deliberation because the decisions that affect a polity ought to emerge from careful and informed judgment, rather than from tyrannical assertion, arbitrary choice, or ignorance. We value public discourse because we believe that at least some decisions in a democracy ought to be deliberated in open exchanges between citizens as well as between citizens and their elected leaders. Even when leaders exercise discretion in the absence of democratic deliberation, we still value public discourse for the justification of these decisions to those burdened by their authority. Deliberation is meaningful and justification legitimate only when substantive arguments are adduced.

To be sure, the *degree* to which democratic theorists worry about the hollowing out of presidential and public discourse turns on their specific conceptions of democracy and the role they assign to citizens. Certainly, almost all theorists have ceded the literal interpretation of "popular sovereignty," in which every citizen ruled on every issue of government and therefore had to possess a maximal degree of political knowledge and evaluative competence. But whether or not we adopt a classical deliberative or agonistic view of democracy; whether we adopt an active, participation-based or a more passive, consent-based view of democracy; even if we adopt a radically proceduralist conception of democracy, such as the Schumpeterian conception which reduces a citizen's duty to just that of a voter—democratic government cannot reflect the will of the people in any meaningful sense if citizens are politically ignorant.[29]

The Democratic Acquiescence

If these justifications and defenses of anti-intellectualism do not work, where does the phenomenon draw its energy from? I propose that the demagogic deification of "common sense," fueled in part by a somewhat triumphalist cultural history of American democracy, has served as a powerful philosophical foundation for the anti-intellectual presidency. Thus, in the 1970s, Daniel Boorstin noted that America is driven by the "democratic temptation."[30] Similarly, James Morone argued that American political culture expresses a "democratic wish," the belief that the people are wiser than their governors and will always possess the innate ability to solve the problems that plague a nation.[31] Appropriating this "wish," anti-intellectual presidents have placed common sense on a pedestal. And so a former Reagan speechwriter opines:

> The public is smarter than the elites. It has a sounder moral and spiritual sense. And in a way it is much better at paradoxical thinking than the intelligentsia of the twentieth and twenty-first century. Most of them have cut themselves off from the Judeo-Christian perspective of the world, which is one of nuance and sophistication. It is not either/or, right or wrong. Even though the intelligentsia's thinking that they're the ones who are against black and white. Actually they're the ones who do it. The truth is too simple for the intellectual[s]; it is also too complex for the intellectuals.[32]

The deification of the wisdom of the common person, or common sense, as I discussed in chapter 4—*vox populi, vox Dei*—represents the demagogy at the heart of presidential anti-intellectualism. As James Cooper wrote, "The man who is constantly telling people that they are unerring in judgment, and that they have all power, is a demagogue."[33] Paradoxically, citizens are not actually empowered by anti-intellectual presidents who foist their understanding of common sense onto them, though they are courted and may feel subjectively empowered.

We may be transitioning from Boorstin's "democratic temptation" to what may be called a "democratic acquiescence." With the untrammeled valorization of common sense, our founders' reservations toward democracy have been all but forgotten. For anti-intellectualists, the republican principles guiding the founding perspective are often depicted as antiquated at best and elitist at worst. But this perspective is worth repeating. For James Madison, writing in the *Federalist* No. 10, democracy meant "pure democracy": "a society consisting of a small number of citizens, who assemble and administer the government in person." This was not possible in the United States. Hence, as Madison continued, the founders preferred a democratic "republic," where a "scheme of representation takes place," which serves "to refine and enlarge the public views, by passing them through the medium of a chosen body of citizens, whose wisdom may best discern the true interest of their country, and whose patriotism and love of justice will be least likely to sacrifice it to temporary or partial considerations." Thus, in a democratic republic, while the people are the source of political authority, they do not rule; rather, their authority is embedded in a constitution which articulates the manner in which some among them are selected to rule on their behalf. By deifying common sense, anti-intellectualism is a recipe for civic complacency. If the people can know no wrong, then they do not need to gather information nor reflect on their views on public policy questions. As Hannah Arendt noted of Adolph Eichmann, the "Grand Inquisitor" of European Jewry, his deeds revealed "not stupidity but *thoughtlessness*."[34] It is this thoughtlessness that the democratic acquiescence engenders.

The founders were clear that the people's elected representatives were charged to deliberate and act in advancement of their general welfare, and not to pander to them. In the *Federalist* No. 71, Alexander Hamilton emphasized:

> The republican principle demands that the deliberate sense of the community should govern the conduct of those to whom they intrust the management of their affairs; but it does not require an unqualified complaisance to every sudden breeze of passion, or to every transient impulse which the people may receive from the arts of men, who flatter their prejudices to betray their interests.

In fact, Hamilton continued, "it is the duty of the persons whom they have appointed to be the guardians of those interests, to *withstand* the temporary delusion, in order to give them time and opportunity for more cool and sedate reflection" (my emphasis). Madison's fear of demagogy, though

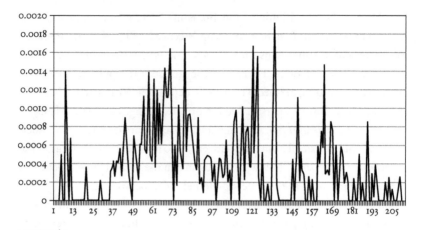

FIGURE 6.1

Occurrence of "Republic" by Annual Message, 1790–2000

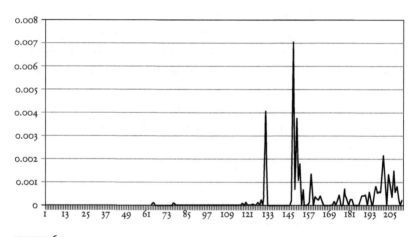

FIGURE 6.2

Occurrence of "Democracy" by Annual Message, 1790–2000

directed toward the tendency of what was then perceived to be the more "popular" branch, congress, has proven prescient as regards the presidency.

All of these are familiar arguments, but they are arguments which have been occluded by the anti-intellectual president's repudiation of the founders' republican principles. Tellingly, the word "democracy" was only introduced into the presidential lexicon in the twentieth century. Figures 6.1 and 6.2 reveal the transformation of this country's self-identification, where there is much less presidential talk today of the American "republic" than of "democracy."

Indicting the Anti-Intellectual Presidency

It is important to disassemble the intellectual embellishments and popular political "theories" that now justify the anti-intellectual presidency. While these justifications are politically seductive, they carry little weight. And our reluctance to spurn them reveals something of the insidious nature of anti-intellectualism in its seductive but disingenuous appeals to our democratic ideals. My objection to presidential anti-intellectualism is not a knee-jerk moral panic provoked by an elite suspicion of mass involvement in politics, but it emerges from the assessment that the theories of the anti-intellectual presidency are, at multiple levels, impoverished. Americans need to be politically educated so that they develop the intellectual and moral capacities that are necessary for competent citizenship, among them, a capacity to look beyond individual interests toward collective interests, and an ability to think through and adjudicate the various policy options that their leaders propose. While we do not expect democratic citizens to be policy experts, there is a threshold level of political knowledge below which their ability to make informed and competent civic judgments is impaired. Presidents are not doing much to elevate this ever-receding threshold.

The hollowing out of our public discursive sphere may be welcome news to some civil libertarians, but it is sorry news for anyone who values civic deliberation and participation. Indeed, the substance of political rhetoric is a barometer of the health of and meaning of our politics. "The quality of the making and of the defending of claims in the public sphere can be seen as a measure of society's success," Mark Kingswell has argued.[35] A state whose leaders perpetually speak with a language filtered of arguments and details can be safe from misgovernment only if the people can truly trust their leaders to always make sound decisions on complex policies, since in that instance citizens are not in an informed position to seriously critique government decisions. But if this were the case, then why should presidents even go public? If citizens are addressed not to be informed or consulted but only to act as unthinking rubber stamps, their "consent" is meaningless. Even if leaders correctly intuit the people's will, it is difficult to see the legitimacy of these intuitions if they are based on an uninformed general will. As James Fishkin has argued, "Without deliberation, democratic choices are not exercised in a meaningful way. If the preferences that determine the results of democratic procedures are unreflective or ignorant, then they lose their claim to political authority over us."[36]

Anti-intellectual rhetoric is a poor surrogate for genuine democratic responsiveness. It substitutes substantive responsiveness with rhetorical responsiveness while at the same time exploiting the public's susceptibility to simplistic slogans to serve the president's political purposes. Succumbing to the locution of "the people" buys short-term popularity at the cost of their intellectual impoverishment. The tabula rasa of citizens and their champions who are allegedly untainted by the ways of Washington or uninhibited by their knowledge of the nitty-gritty details of public policy represents both innocence *and* ignorance.

7

Reforming the Anti-Intellectual Presidency

Mend your speech a little
Lest it may mar your fortunes.
—*King Lear,* Act I, scene 1

This book is being finished as we enter another presidential election year, and Americans will be asked, as they were asked in 2004, if the simplistic slogans that have defined the policies of the Bush administration—the equation of the "war on terror" with the war in Iraq, the unflinching promise to "stay the course" and not to "cut and run," and so forth—have been persuasive. And they will likely be presented with a fresh set of campaign simplifications—such as the ambiguous idea of a "strategic redeployment" in Iraq or a "return on success"—from both political parties to whet their voting appetites. As the 2008 campaign season ensued, John McCain began his tours on the "straight talk express" to address his "friends"—tapping the age-old presidential rhetorical strategy of linguistic imitation and affiliation. But not everyone thought the senator talked straight about something as fundamental as his religious affiliation with either the Episcopalian or the Baptist church, or his position on immigration. John Edwards continued his recurring anthem of "two Americas"—a mawkish simplification of us versus them that does little to express or confront the real and legitimate differences that prevent consensual politics in our time. Fred Thompson declined participation in a Republican presidential debate because he thought his time was better spent chatting on *The Tonight Show* with Jay Leno, where he finally declared his candidacy. Barack Obama waxed poetic about his theme of "change," while leaving details of his inspirational rhetoric unspecified. Tellingly, he drew support from both ultra liberals (such as supporters of MoveOn.org) *and* moderate Republicans with this strategy.

If these rhetorical tricks seem familiar and unimpressive, it is because these candidates are campaigning for the anti-intellectual presidency, and we are in urgent need of a better model of leadership. In diagnosing the problem of presidential rhetoric as a matter of quality rather than of quantity, I have suggested, throughout this book, the type and purpose of rhetoric that befits a president. If, as Simone Chambers has argued, only the "force of the better argument" should be the basis of decision making, then we urgently need to "set conditions such that only rational, that is, argumentative, convincing is allowed to take place."[1] Simplistic language, applause-rendering platitudes, partisan slogans, and a heavy reliance on emotional and human appeals simply will not do. Only when reasons and arguments are precisely laid out can citizens, members of congress, and journalists dissect them and offer endorsements, objections, and alternative proposals in a healthy process of rational disputation. If intellectual rhetoric aims to promote rather than preempt deliberation, then logos, or the weighing and judging of reasons, should lie very near to the heart of the intellectual presidential rhetorical formula.

In these concluding pages, I pull my observations together to propose a corrective account of rhetorical leadership premised on pedagogy, rather than demagogy. I offer these tentative thoughts as an invitation for us to start, rather than to conclude, a new debate about the substance of presidential rhetoric rather than its quantity.

Attending to the Substance of Presidential Rhetoric

Theorists of deliberative democracy have furnished many accounts of what deliberative rhetoric among citizens should sound like, but these accounts have not focused specifically on what *presidential* rhetoric should sound like.[2] Indeed, there has been little scholarly attention paid to the structure and substance of deliberative speech between asymmetric interlocutors—where one speaks far louder, with greater publicity, and more often than others—in part because it is admittedly difficult to characterize such indirect speech situations as typically "deliberative." Yet while we do not usually think of Benito Mussolini's or Eva Perón's speeches off a palace balcony as constituting or facilitating deliberation, we do (want to) think of Theodore Roosevelt's swings round the circle or Franklin Roosevelt's Fireside Chats as doing just that. If so, then we do think that indirect communication between asymmetric interlocutors can nevertheless promote deliberation, though we urgently need a theory that will discriminate between these different types of rhetoric. The key, again, is to attend to the substance of what transpires. As long as we expect presidents to monopolize our public sphere, and as long as we want to insist or expect that their speeches contribute constructively rather than deleteriously to our public deliberative sphere, then we need to examine what qualitatively distinguishes the rhetoric of TR and FDR from that of Mussolini and Perón.

To be sure, quantitative critics of presidential rhetoric have resisted this direction of inquiry precisely because they have preferred an alternative solution in terms of a restoration of the rhetorical balance of power between the president and congress. But this alone will not guarantee the rehabilitation of our public sphere. Even if reducing the quantity of presidential rhetoric to the public may increase interbranch deliberation between presidents and congress, there is no guarantee that the substance of this rhetoric will be conducted at a level that facilitates deliberation. For all we know, presidents may be just as likely to fling platitudes and partisan slogans at congress as they appear to be doing in their State of the Union addresses today. It is unclear that less talk meant more substance for Presidents Ford and George H. W. Bush, and more was necessarily less for Theodore Roosevelt and Franklin Roosevelt. Instead, I suggest that the constitutional imbalance of rhetorical power can be partially righted if presidents conduct their rhetoric in a way that achieves some of the same purposes as interbranch deliberation. To paraphrase the *Federalist*, if congressional rhetorical ambition will not counteract presidential ambition, then presidential rhetoric must rise above the anti-intellectual fray to promote deliberation in the public sphere.

Note, however, that I am not advocating or endorsing an institutionally partisan proposal for a dominant executive just because I acknowledge its loquaciousness. Congress is free to talk back as much as it cares to—indeed, I welcome this. But we corner ourselves into an orthogonal solution if we continue to frame the problem and its solution in terms of congress's failure to speak up. After all, we are the intended audience of the anti-intellectual presidency, so we can demand more of our presidents. Rather than defer our responsibility and expect congress to tame the anti-intellectual presidency, we should step up to the task of taking presidents to account for what they say. Since we have permitted the rise of the anti-intellectual presidency, we can also quash it.

Leadership as Pedagogy

The first duty of government is to see that people have food, fuel, and clothes.
The second, that they have means of moral and intellectual education.
—John Ruskin's *Fors Clavigera*, letter 67, 1876

Rather than go on to flesh out the details of a positive account of presidential rhetoric that is not anti-intellectual, which should take the length of at least another book, let me instead address the purpose of rhetoric so as to clarify the thrust that underpins these rhetorical prescriptions. Democratic leaders face a peculiar tension in their rhetorical appeals to the public. They need both to seek the public's permission, as well as to guide it. The former goal requires that leaders faithfully represent the relevant facts of the political issue under consideration in a manner that facilitates an informed decision; the latter goal requires a degree of rhetorical manipulation to direct citizens toward a preferred conclusion. The anti-intellectual president leans immoderately on the latter end of this dilemma, making him more similar to a Mussolini than to a Roosevelt. I suggest, then, that what separates Mussolini from Roosevelt are the different models of leadership they represent. While Mussolini was a demagogue who stoked the people's prejudices and passions toward his particular ends, Roosevelt was a pedagogue who, while having a political agenda, as we would expect of all politicians, also tried to educate the audience in the hope that citizens would come down on his side. We prefer the latter to the former because we want presidents to be statesmen not propagandists, teachers not salesmen.

As presidents and speechwriters in the last half century have killed oratory and gone anti-intellectual, they have made extinct not merely a style of talking, but an entire conception of leadership that emphasized pedagogy over demagogy.[3] Even though Plato was wary of rhetoric, the relationship between leadership and pedagogy is as old as his idea of the philosopher-king. Cicero, perhaps the fiercest champion of rhetoric, celebrated it as an instrument that transformed men from brutes into citizens:

> To come, however at length to the highest achievements of eloquence,
> and what other power could have been strong enough either to
> gather scattered humanity into one place, or to lead it out of its brutish
> existence in the wilderness up to our present condition of civilization
> as men and citizens.[4]

The founders understood leadership as education. The authors of the *Federalist Papers* were not against rhetoric but against the wrong type of rhetoric, and thus created institutions that should divert and guide rhetorical energies in order to encourage deliberation over demagogy.[5] In a letter to John Adams, Thomas Jefferson noted his belief in a "natural aristocracy among men," which was to him, "the most precious gift of nature, for the *instruction*, the trusts, and government of society" (my emphasis).[6]

The ideal of rhetorical pedagogy pervades scholarly conceptions of leadership. For Arthur Schlesinger, "politics in a democracy is essentially a part of an educational process, and the speech is a great instrument of education."[7] Erwin Hargrove defines leadership as the ability to "teach reality."[8] William Muir argues that "a president leads well when he teaches."[9] The model of rhetorical leadership as pedagogy is also implied in scholarly criticisms of presidential rhetoric. Fred Greenstein notes that presidents consistently give "short shrift to the teaching and preaching style of presidential leadership."[10] Mary Stuckey argues that Reagan's speeches "function[ed] to impede the rational discussion of issues and the educative possibilities of communication."[11] The anti-intellectual president is the anti-pedagogical president because rather than educating citizens or promoting rational discussion, he panders to the politically ignorant and harnesses their baser instincts.

The strongest case for the pedagogical presidency can be made with the theories and practices of the founding rhetorical presidents, Theodore Roosevelt, Woodrow Wilson, and Franklin Roosevelt, all of whom talked a lot, but all of whom refrained from anti-intellectualism and understood well the pedagogical responsibilities of leadership.[12] In praising Theodore Roosevelt's successful rhetorical tours, designed to win public support for the Hepburn Bill, Jeffrey Tulis explained that a condition for his success was that the president "articulated public principles with sufficient clarity to educate, not simply arouse public opinion."[13] Similarly, Wilson believed that leadership entailed a "didactic function."[14] According to John Cooper, "Wilson regarded education of the public as the most important ingredient in political leadership."[15] If anything, Wilson saw the corruption of the Gilded Age as intimately related to the degeneration of rhetorical leadership. While he was a founder of the rhetorical presidency, he was really trying to rehabilitate a lost tradition of oratory rather than to end it.[16]

Like his cousin, Franklin Roosevelt believed that it is from the pulpit of the White House that citizens are politically educated:

> Government includes the art of formulating a policy and using the
> political technique to attain so much of that policy as will receive
> general support; persuading, leading, sacrificing, teaching always,
> because the greatest duty of a statesman is to educate.[17]

Franklin Roosevelt did not just talk the talk. As we saw in chapter 2, of the last 12 presidents, Roosevelt's *Public Papers* scored the lowest on the Flesch scale. Even though the conventional wisdom—sustained in no small part by Roosevelt himself—has held that Roosevelt's legendary Fireside Chats were "elemental recitals" to the American public, the average Flesch scores of the chats was 57.5, much lower than the average scores of prime-time presidential addresses today.[18] FDR took his didactic responsibility seriously, calling the press meeting room in the White House the "schoolroom."[19] He even played the role of history teacher in his public speeches. Before his Fireside Chat in February 1942, he asked the people to have a world map at hand, and he then asked his listeners to follow along during his speech.[20] In all of this, Roosevelt did not cease to be a politician, but he did see the political and moral merits of pedagogy over demagogy. Responding to his Fireside Chats, Roosevelt's audiences consistently praised him for being "instructive," "illuminating and constructive," "highly informative," "explanatory and advisory," and "instructive and enlightening."[21] Another citizen put it like this: "You are more than a President, more than a leader, you are an educator."[22] Historians would later praise Roosevelt's leadership for his conduct of "high politics—not politics as intrigue, but politics as education" and for the fact that he emerged as the "country's foremost civic educator."[23] If we are to hold on to Roosevelt as an oratorical exemplar, we should also remember that he was a rhetorical president who acknowledged that the first purpose of rhetoric is to educate.

Rehabilitating Presidential Rhetoric

When we ask what is wrong with American politics today, we observe a cluster of problems for which presidential anti-intellectualism is both a symptom and a cause: our leaders lie to us or mislead us, campaigns are focused on personalities and negative attacks rather than on substantive issues, and citizens are becoming increasingly cynical, ignorant, and disengaged from politics. These problems may not necessarily be routed if presidents stop talking. But if we demand that presidents infuse their rhetoric with arguments and substance, it will be a lot harder for them to deceive us. If candidates focus on the issues, they will compete on ideas that actually matter rather than spend their time discrediting each other. We can hope to bridge the credibility gap in Washington—one that has widened as a result of massaged truths or outright perjury—if we demand that presidents eschew the rhetorical apparatus of anti-intellectualism and speak with reasons and arguments, rather than with unhelpful verisimilitudes. When words carry substantive and refutable content, presidents will once again account for their words. Rhetoric will no longer be mere rhetoric, and citizens might be more likely to tune into politics, examine the issues, and even vote. As we rehabilitate presidential rhetoric, we can hope to restore and enhance the health of our republic.

How may we attend to and elevate the quality of presidential rhetoric to serve pedagogical rather than demagogical purposes? For a start, we must revise our understanding of presidential rhetoric on three integrally related dimensions. The first is to begin a conversation that challenges many taken-for-granted precepts of presidential communication and to come to terms with the pernicious side of many rhetorical practices hitherto thought to be benign. We need to chip at the entrenched opinion that rhetorical simplification is always good and that simplification only facilitates communication but does not also distort the message. We need to trouble the narrative that the public cannot embrace logos, or that public deliberation is best promoted with platitudinous declarations or partisan assertions rather than with nuanced arguments. We need to challenge the groupthink that simple truths are simply put, or that which is commonsensically phrased must be true. We need to interrogate the assumption that American democracy can continue apace with the hollowing out of its public sphere by its principal spokesperson. This book has taken a small step in these endeavors.

Second, to achieve the aforementioned, we need to recast our understanding and characterization of presidential rhetoric as a personal rather than a community resource. We need to drop the idea that the president should only speak for his party, administration, or himself. The White House speechwriting and public relations machine should not be dedicated to executing the president's persuasive task because presidential words should instead be conscientiously chosen to advance the public debate rather than a private or partisan agenda. We need, in short, to stop looking for the great communicator, or at least the type that Washington has become used to. Why should we remember Ronald Reagan as the Great Communicator when, according to Stuckey, 80 percent of his responses to reporters' questions in his press conferences were evasive and ambiguous, and only 20 percent were direct answers?[24] It would appear that the greatest communicators in recent memory—Reagan and Clinton—were also among the most anti-intellectual. Yes, they connected well with the people—and perhaps that is what great communication amounts to in our time—but did they educate us or help to promote deliberation in the public sphere? There is nothing inherently laudatory about a president who communicates well. Rather, let us either congratulate or condemn presidents for *what* they have said.

Third, we need to distinguish instrumental persuasion from pedagogical leadership, a great communicator from a great teacher. Persuasion does not require that new information be transmitted. It does not require the imparting of objective or verifiable facts or arguments. Its aim is to convert someone to a particular point of view, regardless of its veracity. Its purpose is immediately instrumental. To educate a citizen is to tell her something that she does not already know. It is to provide her with a store of information that is not necessarily tailored to engender a particular opinion. It is to train a citizen and to equip her with certain skills that she can use in the long run. The persuader seeks to expand his influence on his audience; the educator seeks to inform his student. There is something objective, nonpartisan, long-sighted, and edifying about education, while there is something subjective, partisan, short-sighted, and insidious about mere persuasion.

Coda

The assumption behind the quantitative critique of the rhetorical presidency is that less presidential talk will lead to more interbranch deliberation, governance, and action. The conventional diagnosis of presidential rhetoric suggests, correspondingly, that we simply need a president who will talk less. There is nothing, however, in presidential loquaciousness that forces congressional reticence. Indeed, presidential reticence is at best a passive model of presidential leadership. It does not tell us *what* a president should say on those rare occasions on which he should speak. Once we stop fixating on the quantity of presidential rhetoric and redirect our attention to its deteriorating quality, it becomes clear that we need a president who will do much more than talk less. We urgently need to attend to the substance of presidential rhetoric precisely because presidents are responsible for the lion's share of what transpires in the American public sphere.

The modern executive's loquaciousness is perhaps a developmental extension of a nation liberated, conceived, and protected by words—by a Declaration of Independence, the first complete written national constitution, and a Bill of Rights—so the perceived surfeit of words from the White House is not necessarily at odds with the constitution or the spirit in which it was enacted. Rather, the problem resides in the degeneration and trivialization of presidential rhetoric, which stands in stark contrast to the precision and seriousness of the words that first constituted this nation. The threat to American democracy is not a rhetorical presidency, but an anti-intellectual presidency; and so the solution to bad rhetoric is not less rhetoric, but better rhetoric.

APPENDIX I

The General Inquirer (GI)

The version of the *GI* I use in this book maps every word in a text to tabulate its content according to 182 predetermined categories of 11,790 words designated by the Harvard IV-4 psychosociological and Lasswell value dictionaries.[1] Once a corpus of text is digitally loaded in a computer folder, the *GI* can be executed to scan the texts for every word that is assigned to a category and produces a score for each category as a percentage of the total number of words in the text; this can then be compared with other texts. For instance, in a three-word text document "$Word_1$, $Word_2$, $Word_3$" in which "$Word_1$" belongs in $Category_1$, $Word_2$ belongs in $Category_2$ and $Word_3$ does not belong in any category, the *GI* will report the scores of $Category_1 = .33$ and $Category_2 = .33$.

Each category is formally a cluster of words, but analytically it gives us a reading of a specific dimension of meaning, defined by the rule governing a word's membership in that category, inherent in the text being examined. For instance, the degree of negativity of a text can be measured by the Harvard IV-4 category *Negativ*, which is a predetermined list of 2,291 words (such as "abhor," "condemn," and "hatred") that register negativity.[2] I have chosen an externally derived dictionary to avoid inferential circularity (insofar as the rules governing any particular word's membership in a particular category were externally defined and validated), and because these categories were developed to capture social scientific concepts developed in established scholarship. The definitions of the 10 *GI* categories used for this book can be found in appendix II.

The *GI* does make some simplifying assumptions, namely, that all words are equally weighted, and it only performs basic root word analysis ("great," "greater," and "greatest" are all recognized as the same word). That said, the *GI* does disambiguate different uses of the same word, where meaning—which is what we are most concerned with—does change. For example, it distinguishes between four usages of "race": as a contest, as moving quickly, as an indicator of a group of people of common descent, and as in the idiom "rat race." Set up to recognize 11,790 words, the *GI* typically maps all but less than 3 percent of the words in a text into 182 categories, so there are rarely problems of uncounted data.[3]

The Rhetoric of President George W. Bush

To provide a sense of what quantitative content analysis alone can tell us, I will tell a brief illustrative story of George W. Bush's first year in office, using three *GI* categories. I collected every word published in the *Weekly Compilation of Presidential Documents* ($N \approx 1,075,748$) from January 20, 2001, to January 19, 2002, and coded all of the relevant words in these documents according to three content analytic categories taken from the Harvard IV-4 and Lasswell psychosociological dictionaries to produce a weekly time series.

Imagine the quantitative content analyst isolated from the world on a remote island with no access either to the texts of Bush's speeches or to third-party (media) accounts of these speeches. All the analyst possesses is a series of content analytic data derived from Bush's speeches. Even in this isolated world, an analyst looking at these data cannot but suspect that something very significant occurred in the 35th week of President's Bush first year in office. As figures A.1 and A.2 show, the president suddenly became discernibly more negative and hostile in his rhetoric at week 35 and continued to be so for at least another 10 weeks.[4] Despite the chaos of politics, these distinct patterns managed to emerge amid the deluge of presidential words.

Since we lived through the terrorist attacks of September 11, 2001, these charts are less interesting in confirming what we already expected than in showing that presidential rhetoric creates a permanent footprint of events and of presidential responses to events that researchers can fruitfully examine. We are accustomed to thinking that presidents, together with their wordsmiths, are masters of their rhetorical fortunes. But figures A.1 and A.2 reveal that

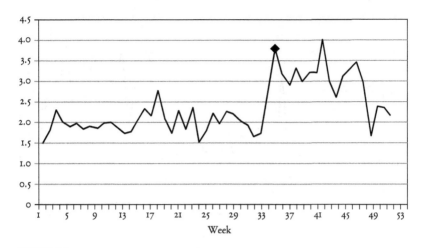

FIGURE A.1

President G. W. Bush's *Negativ* Score by Week (2001–2002)

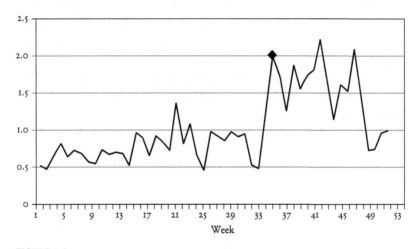

FIGURE A.2

President G. W. Bush's *Hostile* Score by Week (2001–2002)

presidential words are very responsive to exogenous shocks, and these shocks are revealed in the deluge of words that presidents produce. That is why presidential rhetoric can tell us not only about the presidency, but also about the political and cultural tectonics in which it is embedded.

Quantitative content analysis does not only reliably confirm what is obvious and expected. It can often uncover unexpected textual traits not

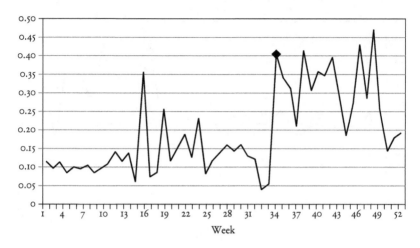

FIGURE A.3

President G. W. Bush's *PowLoss* Score by Week (2001–2002)

immediately apparent to the unaided human eye and ear contemplating a deluge of words. This is where it becomes most useful. Figure A.3 shows that, despite his efforts to project an image of strength in adversity in order to galvanize the nation, Bush's words, measured en masse, registered a loss of power or an insecurity that even his crafted words could not hide.[5] This is not an obvious conclusion that traditional content analysis would have necessarily yielded.

APPENDIX II

Definitions of General Inquirer *Categories Used*

Category Name	Definition	Example Words	Number of Words	Source Dictionary
AffGain	Words denoting the reaping of affect	care, devote, heart, like, love	35	Lasswell
Causal	Words denoting presumption that occurrence of one phenomenon is necessarily preceded, accompanied, or followed by the occurrence of another	consequence, depend, effect, hence, likely	112	Harvard IV-4
Hostile	Words indicating an attitude or concern with hostility or aggressiveness	afflict, execute, fight, oust, raid	833	Harvard IV-4
Kin@	Words denoting kinship	aunt, brother, family, parent, relative	50	Harvard IV-4
Know	Words indicating awareness or unawareness, certainty or uncertainty, similarity or difference, generality or specificity, importance or unimportance, presence or absence, as well as components of mental classes, concepts, or ideas	analysis, calculation, definition, fact, generalization	348	Harvard IV-4

(*continued on next page*)

(continued)

Category Name	Definition	Example Words	Number of Words	Source Dictionary
Negativ	Words indicating negativity	abhor, condemn, hatred, punish, shame	2,291	Harvard IV-4
Nonadlt	Words associated with infants through adolescents	baby, children, girl, grandchild, teenager	25	Harvard IV-4
PowLoss	Words indicating a decrease of power	concede, dismiss, expel, loss, overwhelm	109	Lasswell
Say	Words indicating direct verbal communication	said, say, tell, told	4	Harvard IV-4
Think	Words referring to the presence or absence of rational thought processes	foresight, mindful, prudence, revelation, senseless	81	Harvard IV-4

APPENDIX III

Annual Messages, 1790–2006

	President	Number	Annual	Date
1.	George Washington	1	1st	1/8/1790
		2	2nd	12/8/1790
		3	3rd	10/25/1791
		4	4th	11/6/1792
		5	5th	12/3/1793
		6	6th	11/19/1794
		7	7th	12/8/1795
		8	8th	12/7/1796
2.	John Adams	9	1st	11/23/1797
		10	2nd	12/8/1798
		11	3rd	12/3/1799
		12	4th	11/22/1800
3.	Thomas Jefferson	13	1st	12/8/1801
		14	2nd	12/15/1802
		15	3rd	11/17/1803
		16	4th	11/8/1804
		17	5th	12/3/1805
		18	6th	12/2/1806
		19	7th	10/27/1807
		20	8th	11/8/1808
4.	James Madison	21	1st	11/29/1809
		22	2nd	12/5/1810

(*continued on next page*)

(*continued*)

	President	Number	Annual	Date
		23	3rd	11/5/1811
		24	4th	11/4/1812
		25	5th	12/7/1813
		26	6th	9/20/1814
		27	7th	12/5/1815
		28	8th	12/3/1816
5.	James Monroe	29	1st	12/4/1817
		30	2nd	11/16/1818
		31	3rd	12/7/1819
		32	4th	11/14/1820
		33	5th	12/3/1821
		34	6th	12/3/1822
		35	7th	12/2/1823
		36	8th	12/7/1824
6.	John Quincy Adams	37	1st	12/6/1825
		38	2nd	12/5/1826
		39	3rd	12/4/1827
		40	4th	12/7/1828
7.	Andrew Jackson	41	1st	12/8/1829
		42	2nd	12/6/1830
		43	3rd	12/6/1831
		44	4th	12/4/1832
		45	5th	12/3/1833
		46	6th	12/1/1834
		47	7th	12/7/1835
		48	8th	12/5/1836
8.	Martin Van Buren	49	1st	12/5/1837
		50	2nd	12/3/1838
		51	3rd	12/2/1839
		52	4th	12/5/1840
10.	John Tyler	53	1st	12/7/1841
		54	2nd	12/6/1842
		55	3rd	12/1843[1]
		56	4th	12/3/1844
11.	James K. Polk	57	1st	12/2/1845
		58	2nd	12/8/1846
		59	3rd	12/7/1847
		60	4th	12/5/1848
12.	Zachary Taylor	61	1st	12/4/1849
13.	Millard Fillmore	62	1st	12/2/1850
		63	2nd	12/2/1851

		64	3rd	12/6/1852
14.	Franklin Pierce	65	1st	12/5/1853
		66	2nd	12/4/1854
		67	3rd	12/31/1855
		68	4th	12/2/1856
15.	James Buchanan	69	1st	12/8/1857
		70	2nd	12/6/1858
		71	3rd	12/19/1859
		72	4th	12/3/1860
16.	Abraham Lincoln	73	1st	12/3/1861
		74	2nd	12/1/1862
		75	3rd	12/8/1863
		76	4th	12/6/1864
17.	Andrew Johnson	77	1st	12/4/1865
		78	2nd	12/3/1866
		79	3rd	12/3/1867
		80	4th	12/9/1868
18.	Ulysses S. Grant	81	1st	12/6/1869
		82	2nd	12/5/1870
		83	3rd	12/4/1871
		84	4th	12/2/1872
		85	5th	12/1/1873
		86	6th	12/7/1874
		87	7th	12/7/1875
		88	8th	12/5/1876
19.	Rutherford B. Hayes	89	1st	12/3/1877
		90	2nd	12/2/1878
		91	3rd	12/1/1879
		92	4th	12/6/1880
21.	Chester A. Arthur	93	1st	12/6/1881
		94	2nd	12/4/1882
		95	3rd	12/4/1883
		96	4th	12/1/1884
22.	Grover Cleveland	97	1st	12/8/1885
		98	2nd	12/6/1886
		99	3rd	12/6/1887
		100	4th	12/3/1888
23.	Benjamin Harrison	101	1st	12/3/1889
		102	2nd	12/1/1890
		103	3rd	12/9/1891
		104	4th	12/6/1892
24.	Grover Cleveland	105	1st	12/4/1893
		106	2nd	12/3/1894

(*continued on next page*)

(*continued*)

	President	Number	Annual	Date
		107	3rd	12/2/1895
		108	4th	12/7/1896
25.	William McKinley	109	1st	12/6/1897
		110	2nd	12/5/1898
		111	3rd	12/5/1899
		112	4th	12/3/1900
26.	Theodore Roosevelt	113	1st	12/3/1901
		114	2nd	12/2/1902
		115	3rd	12/7/1903
		116	4th	12/6/1904
		117	5th	12/5/1905
		118	6th	12/3/1906
		119	7th	12/3/1907
		120	8th	12/8/1908
27.	William H. Taft	121	1st	12/7/1909
		122	2nd	12/8/1910
		123	3rd	12/5/1911
		124	4th	12/3/1912
28.	Woodrow Wilson	125	1st	12/2/1913
		126	2nd	12/8/1914
		127	3rd	12/7/1915
		128	4th	12/5/1916
		129	5th	12/4/1917
		130	6th	12/2/1918
		131	7th	12/2/1919
		132	8th	12/7/1920
29.	Warren G. Harding	133	1st	12/6/1921
		134	2nd	12/8/1922
30.	Calvin Coolidge	135	1st	12/6/1923
		136	2nd	12/3/1924
		137	3rd	12/8/1925
		138	4th	12/7/1926
		139	5th	12/6/1927
		140	6th	12/4/1928
31.	Herbert Hoover	141	1st	12/3/1929
		142	2nd	12/2/1930
		143	3rd	12/8/1931
		144	4th	12/6/1932
32.	Franklin D. Roosevelt	145	1st	1/3/1934
		146	2nd	1/4/1935
		147	3rd	1/3/1936

		148	4th	1/6/1937
		149	5th	1/3/1938
		150	6th	1/4/1939
		151	7th	1/2/1940
		152	8th	1/6/1941
		153	9th	1/6/1942
		154	10th	1/7/1943
		155	11th	1/11/1944
		156	12th	1/6/1945
33.	Harry S Truman	157	1st	1/14/1946
		158	2nd	1/6/1947
		159	3rd	1/7/1948
		160	4th	1/5/1949
		161	5th	1/4/1950
		162	6th	1/8/1951
		163	7th	1/9/1952
		164	8th	1/7/1953
34.	Dwight D. Eisenhower	165	1st	2/2/1953
		166	2nd	1/7/1954
		167	3rd	1/6/1955
		168	4th	1/5/1956
		169	5th	1/10/1957
		170	6th	1/9/1958
		171	7th	1/9/1959
		172	8th	1/7/1960
		173	9th	1/12/1961
35.	John F. Kennedy	174	1st	1/30/1961
		175	2nd	1/11/1962
		176	3rd	1/14/1963
36.	Lyndon B. Johnson	177	1st	1/8/1964
		178	2nd	1/4/1965
		179	3rd	1/12/1966
		180	4th	1/10/1967
		181	5th	1/17/1968
		182	6th	1/14/1969
37.	Richard M. Nixon	183	1st	1/22/1970
		184	2nd	1/22/1971
		185	3rd	1/20/1972
		186	4th	2/22/1973[2]
		187	5th	1/30/1974
38.	Gerald Ford	188	1st	1/15/1975
		189	2nd	1/19/1976
		190	3rd	1/12/1977

(*continued on next page*)

(continued)

	President	Number	Annual	Date
39.	James E. Carter	191	1st	1/19/1978
		192	2nd	1/23/1979
		193	3rd	1/23/1980
		194	4th	1/16/1981
40.	Ronald Reagan	195	1st	1/26/1982
		196	2nd	1/25/1983
		197	3rd	1/25/1984
		198	4th	2/6/1985
		199	5th	2/4/1986
		200	6th	1/27/1987
		201	7th	1/25/1988
41.	George H. W. Bush	202	1st	1/31/1990
		203	2nd	1/29/1991
		204	3rd	1/28/1992
42.	William J. Clinton	205	1st	1/25/1994
		206	2nd	1/24/1995
		207	3rd	1/30/1996
		208	4th	2/4/1997
		209	5th	1/27/1998
		210	6th	1/19/1999
		211	7th	1/27/2000
43.	George W. Bush	212	1st	1/29/2002
		213	2nd	1/28/2003
		214	3rd	1/20/2004
		215	4th	2/2/2005
		216	5th	1/31/2006

Two presidents did not deliver any annual messages at all: William Henry Harrison (the 9th president) died of pneumonia a month after his inauguration, and James Garfield (the 20th) was assassinated 200 days after his.

1. Specific date not recorded in the *Messages and Papers of John Tyler*.
2. Nixon presented his fourth State of the Union in six written parts to Congress. The date here indicates the date of submission of part III.

APPENDIX IV

Inaugural Addresses, 1789–2005

	President	Inaugural	Date
1.	George Washington	1st	3/30/1789
		2nd	3/4/1793
2.	John Adams	1st	3/4/1797
3.	Thomas Jefferson	1st	3/4/1801
		2nd	3/4/1805
4.	James Madison	1st	3/4/1809
		2nd	3/4/1813
5.	James Monroe	1st	3/4/1817
		2nd	3/5/1821
6.	John Quincy Adams	1st	3/4/1825
7.	Andrew Jackson	1st	3/4/1829
		2nd	3/4/1833
8.	Martin Van Buren	1st	3/4/1837
9.	William Henry Harrison	1st	3/4/1841
11.	James K. Polk	1st	3/4/1845
12.	Zachary Taylor	1st	3/5/1849
14.	Franklin Pierce	1st	3/4/1853
15.	James Buchanan	1st	3/4/1857
16.	Abraham Lincoln	1st	3/4/1861
		2nd	3/4/1865
18.	Ulysses S. Grant	1st	3/4/1869
		2nd	3/4/1873

(continued on next page)

(*continued*)

	President	Inaugural	Date
19.	Rutherford B. Hayes	1st	3/5/1877
20.	James A. Garfield	1st	3/4/1881
22.	Grover Cleveland	1st	3/4/1885
23.	Benjamin Harrison	1st	3/4/1889
24.	Grover Cleveland	1st	3/4/1893
25.	William McKinley	1st	3/4/1897
		2nd	3/4/1901
26.	Theodore Roosevelt	1st	3/4/1905
27.	William H. Taft	1st	3/4/1909
28.	Woodrow Wilson	1st	3/4/1913
		2nd	3/5/1917
29.	Warren G. Harding	1st	3/4/1921
30.	Calvin Coolidge	1st	3/4/1925
31.	Herbert Hoover	1st	3/4/1929
32.	Franklin D. Roosevelt	1st	3/4/1933
		2nd	1/20/1937
		3rd	1/20/1941
		4th	1/20/1945
33.	Harry S Truman	1st	1/20/1949
34.	Dwight D. Eisenhower	1st	1/20/1953
		2nd	1/21/1957
35.	John F. Kennedy	1st	1/20/1961
36.	Lyndon B. Johnson	1st	1/20/1965
37.	Richard M. Nixon	1st	1/20/1969
		2nd	1/20/1973
39.	James E. Carter	1st	1/20/1977
40.	Ronald Reagan	1st	1/20/1981
		2nd	1/21/1985
41.	George H. W. Bush	1st	1/20/1989
42.	William J. Clinton	1st	1/21/1993
		2nd	1/20/1997
43.	George W. Bush	1st	1/20/2001
		2nd	1/19/2005

Five presidents did not deliver any inaugural addresses: John Tyler (the 10th president), Millard Fillmore (13th), Andrew Johnson (17th), Chester Arthur (21st), and Gerald Ford (38th). I do not include their acceptance speeches upon taking the oath of office because these speeches are delivered under exceptional circumstances and do not fit comfortably into the inaugural genre.

APPENDIX V

Presidential Speechwriters Interviewed

Name	Title	Administration	Date
Kayle, Milton P.	special assistant, 1951–1953	Truman	9/9/2002
Neustadt, Richard	special assistant, 1950–1953	Truman	6/13/2003
Benedict, Stephen	assistant staff secretary, 1953–1955	Eisenhower	9/3/2002
Ewald, William B. (Jr.)	special assistant, 1954–1956	Eisenhower	9/10/2002
Hess, Stephen	special assistant, 1959–1961	Eisenhower	8/12/2002
Kieve, Robert S.	special assistant, 1953–1955	Eisenhower	9/2/2002
Feldman, Myer	deputy special counsel, 1961–1963; counsel to LBJ, 1963–1965	Kennedy	8/20/2002
Schlesinger, Arthur (Jr.)	special assistant and speechwriter, 1961–1963	Kennedy	9/7/2002
Sorensen, Theodore	special counsel, 1961–1963	Kennedy	9/6/2002
McPherson, Harry	special assistant and counsel, 1965–1966; special counsel, 1966–1969	Johnson	8/21/2002
Middleton, Harry	assistant, 1967–1968	Johnson	9/20/2002
Valenti, Jack	special assistant, 1963–1966	Johnson	8/22/2002

(*continued on next page*)

(*continued*)

Name	Title	Administration	Date
Andrews, John	deputy special assistant, 1971–1973	Nixon	10/4/2002
Gavin, William	staff assistant, 1969–1970	Nixon	8/14/2002
Gergen, David	special assistant, 1973–1974	Nixon	8/29/2002
Huebner, Lee	special assistant, deputy director of the White House writing and research staff, 1969–1973	Nixon	9/27/2002
Keogh, James	special assistant in charge of the research and writing office, 1969–1970	Nixon	9/18/2002
Lezar, Tex	staff assistant, 1971–1974	Nixon	9/18/2002
Price, Ray	special assistant, 1969–1972 (head of writing staff, 1971–1972); special consultant, 1973–1974	Nixon	9/10/2002
Boorstin, David	associate editor of the editorial office, 1976–1977	Ford	9/4/2002
Butler, Patrick H.	speechwriter, 1975–1977	Ford	7/31/2002
Hartmann, Robert T.	counselor, supervisor of the speech and editorial office, 1974–1976	Ford	9/16/2002
Theis, Paul	executive editor, White House editorial office, 1974–1975	Ford	8/23/2002
Hertzberg, Hendrik	chief speechwriter, 1979–1981	Carter	9/13/2002
Shapiro, Walter	speechwriter, 1979	Carter	9/2/2002
Stewart, Gordon	deputy chief speechwriter, 1978–1981	Carter	9/30/2002
Bakshian, Aram (Jr.)	special assistant and director of the speechwriting office, 1981–1983	Reagan	7/30/2002

Dolan, Anthony	speechwriter and special assistant, 1981–1986; director of speechwriting, 1986–1989	Reagan	10/3/2002
Gilder, Joshua	senior speechwriter, 1985–1988	Reagan	9/2/2002
Judge, Clark	speechwriter and special assistant, 1986–1989	Reagan	8/6/2002
Parvin, Landon	speechwriter, 1981–1983	Reagan	9/4/2002
Robinson, Peter	speechwriter and special assistant, 1983–1988	Reagan	9/27/2002
Cary, Mary Kate	speechwriter, 1989–1992	G. H. W. Bush	9/6/2002
McGroarty, Daniel	special assistant to the president and deputy director of White House speechwriting, 1989–1993	G. H. W. Bush	8/23/2002
Baer, Donald A.	assistant to the president for speechwriting and chief speechwriter, 1994–1995; assistant to the president and White House director of strategic planning and communications, 1995–1997	Clinton	8/18/2002
Boorstin, Robert	senior director of the National Security Council, 1994–1995	Clinton	9/27/2002
Curiel, Carolyn	senior speechwriter, 1993–1997	Clinton	9/6/2002
Glastris, Paul	special assistant and senior speechwriter, 1998–2001	Clinton	8/21/2002
Kusnet, David	chief speechwriter, 1993–1994	Clinton	8/2/2002
Shesol, Jeff	deputy assistant to the president and deputy director of presidential speechwriting, 1998–2001	Clinton	9/6/2002

(*continued on next page*)

(continued)

Name	Title	Administration	Date
Waldman, Michael	director of speechwriting, 1995–1999	Clinton	9/9/2002
Gerson, Michael	deputy assistant to the president and director of presidential speechwriting, 2001–2002; assistant to the president for speechwriting and policy advisor, 2002–2005; assistant to the president for policy and strategic planning, 2005–2006	G. W. Bush	4/30/2002

This list constitutes almost two-thirds of the membership of the Judson Welliver Society. Twenty-seven speechwriters were either unavailable or declined to offer time for an interview.

APPENDIX VI

The Flesch Readability Score

The Flesch Readability score is the most widely used index of readability. It is calculated by the following formula:

$$\text{Flesch Readability} = 206.835 - (1.015 \times \text{ASL}) - (84.6 \times \text{ASW}),$$

where ASL = average sentence length (the number of words divided by the number of sentences) and ASW = average number of syllables per word (the number of syllables divided by the number of words). The resulting scores normally range on a 100-point scale (although this is not mathematically necessary), with a higher score indicating greater readability or simplicity.

The basic rule that underpins the Flesch formula is that simplicity correlates with economy or concision. Each sentence, which is a basic unit of the English language, conveys a coherent unit of thought. We explain each unit of thought more fully by adding phrases that act as qualifiers, summarizers, and magnifiers. Short sentences are shorn of such complexities, which is why they are easier to understand but also bereft of nuance. Similarly, long words typically contain within them a combination of modifying referents built on a basic word (often identifiable as prefixes or suffixes), and so by the same token, they are more complex and less accessible than short words.

It is worth noting that another widely used index, the Flesch-Kincaid formula, which rates the readability of a text on U.S. grade-school levels, is derived from and built on the same principles as the Flesch Readability score. I have chosen to use the Flesch Readability rather than the Flesch-Kincaid formula because the former produces a scaled (and not an ordinal) variable output. The Flesch-Kincaid formula is the U.S. Department of Defense standard (DOD MIL-M-38784B), and the federal government requires its use by contractors producing manuals for the armed services.[1] The formula also accompanies the spelling- and grammar-check functions in Microsoft Word and is expressed as:

$$\text{Grade Level} = (.39 \times \text{ASL}) + (11.8 \times \text{ASW}) - 15.59$$

Sample of Average Flesch Readability Scores	
Textual Sample	Score
Comics	92
Consumer advertisements in magazines	82
Movie Screen	75
Seventeen	67
Reader's Digest	65
Sports Illustrated	63
New York Daily News	60
Atlantic Monthly	57
Time	52
Newsweek	50
Wall Street Journal	43
Harvard Business Review	43
New York Times	39
New York Review of Books	35
Harvard Law Review	32
Standard auto insurance policy	10
Internal Revenue Code	−6

Flesch Readability Scores Translated into School Grades	
School Level	Score
5th grade	90–100
6th grade	80–90
7th grade	70–80
8th–9th grade	60–70
10th–12th grade (high school)	50–60
college	30–50
college graduate	0–30

NOTES

Preface

1. Henry L. Mencken, *A Carnival of Buncombe* (Baltimore, MD: Johns Hopkins University Press, 1956), 56.
2. Plato, *Georgias*, trans. Walter Hamilton (London: Penguin, 1960), 44; Jeffrey K. Tulis, *The Rhetorical Presidency* (Princeton, NJ: Princeton University Press, 1987).
3. Samuel Kernell, *Going Public: New Strategies of Presidential Leadership* (Washington, DC: CQ Press, 1997).
4. Mencken, *A Carnival of Buncombe*, 5; Oliver Wendell Holmes, cited in Raymond Moley, *The First New Deal* (New York: Harcourt, Brace & World, 1966), 4.
5. Tevi Troy, *Intellectuals and the American Presidency: Philosophers, Jesters or Technicians? 1960 to Present* (Lanham, MD: Rowman & Littlefield, 2002).
6. David Gergen, *Eyewitness to Power: The Essence of Leadership: Nixon to Clinton* (New York: Simon & Schuster, 2000), 217.
7. Richard E. Neustadt, *Presidential Power and the Modern Presidents: The Politics of Leadership from Roosevelt to Reagan* (New York: Free Press, 1990).
8. Tulis, *Rhetorical Presidency*, 9.
9. Michael B. Grossman and Martha J. Kumar, *Portraying the President: The White House and the News Media* (Baltimore, MD: Johns Hopkins University Press, 1981); John A. Maltese, *Spin Control: The White House Office of Communications and the Management of Presidential News* (Chapel Hill: University of North Carolina Press, 1994).

10. Sheryl G. Stoleberg, "Clandestine, or at Least He Was until Yesterday," *New York Times*, 4/15/2004, A23.

Chapter 1

1. *Public Papers of Herbert Hoover*, "Address to the Gridiron Club," 4/9/1932.
2. *Public Papers of Dwight D. Eisenhower*, "Remarks at the Breakfast in Los Angeles Given by Republican Groups of Southern California," 9/24/1954.
3. *Public Papers of Lyndon B. Johnson*, "Remarks in San Antonio at the Signing of the Medicare Extension Bill," 4/8/1966.
4. Allan D. Bloom, *The Closing of the American Mind: How Higher Education Has Failed Democracy and Impoverished the Souls of Today's Students* (New York: Simon & Schuster, 1987); Robert D. Cross, "The Historical Development of Anti-Intellectualism in American Society: Implications for the Schooling of African Americans," *Journal of Negro Education* 59 (1990): 19–28; Craig B. Howley, Aimee Howley, and Edwina D. Pendarvis, *Out of Our Minds: Anti-Intellectualism and Talent Development in American Schooling* (New York: Teachers College Press, 1995); Deborah M. De Simone, "The Consequences of Democratizing Knowledge: Reconsidering Richard Hofstadter and the History of Education," *History Teacher* 34 (2001): 373–82. An important exception to the scholarly gap within political science is Colleen Shogan, "Anti-Intellectualism in the Modern Presidency: A Republican Populism," *Perspectives in Politics* 5 (2007): 295–304.
5. George Orwell, "Politics and the English Language," in George Orwell, *Collected Chapters* (London: Secker & Warburg, 1961), 362–63.
6. Murray Edelman, "Political Language and Political Reality," *PS: Political Science & Politics* 18 (1985): 10–19, 14.
7. Kenneth Burke, *A Grammar of Motives* (New York: Prentice-Hall, 1945), 393.
8. Mark C. Miller, *The Bush Dyslexicon: The Sayings of President Dubya* (London: Bantam, 2001), 14; Arthur Schlesinger, Jr. (ed.), *The Chief Executive: Inaugural Addresses of the Presidents of the United States from George Washington to Lyndon B. Johnson* (New York: Crown, 1965), vi; Henry L. Mencken, *A Carnival of Buncombe* (Baltimore, MD: Johns Hopkins University Press, 1956), 56; James W. Ceaser, "The Rhetorical Presidency Revisited," in Marc K. Landy (ed.), *Modern Presidents and the Presidency* (Lexington, MA: Lexington, 1985), 15–34, 32; Roderick P. Hart, *The Sound of Leadership: Presidential Communication in the Modern Age* (Chicago: University of Chicago Press, 1987), 195.
9. Hugh Heclo, "Governing and Campaigning: A Conspectus," in Norman Ornstein and Thomas Mann (eds.), *The Permanent Campaign and Its Future* (Washington, DC: American Enterprise Institute and Brookings Institution, 2000), 1–37, 35.
10. Hart, *Sound of Leadership*, 195.

11. Bruce Miroff, "The Presidential Spectacle," in Michael Nelson (ed.), *The Presidency and the Political System* (Washington, DC: CQ Press, 2003), 278–303, 302.

12. Robert E. Denton, *The Symbolic Dimensions of the American Presidency* (Prospect Heights, IL: Waveland, 1982), 97.

13. George C. Edwards, *The Public Presidency* (New York: St. Martin's, 1983), 199.

14. James W. Ceaser, Glen E. Thurow, Jeffrey K. Tulis, and Joseph M. Bassette, "The Rise of the Rhetorical Presidency," in Thomas E. Cronin (ed.), *Rethinking the Presidency* (Boston: Little, Brown, 1982), 233–52, 237, 242.

15. Peggy Noonan, *Simply Speaking: How to Communicate Your Ideas with Style, Substance, and Clarity* (New York: Regan, 1998), 70.

16. Interview with Harry Middleton, assistant (Johnson), 1967–1968, 9/20/2002.

17. Interview with Landon Parvin, speechwriter (Reagan), 1981–1983, 9/4/2002.

18. Interview with Tex Lezar, staff assistant (Nixon), 1971–1974, 9/18/2002.

19. Interview with William Gavin, staff assistant (Nixon), 1969–1970, 8/14/2002.

20. Aram Bakshian, in Gage William Chapel, "Speechwriting in the Nixon Administration: An Interview with Presidential Speechwriter Aram Bakshian," *Journal of Communication* 26 (1976): 65–72, 71–72.

21. Peggy Noonan, *What I Saw at the Revolution* (New York: Random House, 1990), 344; Interview with David Gergen, special assistant, 1973–1974 (Nixon), 8/29/2002; Jack Valenti, *A Very Human President* (New York: Norton, 1975), 85; James C. Humes, *Confession of a White House Ghostwriter: Five Presidents and Other Political Adventures* (Washington, DC: Regnery, 1997), 3.

22. Karlyn K. Campbell and Kathleen H. Jamieson, *Deeds Done in Words* (Chicago: University of Chicago Press, 1990).

23. Hart, *Sound of Leadership.*

24. Ornstein and Mann, *Permanent Campaign.*

25. Samuel Kernell, *Going Public: New Strategies of Presidential Leadership* (Washington, DC: CQ Press, 1997).

26. Edwards, *Public Presidency.*

27. Jeffrey K. Tulis, *The Rhetorical Presidency* (Princeton, NJ: Princeton University Press, 1987).

28. Ceaser et al., "Rise of the Rhetorical Presidency."

29. Tulis, *Rhetorical Presidency*, 146, 17.

30. Terri Bimes and Stephen Skowronek, "Woodrow Wilson's Critique of Popular Leadership: Reassessing the Modern-Traditional Divide in Presidential History," in Richard J. Ellis (ed.), *Speaking to the People: The Rhetorical Presidency in Historical Perspective* (Amherst: University of Massachusetts Press, 1998), 134–61; Mel Laracey, *Presidents and the People: The Partisan Story of Going Public* (College Station: Texas A&M University Press, 2002); Karen S. Hoffman, " 'Going Public' in the Nineteenth Century: Grover Cleveland's Repeal

of the Sherman Silver Purchase Act," *Rhetoric & Public Affairs* 5 (2002): 57–77; Richard J. Ellis and Alexis Walker, "Policy Speech in the Nineteenth Century Rhetorical Presidency: The Case of Zachary Taylor's 1849 Tour," *Presidential Studies Quarterly* 37 (2007): 248–69.

31. The central insight of scholars who have challenged the bifurcated frame in Tulis's account, then, is in showing that the older constitution *already* provides for, and sanctions, emergency presidential and presidential rhetoric powers. The ambivalent nature of our constitution has always provided for the restraint and exercise of power, both reticence and rhetoric. For an argument along these lines, see Harvey Mansfield, *Taming the Prince: The Ambivalence of Modern Executive Power* (Baltimore, MD: Johns Hopkins University Press, 1993). If we accept these accounts, then there never was a need for, and there never did emerge, a new constitution to prescribe a more rhetorical presidency in moments of crisis or emergency. It was always right there, embedded within the original constitution.

32. Tulis, *Rhetorical Presidency*, 176.

33. Ibid.

34. Ibid., 178.

35. Ibid., 95–116.

36. Theodore Roosevelt, *Oliver Cromwell*, quoted in John M. Cooper, Jr., *The Warrior and the Priest: Woodrow Wilson and Theodore Roosevelt* (Cambridge, MA: Belknap, 1983), 43.

37. John D. Long to Pierce Long, 12/5/1901, John D. Long Papers, Massachusetts Historical Society.

38. *Messages and Papers of the Presidents*, Theodore Roosevelt, First Annual Message, 12/3/1901.

39. "The President's Message," *New York Times*, 12/4/1901, 8.

40. "A Roosevelt Day," *New York Times*, 2/1/1905, 8.

41. Woodrow Wilson, "Cabinet Government in the United States," in Mario R. DiNunzio (ed.), *Woodrow Wilson: Essential Writings and Speeches of the Scholar-President* (New York: New York University Press, 2006), 218–31, 224.

42. Woodrow Wilson, *Congressional Government: A Study in American Politics* (Mineola, NY: Dover, 2006 [1885]), 184.

43. This helpful distinction between the rhetorical presidency and presidential rhetoric was first clarified in Martin J. Medhurst, "A Tale of Two Constructs: The Rhetorical Presidency versus Presidential Rhetoric," in Martin J. Medhurst (ed.), *Beyond the Rhetorical Presidency* (College Station: Texas A&M University Press, 1996), xi–xxv.

44. Lyn Ragsdale, "The Politics of Presidential Speechmaking, 1949–1980," *American Political Science Review* 78 (1984): 971–84; Dennis M. Simon and Charles W. Ostrom, "The Impact of Televised Speeches and Foreign Travel on Presidential Approval," *Public Opinion Quarterly* 53 (1989): 58–82; Jeffrey Cohen, "Presidential

Rhetoric and the Public Agenda," *American Journal of Political Science* 39 (1995): 87–107; Brandice Canes-Wrone, "The President's Legislative Influence from Public Appeals," *American Journal of Political Science* 45 (2001): 313–29; George C. Edwards, *On Deaf Ears: The Limits of the Bully Pulpit* (New Haven, CT: Yale University Press, 2003); Brandice Canes-Wrone, *Who Leads Whom? Presidents, Policy Making and the American Public* (Chicago: University of Chicago Press, 2005); B. Dan Wood, *The Politics of Economic Leadership: The Causes and Consequences of Presidential Rhetoric* (Princeton, NJ: Princeton University Press, 2007).

45. Even Tulis did not concern himself much with the content of presidential rhetoric. The only place in his book where he engaged in content analysis is in the section "Comparing Rhetoric: Old and New" in chapter 5, and even there he was mostly interested in the "structure of presentation." See Tulis, *Rhetorical Presidency*, 137–44.

46. Kathryn M. Olson, "Rhetoric and the American President," *Review of Communication* 1 (2001): 247–53, 251.

47. Interview with Gavin.

48. Ernest J. Wrage, "Public Address: A Study in Social and Intellectual History," in Martin J. Medhurst (ed.), *Landmark Essays on American Public Address* (Davis, CA: Hermagoras, 1993), 53–60, 47.

49. Theodore Windt (ed.), *Presidential Rhetoric (1961 to the Present)* (Dubuque, IA: Kendall/Hunt, 1983), 2.

50. Medhurst, "A Tale of Two Constructs," xiv.

51. Tulis, *Rhetorical Presidency*, 9.

52. This preoccupation with the persuasive impact of presidential rhetoric rather than its systemic consequences has arisen in part because of a relatively widespread misreading of Richard Neustadt's famous dictum that "presidential power is the power to persuade." See Richard E. Neustadt, *Presidential Power and the Modern Presidents: The Politics of Leadership from Roosevelt to Reagan* (New York: Free Press, 1990 [1960]), 28. Neustadt was referring, by "persuasion," to interbranch bargaining and not to going public. He prioritized and distinguished the deliberative processes of interbranch bargaining from going public, which constitutes an attempt to bypass Congress altogether.

53. Bernard Berelson, *Content Analysis in Communication Research* (Glencoe, IL: Free Press, 1952); Oli R. Holsti, *Content Analysis for the Social Sciences and Humanities* (Reading, MA: Addison-Wesley, 1969); Klaus Krippendorff, *Content Analysis: An Introduction to Its Methodology* (Newbury Park, CA: Sage, 1980).

54. Carl W. Roberts (ed.), *Text Analysis for the Social Sciences: Methods for Drawing Inferences from Texts and Transcripts* (Mahwah, NJ: Erlbaum, 1997); Daniel Riffe, Stephen Lacy, and Frederick G. Fico, *Analyzing Media Messages: Using Quantitative Content Analysis in Research* (Mahwah, NJ: Erlbaum, 1998); Roel Popping, *Computer-Assisted Text Analysis* (Thousand Oaks, CA: Sage, 2000);

Mark D. West (ed.), *Theory, Method, and Practice in Computer Content Analysis* (Westport, CT: Ablex, 2001); Michael Laver, Kenneth Benoit, and John Garry, "Extracting Policy Positions from Political Texts Using Words as Data," *American Political Science Review* 97 (2003): 311–31.

55. While we are accustomed to thinking of rhetoric only as public advocacy, the Aristotelian definition of rhetoric rightly includes all forms of verbal communication, written and spoken. The texts that I use in this book include both the presidents' spoken and written statements, including their public addresses, radio addresses, press conferences, executive orders, and proclamations. I do not attempt any performance analysis in this book, though I am sure that such analyses will offer fresh perspectives and additional insights. Because I want to include all presidential statements in the analysis, I can only rely on content analysis because while texts may be either read or heard, their common denominator is their content.

56. James Fallows, Exit interview, 11/14/1978, Jimmy Carter Library, available at http://www.jimmycarterlibrary.org/library/exitInt/exitFallows.pdf (accessed 1/18/2008).

57. Wilson, *Congressional Government*, 22.

58. In the late 1890s, Congress authorized an extensive retrospective compilation of the messages and papers of the presidents from the period 1789 to 1897. The papers of Presidents Washington to McKinley were compiled in ten volumes in James D. Richardson, *A Compilation of the Messages and Papers of the Presidents, 1789–1897* (Washington, DC: Government Printing Office, 1896–1899). A subsequent 20-volume edition published in 1918 added coverage of all of Taft and much of Wilson. (Wilson's and Coolidge's papers have also been published in private collections.) In fulfilling his commission by the Congressional Joint Committee on Printing, Richardson prefatorily noted, "I have sought to bring together in the several volumes of the series all Presidential proclamations, addresses, messages, and communications to Congress," and "the utmost effort has been made to render the compilation accurate and exhaustive" (v). The only significant gap in coverage is President Warren Harding, who left behind no significant compilation of his papers (thus both reflecting and ensuring his relative historical obscurity). The Office of the Federal Register began publishing the *Public Papers of the Presidents* series in 1957 as the official compilation of presidential public writings, addresses, and remarks. Each *Public Papers* volume contains the documents of the president of the United States that were issued by the Office of the Press Secretary during the specified time period. Hence, the series provides a historical reference covering the administrations of Presidents Hoover, Truman, Eisenhower, Kennedy, Johnson, Nixon, Ford, Carter, Reagan, Bush, and Clinton. (The papers of President Franklin Roosevelt were published privately before the commencement of the official *Public Papers* series.) The full texts of papers from this series and from Richardson's *Messages and Papers*

series are now commercially available in digital format on CD-ROM, as well as (though less comprehensively) on the Internet. President George W. Bush's papers can be found in the *Weekly Compilation of Presidential Documents*, also published by the Office of the Federal Register, which will be equivalent to the *Public Papers* when they are published. (From 1977 onward, all materials appearing in the *Weekly Compilation of Presidential Documents* have been incorporated into the *Public Papers of the Presidents of the United States*.)

59. Bruce Miroff, "Monopolizing the Public Space: The President as a Problem for Democratic Politics," in Thomas Cronin (ed.), *Rethinking the Presidency* (Boston: Little, Brown, 1982), 218–32.

60. Chuck Conconi, "Personalities," *Washington Post*, 4/21/1987, C3; Robert Schlesinger and Philippe Shepnick, "Speechifying: Welliver? Well I Never!" *Hill*, 4/14/1999, 9; Ken Hechler, "Shooting from the Heart: Former White House Speechwriters Reflect on Success," *Charleston Gazette*, 12/5/1995, A5. This society is perhaps one of the most exclusive clubs in Washington, with its membership including such luminaries as Stephen Hess, Ted Sorensen, and David Gergen. Members meet once a year in a jovial and collegiate atmosphere to discuss their craft and politics over dinner. The annual dinner and meeting is held, according to a previous attendee, in a "beautiful physical arrangement, with cocktails [and] hors d'oeuvres ahead of time. The bar is always there. And then there's [a] fabulous dinner" (interview with Milton P. Kayle, special assistant [Truman], 1951–1953, 9/9/2002).

61. The full list of interviews can be found in appendix V.

62. David Gergen, *Eyewitness to Power: The Essence of Leadership: Nixon to Clinton* (New York: Simon & Schuster, 2000).

Chapter 2

1. See the preface of this book for an explanation of my choice of terminology.

2. Voltaire, "Lettres," in T. Besterman (ed.), *Philosophical Dictionary* (New York: Penguin, 1972), 274.

3. Antoine-Nicolas de Condorcet, *Sketches for a Historical Picture of the Progress of the Human Mind*, trans. J. Barraclough (London: Weidenfeld and Nicholson, 1955), 135–37.

4. Richard Hofstadter, *Anti-Intellectualism in American Life* (New York: Knopf, 1963), 7.

5. Ibid., 25. This distinction is more of a widespread belief, itself indicative of anti-intellectual prejudices, than a position that I want to defend philosophically. Whether or not intelligence and intellect are really distinct ontological categories remains philosophically disputable because the separation of intelligence from the intellect piggybacks on the debated idea of a Cartesian homunculus within each mind, which is capable of perceiving its own operations. However, the philosophical basis of this distinction need not be a concern here, because

I do confront the empirical fact that the distinction is customarily embraced and indicative of the anti-intellectualism found in common parlance.

6. Ibid.

7. Ibid., 24.

8. The full text of this speech, delivered on 5/21/2001, can be found at http://www.yale.edu/lt/archives/v8n1/v8n1georgewbush.htm (accessed 8/10/2007).

9. Sentence and word length are the principal variables used in the calculation of the Fog Index (see Robert Gunning, *The Technique of Clear Writing* [New York: McGraw-Hill, 1952]), the SMOG formula (see G. Harry McLaughlin, "Proposals for British Readability Measures," in John Downing and Amy L. Brown [eds.], *Third International Reading Symposium* [London: Cassell, 1968], 186–205], and the ATOS readability formula (see Terrance Paul, *Guided Independent Reading* [Madison, WI: School Renaissance Institute, 2003]).

10. See appendix VI for a methodological note on the Flesch Readability score.

11. See Carol M. Santa and Joan N. Burstyn, "Complexity as an Impediment to Learning: A Study of Changes in Selected College Textbooks," *Journal of Higher Education* 48 (1977): 508–18; Lee Sigelman, "Presidential Inaugurals: The Modernization of a Genre," *Political Communication* 13 (1996): 81–92; Jackie Hill and Hector Bird, "The Development and Evaluation of a Drug Information Leaflet for Patients with Rheumatoid Arthritis," *Rheumatology* 42 (2003): 66–70. The score is so ubiquitous that it is now bundled with most word-processing programs such as KWord, Lotus WordPro, and Microsoft Word.

12. For a further discussion on the rationale behind the formula, see Rudolph Flesch, "A New Readability Yardstick," *Journal of Applied Psychology* 32 (1948): 221–33; Rudolph Flesch, *The Art of Readable Writing* (New York: Harper, 1949); Rudolph Flesch, "Measuring the Level of Abstraction," *Journal of Applied Psychology* 34 (1950): 384–90.

13. Janice C. Redish and Jack Selzer, "The Place of Readability Formulas in Technical Communication," *Technical Communication* 32 (1985): 46–52; Karen Schriver, "Readability Formulas in the New Millennium: What's the Use?" *ACM Journal of Computer Documentation* 24 (2000): 138–40.

14. The texts for this analysis were gratefully obtained from Roderick P. Hart's Campaign Mapping Project at the University of Texas at Austin. "Social science scholarship" consisted of 50 text segments from academic journal articles in communications, political science, and psychology. "Humanities scholarship" consisted of 52 text segments from academic journal articles in classics, comparative literature, and English. "Legal documents" consisted of 50 text segments from federal and state court briefs. "Philosophical essays" consisted of 25 text segments from philosophers such as Derrida, Descartes, Hume, Kant, Leibniz, and Nietzsche. "Science magazines" consisted of 25 text segments from *Scientific American* and *Discover*. "Print editorials" consisted of 50 text segments from editorial opinion pieces in major national and state newspapers. "Celebrity

reporting" consisted of 37 text segments of articles from *Entertainment Weekly* and *TV Guide*. "Sports reporting" consisted of 61 text segments of sports stories from national and state newspapers, the Associated Press, and *Sports Illustrated*. "Email" consisted of 82 samples of personal and business e-mail. "Phone conversations" consisted of the transcripts of 10 personal telephone conversations. "TV ads" consisted of the transcripts of 110 television commercials. "TV drama" consisted of 7 transcribed segments of 4 television series: *My So-Called Life, Northern Exposure, Twin Peaks*, and *The Warrior Princess*. "TV comedy" consisted of 18 transcribed segments of 4 television comedies: *Caroline in the City, Friends, Married with Children*, and *Seinfeld*.

15. William H. DuBay, *The Principles of Readability* (Costa Mesa, CA: Impact Information, 2004).

16. It could be that social science scholarship really is more substantively complex than the philosophical essays sampled here, or the seemingly anomalous result could be an artifact of the Flesch score's reduced reliability when applied to translated texts (which constituted the bulk of the "philosophical essays" genre). Nevertheless, figure 2.1 indicates that there is at least a *general* relationship between rhetorical and substantive simplicity.

17. Refer to appendix II for definitions and examples of words for these and other categories and how the *GI* works.

18. Regressing each of these content analytic scores against the Flesch score, I obtained coefficients of –0.91 and –0.89 for *Know* and *Think*, respectively, at 0.0001 levels of significance. The adjusted R^2 values were 0.82 and 0.77, respectively. These remarkably high coefficients suggest a robust statistical relationship between the Flesch score and each of these categories.

19. Alice Davison, *Readability: The Situation Today* (Champaign, IL: Center for the Study of Reading, University of Illinois at Urbana-Champaign, 1986); Ronald P. Carver, "Predicting Accuracy of Comprehension from the Relative Difficulty of Material," *Learning and Individual Differences* 2 (1990): 405–22; Jeanne S. Chall and Edgar Dale, *Readability Revisited: The New Dale-Chall Readability Formula* (Cambridge, MA: Brookline, 1995).

20. Susan Kemper, "Measuring the Inference Load of a Text," *Journal of Educational Psychology* 75 (1983): 391–401, 399.

21. Walter Kintsch and James R. Miller, "Readability: A View from Cognitive Psychology," in James Flood (ed.), *Understanding Reading Comprehension* (Newark, DE: International Reading Association, 1984), 220–32, 222.

22. Hofstadter, *Anti-Intellectualism in American Life*, 6.

23. David Gergen, *Eyewitness to Power: The Essence of Leadership: Nixon to Clinton* (New York: Simon & Schuster, 2000), 203.

24. Hofstadter, *Anti-Intellectualism in American Life*, 6.

25. Cited in Ralph Ketcham, *Presidents above Party: The First American Presidency* (Chapel Hill: University of North Carolina Press, 1987), 79.

26. Hector de Crèvecoeur, *Letters from an American Farmer* (London: Dent, 1912 [1782]), 49.

27. Cited in Hofstadter, *Anti-Intellectualism in American Life*, 155.

28. See Charles O. Lerche, "Jefferson and the Election of 1800: A Case Study of the Political Smear," *William and Mary Quarterly* 5 (1948): 467–91.

29. The last president who had been a professional academic before coming into office was, tellingly, the progressive Woodrow Wilson, who had taught at Bryn Mawr, Wesleyan, and Princeton. Only two other presidents in American history possessed an academic background. John Quincy Adams was the Boylston Professor of Rhetoric at Harvard, and James Garfield was, first, professor of classics and then president of Western Reserve Eclectic Institute (later Hiram College).

30. Theodore Roosevelt, "Citizenship in a Republic," speech at the Sorbonne, Paris, 4/23/1910.

31. Woodrow Wilson, *A Crossroads of Freedom: The 1912 Campaign Speeches of Woodrow Wilson*, ed. John W. Davidson (New Haven, CT: Yale University Press, 1956), 83–84.

32. Bertrand Russell, "The Role of the Intellectual in the Modern World," *American Journal of Sociology* 44 (1939): 491–98, 495.

33. Tevi Troy, *Intellectuals and the American Presidency: Philosophers, Jesters or Technicians* (Lanham, MD: Rowman & Littlefield, 2002), 2.

34. Hofstadter, *Anti-Intellectualism in American Life*, 229.

35. Cited in Robert Dallek, *Ronald Reagan: The Politics of Symbolism* (Cambridge, MA: Harvard University Press, 1999), 46.

36. Reagan cited in Gerard De Groot, "Reagan's Rise," *History Today*, September 1995, 33. Even his sympathetic biographer, Lou Cannon, argued that while Reagan was in real life in awe of intellectuals, "Reagan, in the long tradition of populism, certainly exploited the anti-intellectual biases of his constituencies." According to Cannon (who saw anti-intellectualism as a form of populism), "Berkeley was Reagan's most effective populist issue" (Lou Cannon, *Governor Reagan: His Rise to Power* [New York: Public Affairs, 2003], 286, 271).

37. Harry McPherson, *A Political Education* (Boston: Little, Brown, 1972), 271–72.

38. Jonathan Chait, "Race to the Bottom: Why, This Year, It's Smart to Be Dumb," *New Republic*, 12/20/1999, 26–29; Diane Roberts, "George W.'s Anti-Intellectualism," *St. Petersburg Times*, 7/31/2000, 8A; Todd Gitlin, "Age of Unenlightenment," *Sydney Morning Herald*, 1/27/2001, 8; Zoe Heller, "Bush Is No Intellectual, but at Least He Is Trying," *Daily Telegraph*, 6/22/2002, 23.

39. Chait, "Race to the Bottom," 26.

40. I refer to the "annual messages" collectively and the "State of the Union addresses" when referring to those speeches that were delivered after 1945. Appendix III lists all of the annual messages and the dates on which they

were delivered. There are seven minor disruptions to the series, all of which occurred at the start of administrations. In four instances, there were no annual messages in a calendar year (1933, 1989, 1993, and 2001); and in three instances (1790, 1953, and 1961), there were two annual messages in a calendar year.

41. No model was presumed for this curve fit in order to obtain a sense of the natural inclination of the data. If we then apply a linear function $[f(x;\beta) = \beta_0 + \beta_1 x]$ to the data, we find that the function explains 68 percent of their variance, where $\beta_0 = -246.35$, $\beta_1 = 0.15$, adjusted $R^2 = 0.68$, F value significant at 0.00001.

42. Interview with Stephen Hess, special assistant (Eisenhower), 1959–1961, 8/12/2002.

43. Daniel Galvin and Colleen Shogan, "Presidential Politicization and Centralization across the Modern-Traditional Divide," *Polity* 36 (2004): 477–504.

44. Applying a linear model $[f(x; \beta) = \beta_0 + \beta_1 x]$ for the annual messages delivered from 1790 to 1912: $\beta_0 = -144.56$, $\beta_1 = 0.10$, adjusted $R^2 = 0.27$, F value significant at 0.00001. For the annual messages delivered from 1913 to 2003: $\beta_0 = -356.17$, $\beta_1 = 0.21$, adjusted $R^2 = 0.38$, F value significant at 0.00001.

45. Ceaser et al., "Rise of the Rhetorical Presidency," 241.

46. Cynthia Ozick, "The Question of Our Speech: The Return to Aural Culture," in Katherine Washburn and John Thornton (eds.), *Dumbing Down: Essays on the Strip-mining of American Culture* (New York: Norton, 1996), 68–87.

47. Appendix IV lists all of the inaugural addresses and the dates on which they were delivered. There are five disruptions to this quadrennial series: Presidents John Tyler, Millard Fillmore, Andrew Johnson, Chester Arthur, and Gerald Ford did not deliver inaugural addresses. As shown in figure 2.4, a lowess curve was fitted to depict the natural inclination of the data. Applying the linear function to the inaugural scores produced even more robust results than on the annual messages, where $[f(x;\beta) = \beta_0 + \beta_1 x]$, and $\beta_0 = -393.02$, $\beta_1 = 0.23$, adjusted $R^2 = 0.71$, F value significant at 0.00001.

48. Arthur Schlesinger, Jr. (ed.), *The Chief Executive: Inaugural Addresses of the Presidents of the United States from George Washington to Lyndon B. Johnson* (New York: Crown, 1965), vi–vii. Schlesinger continued: "It [the inaugural address] is rarely an occasion for original thought or stimulating reflection. The platitude quotient tends to be high, the rhetoric stately and self-serving, the ritual obsessive, and the surprises few."

49. See Shanto Iyengar and Douglas Kinder, *News That Matters: Agenda-Setting and Priming in a Television Age* (Chicago: University of Chicago Press, 1987); John Zaller and Stanley Feldman, *The Nature and Origins of Mass Opinion* (New York: Cambridge University Press, 1992).

50. Kiku Adatto, "Sound Bite Democracy: Network Evening News Presidential Campaign Coverage, 1968 and 1988," Research Paper R-2, Joan Shorenstein Barone Center for Press, Politics, and Public Policy, June 1990; Stephen Hess,

"Dwindling TV Coverage Fell to New Low," 11/7/2002, available at http://www.brookings.edu/GS/Projects/HessReport/week9.htm (accessed 1/19/2008).

51. Ozick, "The Question of Our Speech: The Return to Aural Culture"; Daniel J. Boorstin, *The Americans: The Democratic Experience* (London: Phoenix, 2000 [1973]), 451.

52. Henry L. Mencken, *The American Language: An Inquiry into the Development of English in the United States* (New York: Knopf, 1921 [1919]), introduction. Mencken was a founder of the Linguistic Society of America and the journal *American Speech*. His pioneering scholarship was followed by the monumental works of William A. Graigie and James R. Hulbert (eds.), *A Dictionary of American English on Historical Principles* (Chicago: University of Chicago Press, 1938–1944); and Mitford M. Mathews, *A Dictionary of Americanisms on Historical Principle* (Chicago: University of Chicago Press, 1951).

53. Peter Shaw, *The War against the Intellect* (Iowa City: University of Iowa Press, 1989); Andrew Ross, *No Respect: Intellectuals and Popular Culture* (New York: Routledge, 1989).

54. Philip B. Gove (editor in chief), *Webster's Third New International Dictionary* (Springfield, MA: Merriam, 1961).

55. For a look at the disapprobative reaction to the new dictionary among linguists and the intellectual elite, see the collection of reviews in James Sledd and Wilma R. Ebbitt (eds.), *Dictionaries and That Dictionary: A Casebook on the Aims of Lexicographers and the Targets of Reviewers* (Chicago: Scott, Foresman, 1962).

56. For example, see Martin Cutts, *The Quick Reference Plain English Guide* (Oxford: Oxford University Press, 1999), which advocates simplicity qua short sentences, advising: "Over the whole document, make the average sentence 15 to 20 words" (9).

57. The texts for this analysis were obtained from Roderick P. Hart's Campaign Mapping Project at the University of Texas at Austin. These texts were also the basis of his book *Campaign Talk: Why Elections Are Good for Us* (Princeton, NJ: Princeton University Press, 2000). "Print stories" ($N = 7,838$) about the campaign included articles from the *New York Times, Washington Post, Christian Science Monitor, Atlanta Constitution, Chicago Tribune, Los Angeles Times*, the AP, and UPI. Randomizing techniques were used to ensure that neither feature nor nonfeature stories dominated the sample. The "campaign speeches" ($N = 624$) included all nationally broadcast addresses during the general election as well as a random sample of middle-of-the-week speeches given on the stump. "Television news" coverage of the campaign ($N = 1,369$) was gathered either by photocopying original scripts or by transcribing the nightly news from audiotapes. Five years were represented in the sample (1980, 1988, 1992, 1996, and 2000), with the various news bureaus (ABC, CBS, NBC, CNN, and PBS) represented on an availability basis. "Campaign advertise-

ments" (N = 620) included a broad sample of advertisements produced by the major campaigns in 1960 and every election year from 1976 to 2000.

58. The Office of the Federal Register began publishing the *Public Papers of the Presidents* series in 1957 as an official publication of presidential public writings, addresses, and remarks. Each *Public Papers* volume contains the documents issued by the Office of the Press Secretary during the specified time period. Hence, the series provides a comparable and relatively complete rhetorical record of the presidencies of Hoover through Clinton. Presidents before Hoover had to be omitted from this analysis because the *Public Papers* series only began with him. President George W. Bush's papers were extracted for this study from the *Weekly Compilation of Presidential Documents*, also published by the U.S. Government Printing Office, since his *Public Papers* have not yet been compiled. This is, it should be said, an equivalent source for Bush's papers because from 1977 onward, all materials appearing in the Weekly *Compilation of Presidential Documents* have been incorporated verbatim into the *Public Papers* of each president. For this analysis, I used all of the documents from each president's first full year in office to keep the data manageable, yet comparable. In sum, about 12,000 texts and 10 million words were analyzed by a computer to generate these results, so there is neither selection nor genre bias.

59. Mel Laracey, *Presidents and the People: The Partisan Story of Going Public* (College Station: Texas A&M University Press, 2002), 8.

60. Johnson appears to have been an outlier and well ahead of his time. It is possible that his verbal style emerged out of his own natural writing and speaking style, but it is equally likely that Johnson strove for rhetorical accessibility to distinguish himself from his rhetorically accomplished predecessor. Significantly, the two largest year-to-year increases in figure 2.9 occurred during the Truman and Johnson presidencies. Both came into power because of the untimely deaths of their predecessors in office, and both lived under the oratorical shadows of their larger-than-life predecessors. George H. W. Bush, following Reagan, took the same path as Truman and Johnson. Rather than compete on grounds that guaranteed failure, these presidents actively sought to prove that they were not even trying.

61. National Center for Education Statistics, *The Health Literacy of America's Adults: Results from the 2003 National Assessment of Adult Literacy* (Washington, DC: U.S. Department of Education, 2006), 4, available at http://nces.ed.gov/pubs2006/2006483.pdf (accessed 11/28/2006).

62. Alice Calaprice (ed.), *The Expanded Quotable Einstein* (Princeton, NJ: Princeton University Press, 2000), 314.

Chapter 3

1. Jeffrey K. Tulis, *The Rhetorical Presidency* (Princeton, NJ: Princeton University Press, 1987), 13.

2. Speechwriters' sentiments are not very different from the advice promulgated in modern guides to effective writing. This is not surprising. Modern-day guidelines will naturally affirm what is considered appropriate by others located in the same cross-section of time. Our recognition of *trends*, on the other hand, point us to potentially deleterious ends that may give us reason to recalibrate our temporal biases and to rethink what is linguistically appropriate at any moment in time.

3. Interview with Stephen Benedict, assistant staff secretary (Eisenhower), 1953–1955, 9/3/2002.

4. James C. Humes, *Confession of a White House Ghostwriter: Five Presidents and Other Political Adventures* (Washington, DC: Regnery, 1997), 3. And so, presidents must take the lion's share of the authorial responsibility for their words and their consequences. Speechwriters are hired and fired on the basis of their willingness and capacity to employ whatever literary tools are necessary to help their principal make the most persuasive case to his audience.

5. Interview with Jeff Shesol, deputy assistant to the president and deputy director of speechwriting (Clinton), 1998–2001, 9/6/2002.

6. Interview with Michael Gerson, deputy assistant to the president and director of presidential speechwriting, 2001–2002 (Bush); assistant to the president for speechwriting and policy advisor, 2002–2005; assistant to the president for policy and strategic planning, 2005–2006, 4/30/2002.

7. Cited in Chester J. Pach, Jr., and Elmo Richardson, *The Presidency of Dwight D. Eisenhower* (Lawrence: University Press of Kansas, 1991), 44.

8. Oral history interview, Robert S. Kieve, 4/10/1978, Dwight D. Eisenhower Library. Eisenhower scholars note the same:

> Bolstering the impression that he was removed from political specifics, he was often ambiguous in reply to reporters' questions, sometimes professing ignorance of matters because he believed they were best not discussed. He expressed himself in a homely, idiomatic way that went over well with the public but led many political observers to doubt his political sophistication.

Meena Bose and Fred I. Greenstein, "The Hidden Hand vs. the Bully Pulpit: The Layered Political Rhetoric of President Eisenhower," in Leroy Dorsey (ed.), *The Presidency and Rhetorical Leadership* (College Station: Texas A&M University Press, 2002), 184–99, 187. This "hidden hand" facet of the Eisenhower presidency seems to have resonated through most if not all of the twentieth-century presidencies.

9. Interview with Stephen Hess, special assistant (Eisenhower), 1959–1961, 8/12/2002.

10. Interview with Harry McPherson, special assistant and counsel (Johnson), 1965–1966; special counsel, 1966–1969, 8/21/2002.

11. Interview with Ray Price, special assistant (Nixon), 1969–1972; special consultant, 1973–1974, 9/10/2002.

12. Interview with Lee Huebner, special assistant (Nixon), 1969–1973, 9/27/2002.

13. Chris Matthews, *Hardball: How Politics Is Played—Told by One Who Knows the Game* (New York: Summit, 1988), 219.

14. David Frum, *The Right Man: The Surprise Presidency of George W. Bush* (New York: Random House, 2003), 48.

15. *Public Papers of Dwight D. Eisenhower*, "Remarks at the Breakfast in Los Angeles Given by Republican Groups of Southern California," 9/24/1954.

16. Interview with Tex Lezar, staff assistant (Nixon), 1971–1974, 9/18/2002.

17. Interview with Anthony Dolan, special assistant, 1981–1986, director of speechwriting (Reagan), 1986–1989, 10/3/2002.

18. Anonymity of this source preserved at the author's discretion.

19. Interview with Richard E. Neustadt, special assistant, 1950–1953 (Truman), 6/13/2003.

20. Interview with Robert S. Kieve, special assistant, 1953–1955 (Eisenhower), 9/2/2002.

21. Interview with Myer Feldman, deputy special counsel, 1961–1963 (Kennedy), 8/20/2002.

22. Interview with Jack Valenti, special assistant, 1963–1966 (Johnson), 8/22/2002.

23. Interview with William Gavin, staff assistant, 1969–1970 (Nixon), 8/14/2002.

24. Interview with Benedict.

25. Emmet J. Hughes, *The Ordeal of Power: A Political Memoir of the Eisenhower Years* (New York: Atheneum, 1963), 25.

26. Sorensen cited in William Safire, *Watching My Language* (New York: Random House, 1997), 231.

27. Interview with Arthur Schlesinger, Jr., special assistant, 1961–1963 (Kennedy), 9/7/2002.

28. Interview with Patrick Butler, speechwriter (Ford), 1975–1977, 7/31/2002.

29. Interview with Don Baer, chief speechwriter (Clinton), 1994–1995; director of strategic planning and communications, 1995–1997, 8/18/2002.

30. Sacvan Bercovitch, *The American Jeremiad* (Madison: University of Wisconsin Press, 1978); Carl R. Burgchardt and Robert M. La Follette, Sr., *The Voice of Conscience* (New York: Greenwood, 1992).

31. Elvin T. Lim, "Five Trends in Presidential Rhetoric: An Analysis of Rhetoric from George Washington to Bill Clinton," *Presidential Studies Quarterly* 32 (2002): 328–66.

32. Robert A. Kraig, *Woodrow Wilson and the Lost World of the Oratorical Statesman* (College Station: Texas A&M University Press, 2004), 9.

33. Ken Hechler, *Working with Truman: A Personal Memoir of the White House Years* (New York: Putnam's, 1982), 213; John R. Coyne, *Fall In and Cheer*

(Garden City, NY: Doubleday, 1979), 82; James C. Humes, *My Fellow Americans: Presidential Addresses That Shaped History* (New York: Praeger, 1992), 260; Interview with Paul Glastris, special assistant (Clinton), 1998–2001, 8/21/2002.

34. Noonan, *Simply Speaking*, 50.

35. Interview with Price.

36. Anonymity of this source preserved at the author's discretion.

37. Terrance Paul, *Guided Independent Reading* (Madison, WI: School Renaissance Institute, 2003); Lev S. Vygotsky, Michael Cole, Vera John-Steiner, and Sylvia Scribner, *Mind in Society* (Cambridge, MA: Harvard University Press, 2006).

38. See Alfred E. Kahn, "The Tyranny of Small Decisions: Market Failures, Imperfections, and the Limits of Economics," *Kyklos* 19 (1966): 23–47; William E. Odum, "Environmental Degradation and the Tyranny of Small Decisions," *Bioscience* 32 (1982): 728–29.

39. The opponent need not be a single actor; it can also be a group, such as journalists attacking the president for either his anti-intellectualism or his consorting with eggheads. For illustrative purposes, it will be easiest to think of the opponent as a major personality pitting himself or herself against the president politically. During election years, this is usually another presidential candidate.

40. Bush cited in Walter Isaacson, "My Heritage Is Part of Who I Am," *Time*, 8/7/2000, 55.

41. Mancur Olson, *The Logic of Collective Action* (Cambridge, MA: Harvard University Press, 1965).

42. David Gergen, *Eyewitness to Power: The Essence of Leadership: Nixon to Clinton* (New York: Simon & Schuster, 2000), 237.

43. This notion builds on the idea of an "informational cascade," which is the term used to describe the rapid evolution or transformation of beliefs. The key difference between an escalating sequence and what others call an informational cascade is that their focus is on the increasing number of adopters, whereas my notion sees the increasing number of adopters as incidental to the more important consequence of the intensification of the belief itself. For a discussion of the concept of an informational cascade, see Arthur Denzau and Douglass North, "Shared Mental Models: Ideologies and Institutions," *Kyklos* 47 (1994): 3–31; Susanne Lohmann, "The Dynamics of Informational Cascades: The Monday Demonstrations in Leipzig, East Germany, 1989–91," *World Politics* 47 (1994): 42–101; Timur Kuran, *Private Truths, Public Lies* (Cambridge, MA: Harvard University Press, 1995); Norman Schofield, "Constitutional Political Economy: On the Possibility of Combining Rational Choice Theory and Comparative Politics," *Annual Review of Political Science* 33 (2000): 277–303.

44. Clark Clifford (with Richard Holbrooke), *Counsel to the President: A Memoir* (New York: Random House, 1991), 74.

45. Richard Goodwin, *Remembering America: A Voice from the Sixties* (Boston: Little, Brown, 1988), 422.

46. The idea of punctuated equilibria first appeared in Stephen J. Gould and Niles Eldredge, "Punctuated Equilibria: The Tempo and Mode of Evolution Reconsidered," *Paleobiology* 3 (1977): 115–51, and has since been appropriated by social scientists. See Elaine Romanelli and Michael L. Tushman, "Organizational Transformation as Punctuated Equilibrium: An Empirical Test," *Academy of Management Journal* 37 (1994): 1141–66; Bryan D. Jones, Frank R. Baumgartner, and James L. True, "Policy Punctuations: US Budget Authority, 1947–1995," *Journal of Politics* 60 (1998): 1–33. In biology as in political science, there are proponents of the alternate view that evolutionary change is mostly gradual and that punctuations are trivial on a macroevolutionary scale. Constitutional scholars who have approached the presidency via the lens of its unchanging constitutional attributes, with the view that these "powers" impose fundamental descriptive and normative parameters on the practice of presidential influence, best represent this perspective. In this tradition, see Edward S. Corwin, *The President, Office and Powers 1787–1957* (New York: New York University Press, 1957); Louis Fisher, *Presidential War Power* (Lawrence: University Press of Kansas, 1995).

47. See Stephen Skowronek, *The Politics Presidents Make: Leadership from John Adams to Bill Clinton* (Cambridge, MA: Belknap, 1997), 30, for the conceptual distinction between these two dimensions of time.

48. This implication emerges from the monotonic trends observed in figures 2.4, 2.5, and 2.9 from chapter 2. Recall, for instance, that the only kink observable in figure 2.4, observed in 1913, merely intensified an already existent trend. The periods before and after 1913 were not periods of relative evolutionary stasis—as the theory of punctuated equilibria would predict—but of significant change as well. See Gould and Eldredge, "Punctuated Equilibria," 117; Jones et al., "Policy Punctuations," 1.

49. The insidiousness maps onto something like the "third dimension" of power elaborated in Stephen Lukes, *Power: A Radical View* (New York: Macmillan, 1974), 23. Here, I refer not to the Dahlsian dimension of concrete, observable power, or to the second dimension of agenda-setting power in nonobservable conflicts (such as that exercised by speechwriters, as I will show in chapter 5), but to the third, ideological dimension of power practiced by political agents who are able to preempt conflict altogether by shaping the preferences of those they seek to influence. The virtue of simplicity is reinforced, in this particular regard, by its apparent democratic appeal. This is perhaps why anti-intellectualism is often disguised and usually popular.

Chapter 4

1. Aristotle, *Rhetoric*, book I, chapter 2, 1356b.

2. Robert E. Goodin, "Democratic Deliberation Within," in James S. Fishkin and Peter Laslett (eds.), *Debating Deliberative Democracy* (Oxford: Blackwell, 2003), 54–79, 54.

3. John Rawls, "The Idea of Public Reason Revisited," *University of Chicago Law Review* 64 (1997): 765–807, 768.

4. Philip J. Stone, Dexter C. Dunphy, Marshall S. Smith, and Daniel M. Ogilvie, *The General Inquirer: A Computer Approach to Content Analysis* (Cambridge, MA: MIT Press, 1966); Kelly Stone and Philip J. Stone, *Computer Recognition of English Word Senses* (New York: North-Holland, 1975); J. Zvi Namenwirth and Robert P. Weber, *Dynamics of Culture* (Boston: Allen and Unwin, 1987); Philip J. Stone, "Thematic Text Analysis: New Agendas for Analyzing Text Content," in Carl W. Roberts (ed.), *Text Analysis for the Social Sciences: Methods for Drawing Statistical Inferences from Texts and Transcripts* (Mahwah, NJ: Erlbaum, 1997), 35–54. Refer to appendix II for definitions and examples of words for these specific categories.

5. As described in chapter 2, I used all of the papers from each president's first full year in office to keep the data manageable, yet comparable. Presidents before Hoover had to be omitted because the *Public Papers* series only began with him. President George W. Bush's papers were extracted from the *Weekly Compilation of Presidential Documents*, published by the U.S. Government Printing Office, since his *Public Papers* have not been compiled yet. In sum, about 12,000 texts and 10 million words were analyzed by a computer to generate these results, so there is very limited selection bias and no genre bias.

6. I use the Clinton examples in order consciously to resist the idea that Republicans have a monopoly on anti-intellectualism. In this vein, see Colleen Shogan, "Anti-Intellectualism in the Modern Presidency: A Republican Populism," *Perspectives in Politics* 5 (2007): 295–304.

7. To make for a fair comparison, these are full paragraphs extracted as they appeared in the transcribed texts of Prime Minister Tony Blair's speech in the House of Commons on March 18, 2003, as released by the Prime Minister's Office, and George W. Bush's war ultimatum speech from the White House on the same day as released by the White House Press Office.

8. Richard M. Weaver, *The Ethics of Rhetoric* (Chicago: Henry Regnery, 1965); Wayne C. Booth, *Modern Dogma and the Rhetoric of Assent* (Chicago: University of Chicago Press, 1974). For an example of a rhetoric of perfect assent that has become commonplace in contemporary presidential rhetoric, consider George W. Bush's words in his inaugural: "America has never been united by blood or birth or soil. We are bound by ideals that move us beyond our

backgrounds, lift us above our interests and teach us what it means to be citizens." These words may not seem very contentful, but they do make their speaker utterly unassailable.

9. John Podhoretz, *Bush Country: How Dubya Became a Great President while Driving Liberals Insane* (New York: St. Martin's, 2004), 8. The combination of rhetorical anti-intellectualism and abstraction is easily confused with intellectual seriousness because rhetorical abstraction invites theorizing and explanation, which are usually features of intellectual language. Yet because rhetorical abstraction is seldom a prelude to substantive argument in modern presidential rhetoric, the effect is pontification without explanation. The awkward coexistence of rhetorical abstraction and anti-intellectualism has understandably led some scholars to highlight the embarrassing vacuousness of modern presidential rhetoric. It might be useful to repeat the quote from Schlesinger here. Of presidential rhetoric, he observed, "It is rarely an occasion for original thought or stimulating reflection. The platitude quotient tends to be high, the rhetoric stately and self-serving, the ritual obsessive, and the surprises few." See Arthur Schlesinger, Jr. (ed.), *The Chief Executive: Inaugural Addresses of the Presidents of the United States from George Washington to Lyndon B. Johnson* (New York: Crown, 1965), vi–vii.

10. The Queen's Speech (formally referred to as the "Most Gracious Speech from the Throne") at the state opening of Parliament, like the State of the Union message, details the British government's proposed legislative program. As the president relies on speechwriters to draft the State of the Union address, a government committee known as the "futureleg" puts the Queen's Speech together.

11. Refer to appendix VI for methodological notes on the Flesch Readability score. Because there were some years in which each speech was not delivered, a rolling average trend line connects all available data points for each genre. The results in figure 4.3 are corroborated in the scores for the nineteenth-century speeches as well, even though nineteenth-century annual messages were bureaucratic tracts delivered in written format to the congress and Queen's Speeches were orally delivered.

12. David Gergen, *Eyewitness to Power: The Essence of Leadership: Nixon to Clinton* (New York: Simon & Schuster, 2000), 217.

13. *Public Papers of William J. Clinton*, "Address before a Joint Session of the Congress on the State of the Union," 1/27/2000.

14. Ira Sharkansky, "Slogan as Policy," *Journal of Comparative Policy Analysis* 4 (2002): 75–93, 83–86.

15. Jeffrey K. Tulis, *The Rhetorical Presidency* (Princeton, NJ: Princeton University Press, 1987), 161–72.

16. Interview with Don Baer, chief speechwriter (Clinton), 1994–1995; director of strategic planning and communications, 1995–1997, 8/18/2002; George

Orwell, "Politics and the English Language," in George Orwell, *Collected Chapters* (London: Secker & Warburg, 1961), 353.

17. Clark Clifford (with Richard Holbrooke), *Counsel to the President: A Memoir* (New York: Random House, 1991), 195.

18. Gergen, *Eyewitness to Power*, 54.

19. Interview with Patrick Butler, speechwriter (Ford), 1975–1977, 7/31/2002.

20. Memorandum, Dan McGroarty to Writers/Researchers, 3/2/1992, folder Memorandum Economic 11/91–3/92 (OA/ID 8677), Tony Snow, Subject File, Office of Speechwriting, George Bush Presidential Library.

21. James D. Richardson, *A Compilation of the Messages and Papers of the Presidents, 1789–1897* (Washington, DC: Government Printing Office, 1896–1899, 1918).

22. David Kusnet cited in Chris Jarosch and Julie Van Grinsven, "Speechwriter Assesses Bush's Style," *The Georgetown Voice*, 1/31/2002, available at http://www.georgetownvoice.com/2002-01-31/news/speechwriter-assesses-bushs-style (accessed 1/18/2008).

23. Michael Waldman, *POTUS Speaks: Finding the Words That Defined the Clinton Presidency* (New York: Simon & Schuster, 2000), 44.

24. Interview with Myer Feldman, deputy special counsel (Kennedy), 1961–1963, 8/20/2002.

25. Interview with William Gavin, staff assistant (Nixon), 1969–1970, 8/14/2002.

26. Interview with Michael Gerson, deputy assistant to the president and director of presidential speechwriting, 2001–2002 (Bush); assistant to the president for speechwriting and policy advisor, 2002–2005; assistant to the president for policy and strategic planning, 2005–2006, 4/30/2002.

27. Peggy Noonan, *Simply Speaking: How to Communicate Your Ideas with Style, Substance, and Clarity* (New York: Regan, 1998), 17.

28. Charles O. Jones, "Preparing to Govern in 2001: Lessons from the Clinton Presidency," in Norman Ornstein and Thomas Mann (eds.), *The Permanent Campaign and Its Future* (Washington, DC: American Enterprise Institute and Brookings Institution, 2000), 185–218, 185.

29. James D. Barber, *The Presidential Character* (Englewood Cliffs, NJ: Prentice-Hall, 1985), 503.

30. Ralph Ketcham, *Presidents above Party: The First American Presidency, 1789–1829* (Chapel Hill: University of North Carolina Press, 1987).

31. "Some Thoughts on the Present State of Public Affairs," 1/30/1878, in Arthur S. Link et al. (eds.), *Public Papers of Woodrow Wilson* (Princeton, NJ: Princeton University Press, 1966–1994), 1:347.

32. Elvin T. Lim, "Five Trends in Presidential Rhetoric: An Analysis of Rhetoric from George Washington to Bill Clinton," *Presidential Studies Quarterly* 32 (2002): 328–66.

33. As the "sense" of the "common" gained authority, the two words were also fused for the first time in presidential lingo in 1929 by President Hoover in

his "Memorial Address" to the nation at Arlington National Cemetery on 5/30/1929. The counts here were taken from sweeps of the *Public Papers* of every president using the search terms "common sense" and "commonsense" and standardized by and rounded to years in office. (The data for George Bush are from 1/20/2001 to 7/31/2007.)

34. Woodrow Wilson, "An Address in the City Auditorium in Pueblo, Colorado," 9/25/1919, in J. Michael Hogan, *Woodrow Wilson's Western Tour: Rhetoric, Public Opinion, and the League of Nations* (College Station: Texas A&M University Press, 2006), 1–16, 11.

35. *Public Papers of William J. Clinton*, "Remarks at a Democratic Congressional Campaign Committee Dinner in Boca Raton, Florida," 10/31/1997.

36. Steven M. Teles, *Whose Welfare? AFDC and Elite Politics* (Lawrence: University Press of Kansas, 1996).

37. Cicero, *De Oratore*, book II, 178.

38. *Public Papers of Richard Nixon*, "Annual Message to the Congress on the State of the Union," 1/20/1972.

39. Christopher Matthews, *Kennedy and Nixon: The Rivalry That Shaped Postwar America* (New York: Simon & Schuster, 1996), 84.

40. Interview with Gavin; William Gavin, "Source Material: His Heart's Abundance: Notes of a Nixon Speechwriter," *Presidential Studies Quarterly* 31 (2001): 358–68.

41. Interview with Gavin.

42. *Public Papers of William J. Clinton*, "Address before a Joint Session of the Congress on the State of the Union," 1/24/1995.

43. *Public Papers of William J. Clinton*, "Remarks at a Democratic National Committee Dinner in Stuart, Florida," 3/16/1999.

44. Interview with Lee Huebner, special assistant, deputy director of the White House writing and research staff (Nixon), 1969–1973, 9/27/2002.

45. *Public Papers of William J. Clinton*, "Address before a Joint Session of the Congress on the State of the Union," 1/24/1995.

46. Alan C. Miller, "Democrats Return Illegal Contribution," *Los Angeles Times*, 9/21/1996; Bob Woodward and Brian Duffy, "Chinese Embassy Role in Contributions Probed," *Washington Post*, 2/13/1997.

47. Mark Halperin, "The Hillary and Bill Show," *Time*, 7/4/2007, available at http://www.time.com/time/nation/article/0,8599,1640108-3,00.html (accessed 8/6/2007).

48. Mark Leibovich, "Clinton Shapes Her Image for '08 Race," *New York Times*, 3/6/2007, available at http://www.nytimes.com/2007/03/06/us/politics/06hillary.html?pagewanted=1&ei=5070&en=65b67a161a840c8d&ex=1186545600 (accessed 8/6/2007).

49. Dana Milbank, "Candidate Clinton, Embracing the Trite and the True," *Washington Post*, 3/9/2007, A2, available at http://www.washingtonpost.com/

wp-dyn/content/article/2007/03/08/AR2007030801786.html (accessed 8/6/2007). Along similar lines, see also Anne Applebaum, "Life, Liberty, and Politicians' Maddening Way with Words: The Infuriating Blandness of Political Speech," *Slate*, 6/18/2007, available at http://www.slate.com/id/2168646/nav/tap3 (accessed 8/6/2007).

Chapter 5

1. Kathleen Donald, "Coolidge Was Eloquent without Welliver," *New York Times*, 2/18/1987, 30.
2. William Hopkins, John F. Kennedy Library Oral History Program, 6/3/1964, John F. Kennedy Library, available at http://www.trumanlibrary.org/oralhist/hopkinsw.htm (accessed 1/18/2008)/
3. "President Writes with the Scissors," *New York Times*, 11/3/1932, 8.
4. "Strother Will Retire as Hoover Assistant," *New York Times*, 4/1/1931, 26. The *Times* reported:

   > Mr. Strother's work at the White House has been devoted chiefly to research work for the president, mainly in connection with the preparation of speeches and messages. He devoted some of his time also to the many quasi-official enterprises in which Mr. Hoover is interested, such as the White House Conference on Child Welfare.

5. Charles Walcott and Karen M. Hult, "Management Science and the Great Engineer: Governing the White House during the Hoover Administration," *Presidential Studies Quarterly* 20 (1990): 557–79, 560.
6. William Safire, *The New Language of Politics: An Anecdotal Dictionary of Catchwords, Slogans, and Political Usage* (New York: Random House, 1968), 414–15. There is a poetic irony that the founder of the Judson Welliver Society and the very person who defined him as a prototypical "ghost" should have resurrected Welliver's name from the past.
7. Mitford M. Mathews, *A Dictionary of Americanisms on Historical Principles* (Chicago: University of Chicago Press, 1951).
8. William J. Hopkins, Herbert Hoover Oral History Program, Herbert Hoover Library.
9. Henry L. Mencken, "Mencken Derides Roosevelt Voice," *New York Times*, 10/21/1937.
10. Quoted in John R. Coyne, *Fall In and Cheer* (Garden City, NY: Doubleday, 1979), 55.
11. Bradley H. Patterson, *The White House Staff: Inside the West Wing and Beyond* (Washington, DC: Brookings Institution Press, 2000), 162.
12. Here is how the *New York Times* ("Crawford to Aid Coolidge," 11/28/1925, *New York Times*, 2) described the chief clerk's responsibilities: "[He] will advise the president in political matters, assist him in the preparation of addresses and

messages and furnish statistical and other information for important letters."
The conventional wisdom has now settled on Welliver's title as "literary clerk"
(see Patterson, *White House Staff*, 162). But this was not his official title. White
House correspondence indicates that Welliver's title was "chief clerk." See, for
instance, Letter from R. K. to Judson C. Welliver, 7/12/1924, folder "Accom-
plishments of Calvin Coolidge Administration, 1924–28," Calvin Coolidge
Papers, Library of Congress. Contemporary reports in the *New York Times*
indicate the same. See, for instance, "Harding Gets Mail Chicks," *New York
Times*, 5/21/1922, 20; "Welliver Quits White House Post," *New York Times*,
10/24/1925, 4.

13. Irwin H. Hoover, *Forty-Two Years in the White House* (New York: Houghton
    Mifflin, 1934), 253.

14. "Welliver Quits White House Post," *New York Times*, 10/24/1925, 4; "Craw-
    ford to Aid Coolidge," *New York Times*, 11/28/1925, 2. Welliver's career move
    presaged the commercial possibilities after government service that all speech-
    writers have since enjoyed.

15. Interview with Stephen Hess, special assistant, 1959–1961 (Eisenhower),
    8/12/2002.

16. Roderick P. Hart, *The Sound of Leadership: Presidential Communication
    in the Modern Age* (Chicago: University of Chicago Press, 1987), 8. Eisen-
    hower's successor, John Kennedy, reverted to an average of 22 speeches a
    month.

17. Coyne, *Fall In and Cheer*, 100; John Podhoretz, *Hell of a Ride: Backstage at the
    White House Follies 1989–1993* (New York: Simon & Schuster, 1993), 81.

18. Interview with Richard E. Neustadt, special assistant, 1950–1953 (Truman),
    6/13/2003.

19. George M. Elsey, Oral History Interview, 7/10/1969, Harry S Truman Library,
    available at http://www.trumanlibrary.org/oralhist/elsey9.htm (accessed 1/18/
    2008).

20. Milton P. Kayle, Oral History Interview, 11/9/1982, Harry S Truman Library,
    available at http://www.trumanlibrary.org/oralhist/kayle.htm#oh1 (accessed
    1/18/2008).

21. Theodore Sorensen (ed.), *"Let the Word Go Forth": The Speeches, Statements,
    and Writings of John F. Kennedy* (New York: Delacorte, 1988), 2.

22. Richard Goodwin, *Remembering America: A Voice from the Sixties* (Boston:
    Little, Brown, 1988), 418.

23. James C. Humes, *Confession of a White House Ghostwriter: Five Presidents and
    Other Political Adventures* (Washington, DC: Regnery, 1997), 1.

24. James Keogh, *President Nixon and the Press* (New York: Funk & Wagnall's,
    1972), 39; Joe McGinnis, *The Selling of the President* (New York: Penguin,
    1988), *passim*; Carol Gelderman, *All the Presidents' Words: The Bully Pulpit and
    the Creation of the Virtual Presidency* (New York: Walker & Company, 1997),

76; David Gergen, *Eyewitness to Power: The Essence of Leadership: Nixon to Clinton* (New York: Simon & Schuster, 2000), 54.

25. Interview with Hess.

26. Christopher Matthews, *Kennedy and Nixon: The Rivalry That Shaped Postwar America* (New York: Simon & Schuster, 1996), 148; Gergen, *Eyewitness to Power*, 48.

27. Hendrik Hertzberg, "In Praise of Judson Welliver," *Washington Post*, 10/20/1985, editorial. Perhaps Welliver's only claim to fame is the widespread supposition that he coined the phrase "the founding fathers."

28. Raymond Moley, *The First New Deal* (New York: Harcourt, Brace & World, 1966), 96.

29. Raymond Moley's responsibilities, as FDR specified, were "the foreign debts, the world economic consequences, supervising of the economic adviser's office and such additional duties as the president may direct in the general field of foreign and domestic government" (Raymond Moley Papers, Box 282 [19], "FD Roosevelt, Schedule A" folder, Hoover Institution). Moley was first and foremost a presidential advisor, then also a speechwriter.

30. Samuel I. Rosenman, *Working with Roosevelt: Franklin D. Roosevelt and the Era of the New Deal* (New York: Da Capo, 1972); Raymond Moley, *After Seven Years: Franklin D. Roosevelt and the Era of the New Deal* (New York: Harper, 1939).

31. Ernest Brandenburg, "The Preparation of Franklin D. Roosevelt's Speeches," *Quarterly Journal of Speech* 35 (1949): 214–21, 221.

32. President's Personal File Speeches, Box 66 (1414), Franklin D. Roosevelt Library.

33. Clark M. Clifford, Oral History Interview, 7/26/1971, Harry S Truman Library, available at http://www.trumanlibrary.org/oralhist/cliford5.htm (accessed 1/18/2008).

34. Hart, *Sound of Leadership*, 8. The number of "major" presidential speeches ("live nationally televised and broadcast addresses to the country that pre-empt all major network programming") has remained essentially unchanged at between three and four speeches a year. (See Lyn Ragsdale, *Vital Statistics on the Presidency: Washington to Clinton* [Washington, DC: CQ Press, 1998], 169.)

35. Raymond Moley Papers, Box 1, Diary entry of 2/28/1933, Hoover Institution. Needless to say, Roosevelt loyalists have denied this claim. Rosenman maintains that the inaugural was "one of those few of which the president wrote the first draft in his own hand." See Rosenman, *Working with Roosevelt*, 89.

36. Interview with Hess.

37. Emmet J. Hughes, *The Ordeal of Power: A Political Memoir of the Eisenhower Years* (New York: Atheneum, 1963), 10.

38. James L. Golden, "John F. Kennedy and the 'Ghosts,'" *Quarterly Journal of Speech* 52 (1966): 348–57, 351.

39. Harry McPherson, *A Political Education* (Boston: Little, Brown, 1972), 327.

40. Ernest G. Bormann, "Ghostwriting and the Rhetorical Critic," *Quarterly Journal of Speech* 46 (1960): 284–88; Marie H. Nichols, *Rhetoric and Criticism* (Baton Rouge: Louisiana State University Press, 1964); L. Patrick Devlin, "The Influences of Ghostwriting on Rhetorical Criticism," *Today's Speech* 32 (1981): 7–12; Lois J. Einhorn, "The Ghosts Unmasked: A Review of Literature on Speechwriting," *Communication Quarterly* 30 (1981): 41–47.

41. Robert T. Hartmann, *Palace Politics: An Inside Account of the Ford Years* (New York: McGraw-Hill, 1980), 404.

42. Interview with Hendrik Hertzberg et al., Miller Center Interviews, Carter Presidency Project, vol. VIII, 12/2/1981–12/4/1981, 1, Jimmy Carter Library.

43. Speech draft, "Presidential Address to the Nation, 7/15/1979 [2]" folder, Box 139, President's Handwriting File, Jimmy Carter Library.

44. However, the controversy that followed David Frum's departure from the White House in February 2002 shows how the code of anonymity, when broken, can still lead to retribution. Robert Novak had speculated on CNN's *Inside Politics* on 2/25/2002 that Frum had been dismissed because of his wife's infelicitous e-mail attributing the phrase "axis of evil" to him. Frum has maintained that his resignation from the White House was entirely voluntary. See David Frum, *The Right Man: The Surprise Presidency of George W. Bush* (New York: Random House, 2003), 267.

45. Hughes, *Ordeal of Power*, 21.

46. *Public Papers of Richard Nixon, 1972* (Washington DC: Government Printing Office, 1973), 34–41, 41–74.

47. Peggy Noonan, *What I Saw at the Revolution* (New York: Random House, 1990), 4.

48. Martin J. Medhurst, "Writing Speeches for Ronald Reagan: An Interview with Tony Dolan," *Rhetoric & Public Affairs* 2 (1998): 245–56, 251.

49. Oral history interview, Ben J. Wattenberg, 11/23/1968, Lyndon B. Johnson Library.

50. Coyne, *Fall In and Cheer*, 75–76.

51. Noonan, *What I Saw at the Revolution*, 67.

52. James C. Humes, *My Fellow Americans: Presidential Addresses That Shaped History* (New York: Praeger, 1992), 266.

53. Letter, George Bush to Mark Lange, 1/30/1991, folder SP230-91, State of the Union 1991, WHORM: Subject File, Speeches, George Bush Presidential Library.

54. Hoover, *Forty-Two Years in the White House*, 252; "Crawford to Aid Coolidge," *New York Times*, 11/28/1925, 2; "Strother Will Retire as Hoover Assistant," *New York Times*, 4/1/1931, 26.

55. In 2002, President George W. Bush had already elevated his chief speechwriter, Mike Gerson, to the position of policy advisor, while Gerson retained the title of assistant to the president for speechwriting, thereby blending roles that

previously had been split apart. Then, in 2005, Gerson, who was previously a speechwriter to then Representative Dan Coats (R-IN), was divested of his speechwriting responsibilities to become assistant to the president for policy and strategic planning. Gerson was an exception in the post-Nixon era who serves to prove the institutional rule that prioritizes style over substance for speechwriters in the contemporary White House.

56. Clark Clifford (with Richard Holbrooke), *Counsel to the President: A Memoir* (New York: Random House, 1991), 74.

57. Quoted in Einhorn, "Ghosts Unmasked," 43.

58. Interview with John Andrews, deputy special assistant, 1971–1973 (Nixon), 10/4/2002.

59. Interview with Milton P. Kayle, special assistant, 1951–1953 (Truman), 9/9/2002.

60. Interview with Jack Valenti, special assistant, 1963–1966 (Johnson), 8/22/2002. Today, Bush's chief speechwriter is back in a comfortable (albeit windowless) office in the basement of the West Wing.

61. Interview with Patrick Butler, speechwriter, 1975–1977 (Ford), 7/31/2002.

62. Gergen, *Eyewitness to Power*, 241.

63. William Hillman (ed.), *Mr. President* (New York: Farrar, Straus & Young, 1952), 65.

64. William Gavin, "Source Material: His Heart's Abundance: Notes of a Nixon Speechwriter," *Presidential Studies Quarterly* 31 (2001): 358–68, 365.

65. Humes, *Confession of a White House Ghostwriter*, 175.

66. Interview with Arthur Schlesinger, Jr., special assistant, 1961–1963 (Kennedy), 9/7/2002.

67. Michael Waldman, *POTUS Speaks: Finding the Words That Defined the Clinton Presidency* (New York: Simon & Schuster, 2000), 267.

68. Interview with Michael Gerson, deputy assistant to the president and director of presidential speechwriting, 2001–2002 (Bush); assistant to the president for speechwriting and policy advisor, 2002–2005; assistant to the president for policy and strategic planning, 2005–2006, 4/30/2002.

69. Dana Rohrabacher, quoted in William K. Muir, *The Bully Pulpit: The Presidential Leadership of Ronald Reagan* (San Francisco, CA: ICS, 1992), 34.

70. Memorandum from Joseph Duggan, Curt Smith, Mary Kate Grant, and Robert Simon to George Bush, 12/6/1991, Case No. 291021SS, WHORM: Subject File, Speeches, George Bush Presidential Library.

71. Interview with Peter Robinson, speechwriter and special assistant, 1983–1988 (Reagan), 9/27/2002.

72. Frum, *Right Man*, 267.

73. Interview with Ray Price, special assistant, 1969–1972 (Nixon); special consultant, 1973–1974, 9/10/2002.

74. Hoover, *Forty-Two Years in the White House*, 253.

75. Frum, *Right Man*, 46.

76. Interview with Carolyn Curiel, senior speechwriter, 1993–1997 (Clinton), 9/6/2002.

77. Interview with Gerson.

78. Interview with Aram Bakshian, Jr., special assistant and director of the speechwriting office (Reagan), 1981–1983, 7/30/2002.

79. Hartmann, *Palace Politics*, 384–85.

80. Williams, "Source Material," 364. The speech in question was "America's Natural Resources," which was broadcast by CBS Radio on 10/18/1968.

81. Interview with Robert Boorstin, senior director of the National Security Council (Clinton), 1994–1995, 9/27/2002.

82. Interview with Robinson.

83. Interview with Joshua Gilder, senior speechwriter, 1985–1988 (Reagan), 9/2/2002.

84. See http://www.whitehouse.gov/news/releases/2003/07/20030711-7.html (accessed 9/28/2006).

85. *Report on the U.S. Intelligence Community's Prewar Intelligence Assessments on Iraq*, 7/7/2004, 81, available at http://www.gpoaccess.gov/serialset/creports/iraq.html (accessed 8/19/2007).

86. See http://www.csmonitor.com/2005/1115/p01s04b-uspo.htm (accessed 8/19/2007).

87. George Tenet, *At the Center of the Storm: My Years at the CIA* (New York: HarperCollins, 2007).

88. Robert Baer, "George Tenet's Real Failure," *Time*, 5/3/2007, available at http://www.time.com/time/nation/article/0,8599,1617191,00.html (accessed 8/13/2007); Arianna Huffington, "Why Didn't George Tenet Just Resign?" *Huffington Post*, 4/29/2007, available at http://www.huffingtonpost.com/arianna-huffington/why-didnt-george-tenet-j_b_47226.html (accessed 8/13/2007).

89. Cited in Walter Pincus, "Recantation of Iraq Claim Stirs Calls for Probes," *Washington Post*, 7/9/2003, A20.

90. Cited in Dana Milbank and Mike Allen, "Bush Skirts Queries on Iraq Nuclear Allegation: Aides Have Backed Off State of Union Assertion," *Washington Post*, 7/10/2003, A1.

Chapter 6

1. Marcus Tullius Cicero, *De officiis*, 2.51, in Miriam T. Griffin and E. Margaret Atkins (eds.), *On Duties* (Cambridge: Cambridge University Press, 1991), 82.

2. Jeffrey K. Tulis, *The Rhetorical Presidency* (Princeton, NJ: Princeton University Press, 1987), 13.

3. Ibid., 179.

4. Ron Suskind, "Why Are These Men Laughing?" *Esquire*, January 2003.

5. Cited in ibid.

6. Interview with Gordon Stewart, deputy chief speechwriter, 1978–1981 (Carter), 9/30/2002.

7. Interview with Robert Boorstin, senior director of the National Security Council, 1994–1995 (Clinton), 9/27/2002.

8. Interview with John Andrews, deputy special assistant, 1971–1973 (Nixon), 10/4/2002.

9. David Gergen, *Eyewitness to Power: The Essence of Leadership: Nixon to Clinton* (New York: Simon & Schuster, 2000), 238.

10. Henry Fairlie, "The Decline of Oratory," *New Republic*, 5/28/1984, 19.

11. Stephen E. Bennett, "Know-Nothings Revisited: The Implications of Political Ignorance Today," *Social Science Quarterly* 69 (1988): 476–90; Michael X. Delli Carpini and Scott Keeter, "Stability and Change in the US Public's Knowledge of Politics," *Public Opinion Quarterly* 55 (1991): 583–612.

12. Philip E. Converse, "The Nature of Belief Systems in Mass Publics," in David E. Apter (ed.), *Ideology and Discontent* (New York: Free Press, 1964); Paul M. Sniderman, "The New Look in Public Opinion Research," in Ada Finifter (ed.), *Political Science: The State of the Discipline II* (Washington, DC: American Political Science Association, 1993).

13. Shanto Iyengar and Douglas Kinder, *News That Matters: Agenda-Setting and Priming in a Television Age* (Chicago: University of Chicago Press, 1987); John Zaller and Stanley Feldman, *The Nature and Origins of Mass Opinion* (New York: Cambridge University Press, 1992); Lawrence R. Jacobs and Robert Y. Shapiro, *Politicians Don't Pander: Political Manipulation and the Loss of Democratic Responsiveness* (Chicago: University of Chicago Press, 2000).

14. Jeffrey E. Cohen, "Presidential Rhetoric and the Public Agenda," *American Journal of Political Science* 39 (1995): 102; Jeffrey E. Cohen, *Presidential Responsiveness and Public Policy-Making* (Ann Arbor: University of Michigan Press, 1997), 234.

15. Jacobs and Shapiro, *Politicians Don't Pander*, 49–50.

16. Herbert H. Hyman and Paul B. Sheatsley, "Some Reasons Why Information Commercials Fail," *Public Opinion Quarterly* 11 (1947): 412–23, 415; Robert C. Luskin, "Explaining Political Sophistication," *Public Behavior* 12 (1990): 331–61, 348; Stephen E. Bennett, "Know-Nothings Revisited Again," *Political Behavior* 18 (1996): 219–33, 226.

17. Mancur Olson, *The Logic of Collective Action* (Cambridge, MA: Harvard University Press, 1965).

18. Anthony Downs, *An Economic Theory of Democracy* (New York: Harper, 1957).

19. Garrett Hardin, "The Tragedy of the Commons," in John S. Dryzek and David Schlosberg (eds.), *Debating the Earth: The Environmental Politics Reader* (Oxford: Oxford University Press, 2005), 25–36.

20. John Stuart Mill, *On Liberty*, in Mary Warnock (ed.), *Utilitarianism, On Liberty, Chapter on Bentham* (Glasgow: HarperCollins, 1962), 195–96.

21. William A. Galston, "Liberal Virtues," *American Political Science Review* 82 (1988): 1277–90, 1284.

22. Jeffrey J. Mondak, "Public Opinion and Heuristic Processing of Source Cues," *Political Behavior* 15 (1993): 167–92; Wendy M. Rahn, "The Role of Partisan Stereotypes in Information Processing about Political Candidates," *American Journal of Political Science* 37 (1993): 472–96; Ellen D. Riggle, Victor Ottati, Robert S. Wyer, James Kuklinski, and Norbert Schwartz, "Bases of Political Judgments: The Role of Stereotypic and Nonstereotypic Information," *Political Behavior* 14 (1992): 67–87.

23. James H. Kulinski, Paul J. Quirk, Jennifer Jerit, and Robert F. Rich, "The Political Environment and Citizen Competence," *American Journal of Political Science* 45 (2001): 410–24, 412.

24. Larry M. Bartels, "Uninformed Votes: Information Effects in Presidential Elections," *American Journal of Political Science* 40 (1996): 194–230; Richard R. Lau and David P. Redlawsk, "Advantages and Disadvantages of Cognitive Heuristics in Political Decision Making," *American Journal of Political Science* 45 (2001): 951–71.

25. Michael X. Delli Carpini and Scott Keeter, *What Americans Know about Politics and Why It Matters* (New Haven, CT: Yale University Press, 1996), 397.

26. Lau and Redlawsk, "Advantages and Disadvantages of Cognitive Heuristics in Political Decision Making," 969.

27. Robert P. Putnam, *Bowling Alone: The Collapse and Revival of American Community* (New York: Simon & Schuster, 2000); William Lyons and Robert Alexander, "A Tale of Two Electorates: Generational Replacement and the Decline of Voting in Presidential Elections," *Journal of Politics* 62 (2000): 1014–34; William A. Galston, "Civic Education and Political Participation," *PS: Political Science & Politics* 37 (2004): 263–66.

28. Samuel L. Popkin and Michael A. Dimock, "Political Knowledge and Citizen Competence," in S. K. Eltin and K. E. Soltan (eds.), *Citizen Competence and Democratic Institutions* (University Park: Pennsylvania State University Press, 1999), 117–46, 142.

29. For a specification of the deliberative conception, see Jürgen Habermas, *Moral Consciousness and Communicative Action*, trans. Christian Lenhardt and Shierry W. Nicholson (Cambridge, MA: MIT Press, 1990); Amy Gutmann and Dennis Thompson, *Democracy and Disagreement* (Cambridge, MA: Harvard University Press, 1996). For the agonistic conception, see Hannah Arendt, *The Human Condition* (Chicago: University of Chicago Press, 1958); Robert Dahl, *Polyarchy* (New Haven, CT: Yale University Press, 1971). For a more active, participation-based conception, see Michael Sandel, *Democracy's Discontent: America in Search of a Public Philosophy* (Cambridge, MA: Harvard University Press, 1996); James S. Fishkin,

"The Televised Deliberative Poll: An Experiment in Democracy," *Annals of the American Academy of Political and Social Science* 546 (1997): 132–40. For a consent-based view of democracy that minimizes the responsibility of citizens, see Patrick Devlin, *The Enforcement of Morals* (Oxford: Oxford University Press, 1965); Raoul Berger, *Government by Judiciary* (Cambridge, MA: Harvard University Press). For the classic proceduralist/minimalist conception, see Joseph Schumpeter, *Capitalism, Socialism and Democracy* (New York: Harper & Row, 1950).

30. Daniel Boorstin, *The Americans: The Democratic Experience* (London: Phoenix, 2000 [1973]), 455.

31. James A. Morone, *The Democratic Wish* (New York: Basic, 1990). This is itself a systematic restatement of a more general observation that Tocqueville made before: "The people reign in the American political world as the Deity does in the universe. They are the cause and aim of all things; everything comes from them; and everything is absorbed by them." Alexis de Tocqueville, *Democracy in America*, trans. Henry Reeve and Francis Bowen (New York: Knopf, 1956 [1835]), 58.

32. Interview with Anthony Dolan, speechwriter and special assistant (Reagan), 1981–1986; director of speechwriting, 1986–1989, 10/3/2002.

33. James F. Cooper, *The American Democrat* (Indianapolis, IN: Liberty Classics, 1931 [1838]), 112–13.

34. Hannah Arendt, *Eichmann in Jerusalem: A Report on the Banality of Evil* (New York: Viking, 1963), 6.

35. Mark Kingswell, *A Civil Tongue: Justice, Dialogue and the Politics of Pluralism* (University Park: Pennsylvania State University Press, 1995), 83.

36. James S. Fishkin, *Democracy and Deliberation: New Directions for Democratic Reform* (New Haven, CT: Yale University Press, 1991), 29.

Chapter 7

1. Simone Chambers, *Reasonable Democracy: Jürgen Habermas and the Politics of Discourse* (Ithaca, NY: Cornell University Press, 1996), 99.

2. Jürgen Habermas, *A Theory of Communicative Action*, vols. 1 and 2 (Cambridge, MA: Polity, 1984, 1989); James S. Fishkin, *Democracy and Deliberation: New Directions for Democratic Reform* (New Haven, CT: Yale University Press, 1991); Amy Guttmann and Dennis Thompson, *Democracy and Disagreement* (Cambridge, MA: Harvard University Press, 1996); Seyla Benhabib, *The Rights of Others: Aliens, Residents, and Citizens* (Cambridge: Cambridge University Press, 2004).

3. By presidential pedagogy, I do not refer to the role that some scholars have assigned to the president as the articulator of the nation's "civil religion." This, the president already does, perhaps to excess. Though it need not be so, it is precisely the assumption of such a role that has led many presidents to inspirational, platitudinous rhetoric. See Robert N. Bellah, "Civil Religion in America," *Daedalus* 96 (1967): 1–21; Michael Novak, *Choosing*

Our King: Powerful Symbols in Presidential Politics (New York: Macmillan, 1974).

4. Cicero, *De Oratore*, book I, 8.

5. Robert A. Kraig, *Woodrow Wilson and the Lost World of the Oratorical Statesman* (College Station: Texas A&M University Press, 2004), 6.

6. Cited in Lester J. Cappon (ed.), *The Adams-Jefferson Letters: The Complete Correspondence Between Thomas Jefferson and Abigail and John Adams* (Chapel Hill: University of North Carolina Press, 1988), 387.

7. Interview with Arthur Schlesinger, Jr., special assistant, 1961–1963 (Kennedy), 9/7/2002.

8. Erwin C. Hargrove, *The President as Leader: Appealing to the Better Angels of Our Nature* (Lawrence: University Press of Kansas, 1998), vii.

9. William K. Muir, "The Bully Pulpit," *Presidential Studies Quarterly* 25 (1995): 13–17, 16.

10. Fred I. Greenstein, *The Presidential Difference: Leadership Style from FDR to Clinton* (Princeton, NJ: Princeton University Press, 2000), 195.

11. Mary Stuckey, *Playing the Game: The Presidential Rhetoric of Ronald Reagan* (Westport, CT: Praeger, 1990), 97.

12. I include Franklin Roosevelt in this triumvirate, because he too is widely regarded as a founding rhetorical president who continues to cast his oratorical shadow on his successors. See Halford R. Ryan, *Franklin D. Roosevelt's Rhetorical Presidency* (New York: Greenwood, 1988).

13. Jeffrey Tulis, *The Rhetorical Presidency* (Princeton, NJ: Princeton University Press, 1987), 106.

14. James Ceaser, *Presidential Selection: Theory and Development* (Princeton, NJ: Princeton University Press, 1979), 177.

15. John M. Cooper, Jr., *The Warrior and the Priest: Woodrow Wilson and Theodore Roosevelt* (Cambridge, MA: Belknap, 1983), xii.

16. Kraig, *Woodrow Wilson and the Lost World of the Oratorical Statesman*, 9.

17. *The Public Papers and Addresses of Franklin D. Roosevelt, 1928–1932*, "Campaign Address, Commonwealth Club, San Francisco," 9/23/1932.

18. *The Public Papers of Franklin D. Roosevelt, 1933*, "First Fireside Chat (Banking)," 3/12/1933. For an account of the myth of simplicity that FDR himself helped to engender, see Elvin T. Lim, "The Lion and the Lamb: Demythologizing Franklin Roosevelt's Fireside Chats," *Rhetoric & Public Affairs* 6 (2003): 437–64.

19. Edward S. Corwin, *The President, Office and Powers, 1787–1957: History and Analysis of Practice and Opinion* (New York: New York University Press, 1957), 274.

20. The *New York Times* (2/24/1942, 4) described the talk to the nation as "a geography lesson of a world at war by a teacher who had asked his pupils—the American listening audience—to prepare themselves with maps that they might better understand the import of his message."

21. Letter from George R. Smith, 5/8/1933, Franklin D. Roosevelt Library (hereafter FDRL), President's Personal File (PPF) 200, Box 13; Letter from James H. Devore, 5/9/1933, FDRL, PPF 200, Box 12; Telegram from M. Sigler, 6/24/1938, FDRL, PPF 200, Box 51; Letter from Margaret B. Beaumont, 12/10/1941, FDRL, PPF 200, Box 108; Telegram from James A. Wilson, 7/29/1943, FDRL, PPF 200, Box 73.

22. Letter from D. Mclean, 6/24/1938, FDRL, PPF 200, Box 51.

23. Arthur M. Schlesinger, Jr., *The Age of Roosevelt: The Coming of the New Deal* (London: Heinemann, 1957), 2:539; William Leuchtenburg, *The FDR Years: On Roosevelt and His Legacy* (New York: Columbia University Press, 1995), 15.

24. Stuckey, *Playing the Game*, 14.

Appendix I

1. Philip J. Stone, Dexter C. Dunphy, Marshall S. Smith, and Daniel M. Ogilvie, *The General Inquirer: A Computer Approach to Content Analysis* (Cambridge, MA: MIT Press, 1966); J. Zvi Namenwirth and Robert P. Weber, *Dynamics of Culture* (Boston: Allen and Unwin, 1987). See also http://www.wjh.harvard.edu/inquirer/3JMoreInfo.html.

2. The Harvard IV-4 and Lasswell value dictionary categories were developed to represent social science concepts introduced by Harold Lasswell, Talcott Parsons, David McClelland, and others. Specifically, the *Negativ* category was developed to capture the semantic language universals theorized in Charles Osgood, *Universals of Language* (Cambridge, MA: MIT Press, 1966).

3. Just the 300 most frequently used English words represent roughly 65 percent of all texts. See Edward B. Fry, Jacqueline E. Kress, and Dona Lee Fountoukidis, *The Reading Teacher's Book of Lists*, 5th ed. (New York: Wiley, 2006).

4. *Hostile*, like *Negativ*, is a category derived from one of the semantic language universals theorized in Osgood, *Universals of Language*. The category contains 833 words (such as "afflict," "execute," and "oppress").

5. *PowLoss* is a Lasswell value dictionary category costing of 109 words (such as "concede," "loss," and "overwhelm") in which the author divided language into four deference domains (power, rectitude, respect, affiliation) and four welfare domains (wealth, well-being, enlightenment, skill). See Namenwirth and Weber, *Dynamics of Culture*, 46–53. *PowLoss* is a subcategory within the first of these domains.

Appendix VI

1. See J. P. Kincaid, R. P. Fishburne, R. L. Rogers, and B. S. Chissom, "Derivation of New Readability Formulas (Automated Readability Index, Fog Count and Flesch Reading Ease Formula) for Navy Enlisted Personnel," *Research Branch Report 8–75* (Memphis, TN: Naval Air Station, 1975).

INDEX